LEVEL I PRACTICE EXAMS – VOLUME 1

W9-BFW-407

SCHWESER 2015 CFA LEVEL I PRACTICE EXAMS VOLUME 1

©2014 Kaplan, Inc. All rights reserved.

Published in 2014 by Kaplan, Inc.

Printed in the United States of America.

ISBN: 978-1-4754-2762-2 / 1-4754-2762-X

PPN: 3200-5534

If this book does not have the hologram with the Kaplan Schweser logo on the back cover, it was distributed without permission of Kaplan Schweser, a Division of Kaplan, Inc., and is in direct violation of global copyright laws. Your assistance in pursuing potential violators of this law is greatly appreciated.

Required CFA Institute disclaimer: "CFA Institute does not endorse, promote, or warrant the accuracy or quality of the products or services offered by Kaplan Schweser. CFA® and Chartered Financial Analyst® are trademarks owned by CFA Institute."

Certain materials contained within this text are the copyrighted property of CFA Institute. The following is the copyright disclosure for these materials: "Copyright, 2014, CFA Institute. Reproduced and republished from 2015 Learning Outcome Statements, Level I, II, and III questions from CFA® Program Materials, CFA Institute Standards of Professional Conduct, and CFA Institute's Global Investment Performance Standards with permission from CFA Institute. All Rights Reserved."

These materials may not be copied without written permission from the author. The unauthorized duplication of these notes is a violation of global copyright laws and the CFA Institute Code of Ethics. Your assistance in pursuing potential violators of this law is greatly appreciated.

Disclaimer: The Schweser Notes should be used in conjunction with the original readings as set forth by CFA Institute in their 2015 CFA Level I Study Guide. The information contained in these Notes covers topics contained in the readings referenced by CFA Institute and is believed to be accurate. However, their accuracy cannot be guaranteed nor is any warranty conveyed as to your ultimate exam success. The authors of the referenced readings have not endorsed or sponsored these Notes.

Use Your Schweser Online Access Account

All purchasers of the SchweserNotes™ package are sent login information for Online Access in an email. This is your login to view video volumes in the Schweser Library, use the Schweser Study Calendar, use Performance Tracker, and (if you purchased the Essential Self-Study, Premium, or Premium Plus packages) join Instructor-led Office Hours. Simply login at www.schweser.com and select any of these features from your dashboard.

VOLUME 1 ONLINE FEATURES AT A GLANCE

Links to Curriculum

Within the online answer explanations, we have included page references to the relevant text in both the SchweserNotes and the CFA Institute program texts.

Performance Tracker

When you enter your answers in our Performance Tracker utility, you can request a breakdown of your overall score on any one-half (120 question) exam. See how you performed by topic area, study session, or reading. You can also get the Learning Outcome Statement references for questions you answered incorrectly to help you focus your review efforts.

When you enter your answers in Performance Tracker, you can find out how your score on each half-exam compares to the scores of others who entered their answers.

How to Use This Book

Volume 1 is a very important part of the Schweser Study Program. **Don't skip over it.**

You shouldn't take the Level I CFA® Exam without lots of practice answering questions.

Test yourself with these practice exams only after you have completed all the assigned readings. As on the actual CFA exam, assume International Financial Reporting Standards (IFRS) apply unless a question indicates otherwise.

The purpose of these questions is to make sure that you know all the concepts and ideas that are in the assigned readings. If you truly know the material you will do well on the actual exam. While our practice questions cover all the material, **they are not actual exam questions.** Our practice exams are not designed to predict your score on the actual CFA exam, although we try to match the level of difficulty on the exam. Use them to practice and identify those areas in which you need additional work.

Remember though, that CFA Institute tries very hard every year to come up with new and innovative ways to test you. Your only defense against a good exam writer is to actually know the material. Learning the material and how to pace yourself on the exam is what our practice questions are designed to help you do.

The CFA exam is structured so that the morning and afternoon exams are each independent exams covering all topic areas. So, the three 6-hour practice exams here in Volume 1 are really six 3-hour practice exams. This gives you several opportunities to test your progress.

Our recommendations for using this book are:

- After you have finished your first complete review of the assigned reading material, take the morning portion of Practice Exam 1, paying strict attention to the time constraint. Enter your answers online. Performance Tracker will identify your weak spots and point you toward the material you need to review. Go back and study the material related to your weak areas.
- After you have reviewed that material, take the afternoon portion of Practice Exam 1. Again, pay strict attention to the allotted time and review the material related to your weak areas identified by Performance Tracker.
- During the weeks prior to the exam, set aside two days to take Exams 2 and 3. Complete each of these 6-hour exams on one day with only a lunch break between the two halves. This will get you used to doing what you must do on exam day. Again review your weak areas but also look at the explanation for every problem you missed, so it won't happen again.
- Finally, review all of Study Session 1 on the day before the exam. Ethical and Professional Standards and Global Investment Performance Standards will be approximately 15% of the Level I exam. A final review of this material, including all the text and all the examples in the *Standards of Practice Handbook,* will serve you well on exam day.

Don't plan on passing the exam by memorizing questions and answers. Instead, learn the logic behind each of the questions. CFA Institute isn't going to ask you our questions, but they will ask you questions that address the same concepts, logic, and definitions necessary to answer the practice exam questions.

©2014 Kaplan, Inc.

Exam 1
Morning Session

Calculating Your Score

Topic	Maximum Score	Your Score
Ethical and Professional Standards	18	
Quantitative Methods	14	
Economics	12	
Financial Reporting and Analysis	24	
Corporate Finance	8	
Portfolio Management	9	
Equity Investments	12	
Fixed Income	12	
Derivatives	6	
Alternative Investments	5	
Total	120	

The morning and afternoon exams are identically weighted over the topics and readings. You can therefore treat the morning and afternoon exams as independent exams.

If you took more than three hours (180 minutes) to complete this portion of the exam, you should adjust your score downward by one point for each minute you ran over.

Remember: the real exam *will be more difficult* than these practice exams. The main reason for this is the general anxiety and stress that you will be feeling on exam day, coupled with the time pressure you will be under. Many of the questions on this practice exam and the real exam are not individually difficult, so if you take extra time to answer the questions on this practice exam, your score will go up significantly. However, if you want an accurate measure of your potential performance on the exam, adhere to the 3-hour time limit.

After you have finished grading your practice exam, you may find it useful to use the exam questions and recommended solutions for review. Many of these questions were specifically written for your use as study tools. Once again, I feel I should remind you not to rely on memorizing these questions; you are not likely to see them on the actual exam. What you will see on the exam, though, are the concepts, terms, and procedures presented in these questions.

Your actual exam will most likely look different than what you see in this book. Please remember, no study provider knows the content of the actual exam. These practice exams are our best guess as to the structure, content, and difficulty of an actual exam.

Test Answers

1.	Ⓐ	Ⓑ	Ⓒ		41.	Ⓐ	Ⓑ	Ⓒ		81.	Ⓐ	Ⓑ	Ⓒ
2.	Ⓐ	Ⓑ	Ⓒ		42.	Ⓐ	Ⓑ	Ⓒ		82.	Ⓐ	Ⓑ	Ⓒ
3.	Ⓐ	Ⓑ	Ⓒ		43.	Ⓐ	Ⓑ	Ⓒ		83.	Ⓐ	Ⓑ	Ⓒ
4.	Ⓐ	Ⓑ	Ⓒ		44.	Ⓐ	Ⓑ	Ⓒ		84.	Ⓐ	Ⓑ	Ⓒ
5.	Ⓐ	Ⓑ	Ⓒ		45.	Ⓐ	Ⓑ	Ⓒ		85.	Ⓐ	Ⓑ	Ⓒ
6.	Ⓐ	Ⓑ	Ⓒ		46.	Ⓐ	Ⓑ	Ⓒ		86.	Ⓐ	Ⓑ	Ⓒ
7.	Ⓐ	Ⓑ	Ⓒ		47.	Ⓐ	Ⓑ	Ⓒ		87.	Ⓐ	Ⓑ	Ⓒ
8.	Ⓐ	Ⓑ	Ⓒ		48.	Ⓐ	Ⓑ	Ⓒ		88.	Ⓐ	Ⓑ	Ⓒ
9.	Ⓐ	Ⓑ	Ⓒ		49.	Ⓐ	Ⓑ	Ⓒ		89.	Ⓐ	Ⓑ	Ⓒ
10.	Ⓐ	Ⓑ	Ⓒ		50.	Ⓐ	Ⓑ	Ⓒ		90.	Ⓐ	Ⓑ	Ⓒ
11.	Ⓐ	Ⓑ	Ⓒ		51.	Ⓐ	Ⓑ	Ⓒ		91.	Ⓐ	Ⓑ	Ⓒ
12.	Ⓐ	Ⓑ	Ⓒ		52.	Ⓐ	Ⓑ	Ⓒ		92.	Ⓐ	Ⓑ	Ⓒ
13.	Ⓐ	Ⓑ	Ⓒ		53.	Ⓐ	Ⓑ	Ⓒ		93.	Ⓐ	Ⓑ	Ⓒ
14.	Ⓐ	Ⓑ	Ⓒ		54.	Ⓐ	Ⓑ	Ⓒ		94.	Ⓐ	Ⓑ	Ⓒ
15.	Ⓐ	Ⓑ	Ⓒ		55.	Ⓐ	Ⓑ	Ⓒ		95.	Ⓐ	Ⓑ	Ⓒ
16.	Ⓐ	Ⓑ	Ⓒ		56.	Ⓐ	Ⓑ	Ⓒ		96.	Ⓐ	Ⓑ	Ⓒ
17.	Ⓐ	Ⓑ	Ⓒ		57.	Ⓐ	Ⓑ	Ⓒ		97.	Ⓐ	Ⓑ	Ⓒ
18.	Ⓐ	Ⓑ	Ⓒ		58.	Ⓐ	Ⓑ	Ⓒ		98.	Ⓐ	Ⓑ	Ⓒ
19.	Ⓐ	Ⓑ	Ⓒ		59.	Ⓐ	Ⓑ	Ⓒ		99.	Ⓐ	Ⓑ	Ⓒ
20.	Ⓐ	Ⓑ	Ⓒ		60.	Ⓐ	Ⓑ	Ⓒ		100.	Ⓐ	Ⓑ	Ⓒ
21.	Ⓐ	Ⓑ	Ⓒ		61.	Ⓐ	Ⓑ	Ⓒ		101.	Ⓐ	Ⓑ	Ⓒ
22.	Ⓐ	Ⓑ	Ⓒ		62.	Ⓐ	Ⓑ	Ⓒ		102.	Ⓐ	Ⓑ	Ⓒ
23.	Ⓐ	Ⓑ	Ⓒ		63.	Ⓐ	Ⓑ	Ⓒ		103.	Ⓐ	Ⓑ	Ⓒ
24.	Ⓐ	Ⓑ	Ⓒ		64.	Ⓐ	Ⓑ	Ⓒ		104.	Ⓐ	Ⓑ	Ⓒ
25.	Ⓐ	Ⓑ	Ⓒ		65.	Ⓐ	Ⓑ	Ⓒ		105.	Ⓐ	Ⓑ	Ⓒ
26.	Ⓐ	Ⓑ	Ⓒ		66.	Ⓐ	Ⓑ	Ⓒ		106.	Ⓐ	Ⓑ	Ⓒ
27.	Ⓐ	Ⓑ	Ⓒ		67.	Ⓐ	Ⓑ	Ⓒ		107.	Ⓐ	Ⓑ	Ⓒ
28.	Ⓐ	Ⓑ	Ⓒ		68.	Ⓐ	Ⓑ	Ⓒ		108.	Ⓐ	Ⓑ	Ⓒ
29.	Ⓐ	Ⓑ	Ⓒ		69.	Ⓐ	Ⓑ	Ⓒ		109.	Ⓐ	Ⓑ	Ⓒ
30.	Ⓐ	Ⓑ	Ⓒ		70.	Ⓐ	Ⓑ	Ⓒ		110.	Ⓐ	Ⓑ	Ⓒ
31.	Ⓐ	Ⓑ	Ⓒ		71.	Ⓐ	Ⓑ	Ⓒ		111.	Ⓐ	Ⓑ	Ⓒ
32.	Ⓐ	Ⓑ	Ⓒ		72.	Ⓐ	Ⓑ	Ⓒ		112.	Ⓐ	Ⓑ	Ⓒ
33.	Ⓐ	Ⓑ	Ⓒ		73.	Ⓐ	Ⓑ	Ⓒ		113.	Ⓐ	Ⓑ	Ⓒ
34.	Ⓐ	Ⓑ	Ⓒ		74.	Ⓐ	Ⓑ	Ⓒ		114.	Ⓐ	Ⓑ	Ⓒ
35.	Ⓐ	Ⓑ	Ⓒ		75.	Ⓐ	Ⓑ	Ⓒ		115.	Ⓐ	Ⓑ	Ⓒ
36.	Ⓐ	Ⓑ	Ⓒ		76.	Ⓐ	Ⓑ	Ⓒ		116.	Ⓐ	Ⓑ	Ⓒ
37.	Ⓐ	Ⓑ	Ⓒ		77.	Ⓐ	Ⓑ	Ⓒ		117.	Ⓐ	Ⓑ	Ⓒ
38.	Ⓐ	Ⓑ	Ⓒ		78.	Ⓐ	Ⓑ	Ⓒ		118.	Ⓐ	Ⓑ	Ⓒ
39.	Ⓐ	Ⓑ	Ⓒ		79.	Ⓐ	Ⓑ	Ⓒ		119.	Ⓐ	Ⓑ	Ⓒ
40.	Ⓐ	Ⓑ	Ⓒ		80.	Ⓐ	Ⓑ	Ⓒ		120.	Ⓐ	Ⓑ	Ⓒ

Exam 1
Morning Session

Questions 1 through 18 relate to Ethical and Professional Standards.
(27 minutes)

1. Phil Lich, CFA, has an anonymous social media account with the user name "CFAcharterholder." Lich wishes to enhance the market's perception of the price impact of his recommendations. He posts a message on the social media network that says, "Well-known analyst upgrading SmithCo today?" and later that day emails a research report to all his clients upgrading his recommendation on SmithCo to "Buy." Lich has *most likely* violated the Standards on:
    A. fair dealing and market manipulation.
    B. fair dealing and use of the CFA designation.
    C. market manipulation and use of the CFA designation.

2. While at dinner a member overhears a well-known and influential analyst from a different firm tell his companion that he will be raising his recommendation on Tree Products from hold to buy when he appears on a morning talk show the next day. Before the broadcast, the member buys 1,000 shares of Tree Products for her own account. The member has violated the Standard relating to:
    A. fair dealing.
    B. diligence and reasonable basis.
    C. material nonpublic information.

3. Allen Winkler, CFA, recently had lunch with Kim Thompson, a former professor of his, who told him of a new valuation model she had developed. Winkler recreated Thompson's model with some revisions and back-tested it using data provided by Standard & Poor's (S&P) with impressive results. Winkler's firm launches a mutual fund based on the revised model, and Winkler provides a discussion of the principles underlying the model and the test results. Is Winkler required to credit Thompson for having developed the model and S&P as the source of the data?
    A. Both of these sources must be cited.
    B. Neither of these sources must be cited.
    C. Only one of these sources must be cited.

4. Donald Smith, CFA, has been assigned by his employer to write a report for clients on Braden Corporation. Smith has 1,000 shares of Braden that he bought three years ago and has been discussing a consulting contract with Braden to write guidelines for their investor relations department. If Smith writes the report on Braden Corporation, he must disclose within the report:
   A. both his ownership of Braden shares and his prospective consulting work.
   B. and to his employer his prospective consulting work but not his ownership of Braden shares.
   C. his ownership of Braden shares but need only disclose his prospective consulting work to his employer.

5. Fran Lester, CFA, works for a broker based in a country in which participation in any IPO is permitted with her employer's permission. She lives and works in a country that has no restrictions on her participation in IPOs. If Lester's firm is distributing shares of an oversubscribed IPO through the office Lester works in, can Lester receive shares in the IPO?
   A. No, not under any circumstances.
   B. Yes, but she must obtain permission from her employer.
   C. Yes, because the applicable law is that of her home country.

6. Diane Harris, a CFA Institute member, is a portfolio manager for Worldwide Investments. One of her clients has offered her the use of his condominium in Hawaii if the returns on his U.S. equities account beat their benchmark on a risk-adjusted basis. Harris informed her manager of all terms of this agreement in writing and received verbal consent to the arrangement before accepting the offer. Did Harris violate the Standards?
   A. Yes, because written consent from her employer is required.
   B. No, because bonuses from clients for doing her job well do not create a conflict of interest.
   C. No, because Harris notified and received verbal consent from her employer to enter the arrangement.

7. American Securities wants to prepare a GIPS-compliant performance presentation. Which of the following is *least likely* compliant with GIPS? American Securities:
   A. calculates total firm assets using all fee-paying, non-fee-paying, discretionary, and client-directed accounts.
   B. only provides a compliant presentation to prospects who have not received one during the last 12 months.
   C. provides a compliant presentation for composites that the firm currently offers to clients, to any prospect who requests one.

©2014 Kaplan, Inc.

8. Betty Cantor, CFA, has been finishing a report on high-tech firm HLC Corporation and intends to give it a "market perform" rating. Before releasing the report, she speaks with Donald Watson, her former manager and mentor, who is now with another investment firm and is well known for his great calls on high-tech companies. Watson is bullish on HLC and tells Cantor that "HLC is going to increase for sure over the next year, and we have it as a buy." Cantor changes her rating on HLC to "outperform" based on Watson's comments. Cantor has:
   A. not violated the Standards because she knows the high quality of Watson's analysis.
   B. violated the Standards because she based her rating on material nonpublic information.
   C. violated the Standards because she does not have a reasonable basis for her recommendation.

9. Tom Hayes, CFA, changed firms recently, becoming the senior analyst at Balcom Management. He had earned a great reputation at his old firm with his analysis of Selldex, which doubled in value after his recommendation. Because he still likes Selldex, Hayes recreates from public sources the records and analysis he did at his previous employer and issues a report on Selldex with a "buy" rating. Hayes has:
   A. not violated the Standards.
   B. violated the Standards because the analysis he did for his previous employer belongs to his previous employer.
   C. violated the Standards because his analysis is based on previous research and not independent of his prior analysis.

10. The CFA Institute Code of Ethics *most likely* requires members and candidates to:
   A. not engage in activity which compromises the integrity of CFA Institute.
   B. stay informed on applicable laws and regulations that pertain to their respective areas of business.
   C. act with competence, integrity, and in ethical manner when dealing with the public, clients, employers, employees, and other market participants.

11. Craig Boone, CFA, a fixed-income trader, observes that one of the salesmen on the desk has been allocating his trades at the end of the day, giving better execution to large clients, a practice Boone suspects is illegal. The salesman tells Boone this is a common practice and that the firm's senior management is aware of it. If Boone makes a personal record of the activity, takes it home for his personal files, and subsequently reveals it to regulatory authorities, he would:
   A. not be in violation of any Standards.
   B. be in violation of the Standards for disclosing confidential information.
   C. be in violation of the Standards for breaching his duty of loyalty to his employer.

12. Lynn Black, CFA, is an analyst with the underwriter for an upcoming issue of Mtex Software debentures. Black learns from an employee in Mtex's programming department that there is a serious problem with Mtex's newest software program and that many customers have canceled their orders with Mtex. There is no mention of these problems in the prospectus for the debentures, which has been circulated. According to the CFA Institute Standards of Professional Conduct, Black's *best* course of action is to:
   A. inform her supervisor of her discovery.
   B. take no action because this is material nonpublic information.
   C. notify potential investors of the omission on a fair and equitable basis.

13. Sanctions that may be imposed on members by CFA Institute include:
   A. public censure, suspension of membership, and fines.
   B. suspension of membership, revocation of CFA charter, and fines.
   C. public censure, suspension of membership, and revocation of CFA charter.

14. Mary Walters, CFA, is a bank trust officer who has entered into a referral agreement with Bob Sear, a tax attorney. Sear has told Walters that he will do her tax work in return for referrals. According to the CFA Institute Code and Standards, Walters must disclose:
   A. only the fact that she compensated for referrals, to any clients or prospects she refers to Sear.
   B. only the fact that she is compensated for referrals, to her employer and any clients or prospects she refers to Sear.
   C. the fact that she is compensated for the referrals and the nature of the compensation she is to receive, to her employer and any clients or prospects she refers to Sear.

©2014 Kaplan, Inc.

15. Ronaldo Jenkins, CFA, chief investment officer for Windwatch Advisors, has been helping his local municipality find an investment bank for a bond issue. Jenkins was told in confidence that one investment bank, which is a subsidiary of a commercial bank held in Windwatch client portfolios, is experiencing financial difficulties and will be shut down soon. According to the CFA Institute Standards of Professional Conduct, Jenkins is *least likely* permitted to:
    A. share the information received about the investment bank with his compliance officer.
    B. share the information received about the investment bank with Windwatch's head of equity investments.
    C. approach the investment bank about making public disclosure of the financial difficulties and pending closure.

16. Lam Securities has managed domestic fixed income and equity accounts for many years. Recently they hired two experienced international equity portfolio managers from a firm with a great record of investment success. Mary Woods, CFA, prepares a new marketing piece for Lam, adding information about their international equities capabilities. She states that Lam has expertise in managing international equities and cites the top quartile performance of the new managers at their previous firm. It is *most likely* that Woods has violated the Standard regarding:
    A. fair dealing.
    B. misrepresentation.
    C. performance presentation.

17. While visiting Cassori Company, Mark Ramsey, CFA, overhears management make comments that are not public information but are not really meaningful by themselves. Combining this information with his own analysis and other outside sources, Ramsey decides to change his recommendation on Cassori from "Buy" to "Sell." According to the CFA Institute Standards of Professional Conduct, Ramsey:
    A. must not issue his report until Cassori's management makes their comments public.
    B. may issue his "Sell" report because the facts are nonmaterial, but should maintain a file of the facts and documents leading to this conclusion.
    C. must report these events to his immediate supervisor and legal counsel, since they have become material in combination with his analysis.

18.   Compliance with the Global Investment Performance Standards *least likely* requires firms to:
       A. include all fee-paying and non-fee-paying accounts in at least one composite.
       B. document in writing the policies and procedures used to comply with GIPS.
       C. specifically define what constitutes the firm that is claiming compliance.

Questions 19 through 32 relate to Quantitative Methods. (21 minutes)

19.   Jim Franklin recently purchased a home for $300,000 on which he made a down payment of $100,000. He obtained a 30-year mortgage to finance the balance on which he pays a fixed annual rate of 6%. If he makes regular, fixed monthly payments, what loan balance will remain just after the 48th payment?
       A. $186,109.
       B. $189,229.
       C. $192,444.

20.   An investor purchased a $10,000, 5-year corporate note one year ago for $10,440. The note pays an annual coupon of $600. Over the past year, the note's annual yield-to-maturity has dropped by 1%. What total return did the investor earn over the year?
       A. 8.5%.
       B. 9.0%.
       C. 9.5%.

21.   An investor holds a portfolio consisting of one share of each of the following stocks:

Stock	Price at the Beginning of the Year	Price at the End of the Year	Cash Dividend During the Year
A	$10	$20	$0
B	$50	$60	$1
C	$100	$110	$4

       For the 1-year holding period, the portfolio total return is *closest* to:
       A. 15.79%.
       B. 18.42%.
       C. 21.88%.

  ©2014 Kaplan, Inc.

22. Which of the following measurement scales provides the *least* information?
   A. Ratio.
   B. Ordinal.
   C. Nominal.

23. An analyst observes the following four annual returns: $R_1 = +10\%$, $R_2 = -15\%$, $R_3 = 0\%$, and $R_4 = +5\%$. The average compound annual rate over the four years is *closest* to:
   A. −5.0%.
   B. −0.5%.
   C. 0.0%.

24. Given the observations 45, 20, 30, and 25, the mean absolute deviation is *closest* to:
   A. 0.0.
   B. 7.5.
   C. 13.3.

25. An investor wants to buy a condominium in Florida. The value of her portfolio is currently $1,000,000, and she needs $100,000 in one year for the down payment. She doesn't mind decreasing her capital as long she has $950,000 remaining in her portfolio after the down payment is made. She is considering two new portfolios for her holdings. The details on the two portfolios are:

	Expected Annual Return	Standard Deviation of Returns
Portfolio 1	17%	15%
Portfolio 2	12%	10%
Portfolio 3	8%	6%

According to Roy's Safety-First criterion, the portfolio she would prefer is:
   A. Portfolio 1.
   B. Portfolio 2.
   C. Portfolio 3.

26. A technical analyst is *most likely* to expect an uptrend in prices to continue if:
   A. converging trendlines form a triangle pattern on a price chart.
   B. the 14-day relative strength index increases from 70 to 80.
   C. the uptrend line acts as a resistance level when the price approaches it.

27. Adam Farman has been asked to estimate the volatility of a technology stock index. He has identified a statistic which has an expected value equal to the population volatility and has determined that increasing his sample size will decrease the sampling error for this statistic. Based only on these properties, his statistic can *best* be described as:
   A. unbiased and efficient.
   B. unbiased and consistent.
   C. efficient and consistent.

28. According to Chebyshev's inequality, the minimum proportion of observations falling within three standard deviations of the mean for a negatively skewed distribution is *closest* to:
   A. 68%.
   B. 75%.
   C. 89%.

29. The following table summarizes the results of a poll taken of CEOs and analysts about the economic impact of a pending piece of legislation:

Group	Number of Respondents who Predict Positive Impact	Number of Respondents who Predict Negative Impact
CEOs	40	30
Analysts	70	60

   What is the probability that a randomly selected individual from this group will be either an analyst or someone who thinks this legislation will have a positive impact on the economy?
   A. 0.75.
   B. 0.80.
   C. 0.85.

30. A researcher has investigated the returns over the last five years to a long-short strategy based on mean reversion in equity returns volatility. His hypothesis test led to rejection of the hypothesis that abnormal (risk-adjusted) returns to the strategy over the period were less than or equal to zero at the 1% level of significance. He would *most* appropriately decide that:
   A. his firm should employ the strategy for client accounts because the abnormal returns are positive and statistically significant.
   B. while the abnormal returns are highly significant statistically, they may not be economically meaningful.
   C. as long as the estimated statistical returns are greater than the transactions costs of the strategy, his firm should employ the strategy for client accounts.

©2014 Kaplan, Inc.

31.   An analyst decides to select 10 stocks for her portfolio by placing
       the ticker symbols for all the stocks traded on the New York Stock
       Exchange in a large bowl. She randomly selects 20 stocks and will put
       every other one chosen into her 10-stock portfolio. The analyst used:
       A. dual random sampling.
       B. simple random sampling.
       C. stratified random sampling.

32.   Which of the following tests would generally be considered a
       nonparametric test?
       A. Whether a sample is random or not.
       B. Large sample test of the value of a population mean.
       C. Value of the variance of a normal population.

Questions 33 through 44 relate to Economics. (18 minutes)

33.   Assume the exchange rate between the Trotter (TRT) and the Roeckl
       (RKL) is 5.50 TRT/RKL and the exchange rate between the Roeckl and
       the Passage (PSG) is 8.00 RKL/PSG. The cross rate between the PSG
       and the TRT is *closest* to:
       A. 0.0227 PSG/TRT.
       B. 0.6875 PSG/TRT.
       C. 44.00 PSG/TRT.

34.   Which of the following statements about methods of calculating gross
       domestic product is *most accurate*?
       A. Except for a statistical discrepancy, the income and expenditure
           approaches to calculating GDP should result in the same value for
           economic output.
       B. Because it includes activity at all stages of production, the sum-
           of-value-added method results in a better estimate of GDP than the
           value-of-final-output method.
       C. Value-of-final-output is used to calculate GDP under the
           expenditure approach, while sum-of-value-added is used to
           calculate GDP under the income approach.

35.   The J-curve, in the context of trade between two countries, refers to the
       fact that when the domestic country has a trade deficit:
       A. appreciation of the domestic currency initially leads to a decrease
           in the trade deficit but will increase the trade deficit in the long
           term.
       B. an increase in domestic inflation will initially increase the trade
           deficit but will decrease the trade deficit in the long term.
       C. appreciation of the foreign currency will initially increase the trade
           deficit but will decrease the trade deficit in the long term.

36. Which of the following organizations is the *most* focused on promoting economic growth and reducing poverty by offering both monetary and technical assistance?
   A. World Bank.
   B. World Trade Organization.
   C. International Monetary Fund.

37. The quantity theory of money states that in a full employment economy, any increase in the supply of money in excess of the rate of growth of real GDP will lead to a proportional increase in:
   A. the price level.
   B. velocity.
   C. real GDP.

38. Akor is a country that has chosen to use a conventional fixed peg arrangement as the country's exchange rate regime. Under this arrangement, Akor's exchange rate against the currency to which it pegs:
   A. is market-determined.
   B. will be equal to the peg rate.
   C. may fluctuate around the peg rate.

39. The supply function for a good is: quantity supplied = $-170 + 10 \times$ price. If the market price is 25, the value of producer surplus is:
   A. 320.
   B. 640.
   C. 2,000.

40. Which of the following statements about a monopolist is *most accurate*? A monopolist will:
   A. maximize the average profit per unit sold.
   B. charge the highest price for which it can sell its product.
   C. produce where marginal revenue equals marginal cost.

41. Assume that the supply of ethanol is relatively more elastic than the demand for ethanol. Compared to an initial competitive equilibrium in the market for ethanol, the imposition of a per-gallon tax on producers of ethanol will *most likely* decrease:
   A. producer surplus by the total amount of tax collected.
   B. producer surplus by less than it reduces consumer surplus.
   C. the sum of consumer and producer surplus by the amount of tax collected.

42. Under what conditions is inflation *most likely* to shift wealth from lenders to borrowers?
   A. Only when inflation is unexpected.
   B. Only when inflation is unexpected and negative.
   C. When inflation is either unexpected or expected.

©2014 Kaplan, Inc.

43. The short-run supply curve for a firm under perfect competition is the firm's:
    A. marginal cost curve above average total cost.
    B. marginal cost curve above average variable cost.
    C. average variable cost curve above marginal revenue.

44. Long-run aggregate supply is *least likely* to be affected by changes in the:
    A. prices of raw materials inputs.
    B. quantity of labor in the economy.
    C. level of technology.

Questions 45 through 68 relate to Financial Reporting and Analysis. (36 minutes)

45. In accrual accounting, the matching principle states that:
    A. an entity should recognize revenues only when received and expenses only when they are paid.
    B. transactions and events producing cash flows are allocated only to time periods in which the cash flows occur.
    C. expenses incurred to generate revenue are recognized in the same time period as the revenue.

46. Which of the following statements about revenue recognition methods is *most accurate*?
    A. The completed contract method under U.S. GAAP recognizes long-term contract revenue only as each phase of production is complete.
    B. The percentage of completion method recognizes profit corresponding to the costs incurred as a proportion of estimated total costs.
    C. The installment method recognizes sales when cash is received, but no profit is recognized until cash collected exceeds costs.

47. The independent auditors of Shadydells, Inc., have determined that the company recorded operating leases that should have been capitalized. This is considered to be a material instance of noncompliance with applicable GAAP, but the financial statements are otherwise fairly presented. Which opinion are the auditors *most likely* to issue?
    A. Adverse opinion.
    B. Qualified opinion.
    C. Unqualified opinion.

48. Which of the following transactions increases contributed capital on the balance sheet but does not increase shareholders' equity?
    A. Issuing preferred stock.
    B. Declaring a stock dividend.
    C. Increasing authorized shares.

49. An analyst gathers the following information:
    - Net income $100
    - Decrease in accounts receivable   30
    - Depreciation   25
    - Increase in inventory   17
    - Increase in accounts payable   10
    - Decrease in wages payable   5
    - Increase in deferred taxes   17
    - Sale of fixed assets   150
    - Purchase of fixed assets   340
    - Profit from the sale of fixed assets   5
    - Dividends paid out   35
    - Sale of new common stock   120

    Based on the above information, the company's cash flow from operations under U.S. GAAP is:
    A. $155.
    B. $165.
    C. $182.

50. Which of the following statements about cash flow is *least accurate*? Under U.S. GAAP, cash flow from:
    A. operations includes cash operating expenses and changes in working capital accounts.
    B. financing includes the proceeds of debt issued and from the sale of the company's common stock.
    C. investing includes interest income from investment in debt securities.

51. An analyst gathered the following data about a company:
    - The company had 500,000 shares of common stock outstanding for the entire year.
    - The company's beginning stock price was $40, its ending price was $60, and its average price over the year was $50.
    - The company has 120,000 warrants outstanding for the entire year.
    - Each warrant allows the holder to buy one share of common stock at $45 per share.

    How many shares of common stock should the company use in computing its diluted earnings per share?
    A. 488,000.
    B. 500,000.
    C. 512,000.

©2014 Kaplan, Inc.

52. Books Forever, Inc., uses short-term bank debt to buy inventory. Assuming an initial current ratio that is greater than 1, and an initial quick (or acid test) ratio that is less than 1, what is the effect of these transactions on the current ratio and the quick ratio?
    A. Both ratios will decrease.
    B. Neither ratio will decrease.
    C. Only one ratio will decrease.

53. Which of the following statements regarding the financial statement reporting of leases is *most accurate*?
    A. Under an operating lease, the lessee treats the entire lease payment as a cash outflow from operations.
    B. The lessee's current ratio is the same whether a lease is treated as an operating or finance lease.
    C. At the inception of a direct financing lease, the lessor recognizes gross profit.

54. Which of the following statements about expenses and intangible assets is *least accurate*?
    A. Advertising fees are generally expensed as incurred.
    B. In most countries, research and development costs are capitalized.
    C. Intangible assets are initially entered on the balance sheet at their purchase prices when they are acquired from an outside entity.

55. Which of the following accounting practices is *most likely* to decrease reported earnings in the current period?
    A. Using the straight-line method of depreciation instead of an accelerated method.
    B. Capitalizing advertising expenses rather than expensing them in the current period.
    C. Using LIFO inventory cost methods during a period of rising prices.

56. Which of the following statements about dilutive securities is *most accurate*?
    A. A simple capital structure is one that contains only common stock and antidilutive securities.
    B. A dilutive security is one that will cause earnings per share to decrease if it is converted into common stock.
    C. Warrants are antidilutive if their exercise price is less than the stock price at the end of the period.

57. As of January 1, a company had 22,500 $10 par value common shares outstanding. On July 1, the company repurchased 5,000 shares. The company also has 11,000, 10%, $100 par value preferred shares. If the company's net income is $210,000, its diluted earnings per share is *closest* to:
    A. $5.00.
    B. $7.50.
    C. $10.00.

58. In periods of rising prices and stable or increasing inventory quantities, compared with companies that use LIFO inventory accounting, companies that use the FIFO method will have:
    A. higher COGS and lower taxes.
    B. higher net income and higher taxes.
    C. lower inventory balances and lower working capital.

59. Rowlin Corporation, which reports under IFRS, wrote down its inventory of electronic parts last period from its original cost of €28,000 to net realizable value of €25,000. This period, inventory at net realizable value has increased to €30,000. Rowlin should revalue this inventory to:
    A. €28,000 and report a gain of €3,000 on the income statement.
    B. €30,000 and report a gain of €3,000 on the income statement.
    C. €30,000 and report a gain of €5,000 on the income statement.

60. Under IFRS, remeasurements related to defined benefit pension plans are initially recognized in:
    A. net income in the current period.
    B. other comprehensive income and are not amortized to income.
    C. other comprehensive income and amortized over time to income.

61. During a period when net income is unexpectedly weak, managers who attempt to smooth earnings are *most likely* to:
    A. capitalize an expense.
    B. capitalize a new lease.
    C. classify a nonrecurring gain as recurring income.

62. Which of the following definitions used in accounting for income taxes is *least accurate*?
    A. Income tax expense is current period taxes payable adjusted for any changes in deferred tax assets and liabilities.
    B. A valuation allowance is a reserve against deferred tax assets based on the likelihood that those assets will not be realized.
    C. A deferred tax liability is created when tax expense is less than taxes payable and the difference is expected to reverse in future years.

©2014 Kaplan, Inc.

63. From the extended (5-part) DuPont equation, which of the following components describes the equation EBT / EBIT?
    A. Tax burden.
    B. Interest burden.
    C. Financial leverage.

64. Under U.S. GAAP, which of the following statements about the financial statement effects of issuing bonds is *least accurate*?
    A. Issuance of debt has no effect on cash flow from operations.
    B. Periodic interest payments decrease cash flow from operations by the amount of interest paid.
    C. Payment of debt at maturity decreases cash flow from operations by the face value of the debt.

65. When an increase in the tax rate is enacted, deferred tax:
    A. assets and liabilities both increase in value.
    B. assets decrease in value and deferred tax liabilities increase in value.
    C. liability and asset accounts are maintained at historical tax rates until they reverse.

66. A manufacturing firm shuts down production at one of its plants and offers the facility for rent. Based on the market for similar properties, the firm determines that the fair value of the plant is €500,000 more than its original cost. If this firm uses the cost model for plant and equipment and the fair value model for investment property, should it recognize a gain on its income statement?
    A. Yes, because the plant will be reclassified as investment property.
    B. No, because the increase in value does not reverse a previously recognized loss.
    C. No, because the firm must continue to use the cost model for valuation of this asset.

67. Under U.S. GAAP, an asset is considered impaired if its book value is:
    A. less than its market value.
    B. greater than the present value of its expected future cash flows.
    C. greater than the sum of its undiscounted expected cash flows.

68. Which of the following pairs of general categories are *least likely* to be considered in the formulas used by credit rating agencies to determine the capacity of a borrower to repay a debt?
    A. Operational efficiency; leverage.
    B. Margin stability; availability of collateral.
    C. Leverage; scale and diversification.

Questions 69 through 76 relate to Corporate Finance. (12 minutes)

69. Which of the following statements about the component costs of capital is *least accurate*?
    A. The cost of common equity is the required rate of return on common stock.
    B. The cost of preferred stock is the preferred dividend divided by the preferred's par value.
    C. The after-tax cost of debt is based on the expected yield to maturity on newly issued debt.

70. Project X has an internal rate of return (IRR) of 14%. Project Y has an IRR of 17%. Both projects have conventional cash flow patterns (all inflows after the initial cash outflow). If the required rate of return is:
    A. 14%, the net present value (NPV) of Project Y will exceed the NPV of Project X.
    B. greater than 17%, Project Y will have a shorter payback period than Project X.
    C. 10%, both projects will have a positive NPV, and the NPV of Project Y will exceed the NPV of Project X.

71. AlcoBanc owns a piece of property that is under consideration for a new bank branch. Which of the following is *least likely* a relevant incremental cash flow in analyzing a capital budgeting project? The:
    A. interest costs of a loan for the property purchase.
    B. business gained at other branches due to new customers at the proposed site.
    C. $150,000 AlcoBanc could get if they sold the property instead of building a new branch.

72. Jay Construction Company is considering whether to accept a new bridge-building project. Jay will use the pure-play method to estimate the cost of capital for the project, using Cass Bridge Builders as a comparable company. To calculate the project beta, Jay should:
    A. estimate Cass's cost of equity capital and apply it to the project.
    B. use the CAPM equation, substituting Cass's equity beta for its own.
    C. adjust Cass's equity beta for any difference in leverage between Cass and Jay.

73. Which of the following would *most likely* indicate deterioration of a firm's working capital management?
    A. An increase in days of payables outstanding.
    B. An increase in days of receivables outstanding.
    C. A decreased amount of cash and cash equivalents.

74. Which of the following is *least likely* an important requirement of good corporate governance?
   A. Members of the board should serve staggered, multiple-year terms.
   B. A board should be composed of at least a majority of independent board members.
   C. Board members should have appropriate experience and expertise relevant to the company's business.

75. Pannonia Enterprises, Inc. (PEI) has a target capital structure of 40% debt with 60% equity. PEI's pretax cost of debt will remain at 9% until the firm raises more than $200,000 in new debt capital, at which point its pretax cost of debt will increase to 9.5%. PEI's cost of equity will increase when more than $400,000 in equity capital is raised. PEI's break point for debt capital is *closest* to:
   A. $200,000.
   B. $500,000.
   C. $666,667.

76. For a profitable company, issuing debt in order to retire common stock will *most likely*:
   A. increase both net income and return on equity.
   B. decrease both operating income and net income.
   C. increase both the level and variability of return on equity.

Questions 77 through 85 relate to Portfolio Management. (13.5 minutes)

77. An investment advisor constructs a portfolio that plots on the capital market line but has less risk and a lower return than the market portfolio. This portfolio is *most accurately* described as a(n):
   A. lending portfolio.
   B. leveraged portfolio.
   C. inefficient portfolio.

78. Smith has more steeply sloped risk-return indifference curves than Jones. Assuming these investors have the same expectations, which of the following *best* describes their risk preferences and the characteristics of their optimal portfolios? Smith is:
   A. less risk averse than Jones and will choose an optimal portfolio with a lower expected return.
   B. more risk averse than Jones and will choose an optimal portfolio with a lower expected return.
   C. more risk averse than Jones and will choose an optimal portfolio with a higher expected return.

79. A stock has a beta of 0.9 and an estimated return of 10%. The risk-free rate is 7%, and the expected return on the market is 11%. According to the CAPM, this stock:
   A. is overvalued.
   B. is undervalued.
   C. is properly valued.

80. An analyst gathers the following data about the returns for two stocks.

	Stock A	Stock B
E(R)	0.04	0.09
σ^2	0.0025	0.0064

$Cov_{A,B} = 0.001$

The correlation between the returns of Stock A and Stock B ($\rho_{A,B}$) is *closest* to:

A. 0.25.
B. 0.50.
C. 0.63.

81. In which step of the portfolio management process does an investment manager rebalance the portfolio to its target asset allocation percentages?
   A. Analysis step.
   B. Feedback step.
   C. Execution step.

82. Which of the following possible portfolios cannot lie on the efficient frontier?

Portfolio	Expected Return	Standard Deviation
1	8%	6%
2	10%	6%
3	14%	12%
4	14%	16%

A. Portfolio 3 only.
B. Portfolios 1 and 4.
C. Portfolios 2 and 3.

©2014 Kaplan, Inc.

83. Which of the following pairs refer to the same type of risk?
    A. Total risk and the variance of returns.
    B. Systematic risk and firm-specific risk.
    C. Undiversifiable risk and unsystematic risk.

84. Greenbaum, Inc. stock pays no dividend and currently trades at $54. Based on the CAPM and assuming an expected return on the market of 12% and a risk-free rate of 8%, the expected price for Greenbaum one year from now is $62. The beta of Greenbaum shares is *closest* to:
    A. 1.5.
    B. 1.6.
    C. 1.7.

85. A primary reason for developing a strategic asset allocation is to:
    A. minimize a portfolio's exposure to systematic risk.
    B. prevent the overweighting of any single asset classes.
    C. determine asset classes offering unique risk and return profiles with low correlations to one another.

Questions 86 through 97 relate to Equity Investments. (18 minutes)

86. A financial market is said to be operationally efficient if:
    A. transactions costs are low.
    B. prices adjust quickly to new information.
    C. it results in resources being allocated to their most productive uses.

87. The weak form of the efficient market hypothesis (EMH) implies that:
    A. no one can achieve abnormal returns using market information.
    B. insiders, such as specialists and corporate board members, cannot achieve abnormal returns on average.
    C. investors cannot achieve abnormal returns, on average, using technical analysis, after adjusting for transaction costs and taxes.

88. Which of the following statements about alternative investment indexes is *most accurate*?
    A. An investor can replicate a commodity index by making direct investments in the underlying physical commodities.
    B. Real Estate Investment Trust indexes track the prices of shares of publicly traded companies that invest in mortgages or real property.
    C. Hedge fund indexes accurately represent the investment performance of the hedge fund industry.

89. The present value of an equity security's future cash flows is *most likely* to be significantly different from the company's:
    A. book value per share.
    B. market value per share.
    C. intrinsic value per share.

90.   An analyst is valuing a company's perpetual preferred stock that pays
       a $6 annual dividend. The company's bonds currently yield 7.5%
       and preferred shares are selling to yield 75 basis points below the
       company's bond yield. The value of the preferred stock is *closest* to:
       A. $72.
       B. $80.
       C. $89.

91.   An investor buys a stock at $32 a share and deposits 50% initial
       margin. Assume that the maintenance margin is 25%, the stock pays
       no dividends, and transaction costs and interest on the margin loan are
       zero. The price at which the investor would receive a margin call is
       closest to:
       A. $16.
       B. $21.
       C. $24.

92.   The risk-free rate is 5%, and the expected return on the market index is
       15%. A stock has a:
       •   Beta of 1.0.
       •   Dividend payout ratio of 40%.
       •   Return on equity (ROE) of 15%.

       If the stock is expected to pay a $2.50 dividend, its intrinsic value
       using dividend discount model is *closest* to:
       A. $27.77.
       B. $41.67.
       C. $53.33.

93.   Which of the following industries is *best* described as non-cyclical and
       defensive?
       A. Energy.
       B. Technology.
       C. Consumer staples.

94.   Which of the following scenarios is inconsistent with efficient financial
       markets?
       A. An analyst's buy recommendations have returned 2% more than the
          broad market index, on average.
       B. Johnson, Inc. reports an increase of 8% in its earnings from a year
          earlier, and its stock price declines 5% on the news.
       C. Earl Baker, an investor, earns consistently superior risk-adjusted
          returns by buying stocks when most investment advisors are
          pessimistic and selling stocks when most investment advisors are
          optimistic.

                    ©2014 Kaplan, Inc.

95. The holder of the type of security that has a priority in liquidation less than that of bonds or promissory notes issued by the company but ahead of that of common stock is *most likely* to have:
    A. no voting rights.
    B. statutory voting rights.
    C. cumulative voting rights.

96. Transactions costs incurred from portfolio rebalancing are *most likely* to be highest for funds that track:
    A. price-weighted indexes.
    B. value-weighted indexes.
    C. equal-weighted indexes.

97. A stock that currently does not pay a dividend is expected to pay its first dividend of $1.00 five years from today. Thereafter, the dividend is expected to grow at an annual rate of 25% for the next three years and then grow at a constant rate of 5% per year thereafter. The required rate of return is 10.3%. The value of the stock today is *closest* to:
    A. $20.65.
    B. $22.72.
    C. $23.87.

Questions 98 through 109 relate to Fixed Income. (18 minutes)

98. Asset-backed securities (ABS) may have a higher credit rating than the seller's corporate bonds because:
    A. the special purpose vehicle is a separate entity.
    B. the seller's ABS are senior to its corporate bonds.
    C. ABS are investment grade while corporate bonds may be speculative grade.

99. All else equal, which of the following is *least likely* to increase the interest rate risk of a bond?
    A. A longer maturity.
    B. Inclusion of a call feature.
    C. A decrease in the YTM.

100. One year ago, an investor purchased a 10-year, $1,000 par value, 8% semiannual coupon bond with an 8% yield to maturity. Now, one year later, interest rates remain unchanged at 8%. If the investor sells the bond today (immediately after receiving the second coupon payment, and with no transaction costs), he will have:
    A. a capital gain of $80.
    B. a capital loss of $80.
    C. no capital gain or loss.

101. Which of the following assets is *most likely* to represent high-quality collateral in credit analysis?
    A. Goodwill.
    B. Trademarks.
    C. Deferred tax assets.

102. A company has two $1,000 face value bonds outstanding both selling for $701.22. The first issue has an annual coupon of 8% and 20 years to maturity. The second bond has the same yield to maturity as the first bond but has only five years remaining until maturity. The second issue pays interest annually as well. What is the annual interest payment on the second issue?
    A. $18.56.
    B. $27.18.
    C. $37.12.

103. If a bond has a convexity of 120 and a modified duration of 10, the convexity adjustment (to a duration-based approximation) associated with a 25 basis point interest rate decline is *closest* to:
    A. −2.875%.
    B. −2.125%.
    C. +0.0375%.

104. Recent economic data suggest an increasing likelihood that the economy will soon enter a recessionary phase. What is the *most likely* effect on the yields of lower-quality corporate bonds and on credit spreads of lower-quality versus higher-quality corporate bonds?
    A. Both will increase.
    B. Both will decrease.
    C. One will increase and one will decrease.

105. A supranational bond:
    A. is issued by a multilateral agency.
    B. trades outside the jurisdiction of any one country.
    C. pays coupons in a different currency than its principal.

106. If an investor wants only investment grade bonds in her portfolio, she would be *least likely* to purchase a:
    A. 2-year municipal bond rated A−.
    B. 3-year municipal bond rated BB.
    C. 15-year, semiannual coupon corporate bond rated BBB.

107. If the yield curve is downward-sloping, the no-arbitrage value of a bond calculated using spot rates will be:
    A. equal to the market price of the bond.
    B. less than the market price of the bond.
    C. greater than the market price of the bond.

©2014 Kaplan, Inc.

108. Changes in a fixed-coupon bond's cash flows associated with changes in yield would be reflected in the bond's:
    A. effective duration.
    B. modified duration.
    C. Macaulay duration.

109. Four non-convertible bonds have the indicated yield spreads to Treasury securities:

	Maturity	Government Spread	Zero-Volatility Spread	Option-Adjusted Spread
Bond W	2 years	156 bp	155 bp	130 bp
Bond X	3 years	173 bp	174 bp	199 bp
Bond Y	5 years	188 bp	189 bp	164 bp
Bond Z	10 years	202 bp	201 bp	226 bp

Based on these spreads, it is *most likely* that:
A. Bond X is callable, and Bond Y is putable.
B. Bond W is callable, and Bond Z is putable.
C. Bond Z is callable, and the spot yield curve is inverted.

Questions 110 through 115 relate to Derivatives. (9 minutes)

110. An analyst using a one-period binomial model calculates a probability-weighted average of an option's values following an up-move or a down-move. According to this model, this average is *most likely*:
    A. equal to the option's value today.
    B. less than the option's value today.
    C. greater than the option's value today.

111. Three months ago, Jen Baker purchased one American put option contract on Mechor Corporation for $4 per option share. Baker also owns 100 shares of Mechor. The following data applies to Baker's position:
    • Option strike price $60
    • Stock price on date of option purchase $60
    • Stock price today $52
    • Time to option expiry from today   1 month

    Given only the above data, if Baker exercises her option today, the profit/loss (from the date of the option purchase) on Baker's combined stock/put position is:
    A. −$800.
    B. −$400.
    C. $800.

112. Two Level I CFA candidates are discussing futures and make the following statements:

    Candidate 1: Futures are traded using standardized contracts. They require margin and incur interest charges on the margin loan.

    Candidate 2: If the margin balance falls below the maintenance margin amount due to a change in the contract price for the underlying assets, the investor must add funds to bring the margin back up to the initial margin requirement.

    Are the candidates' statements correct or incorrect?
    A. Both statements are correct.
    B. Neither statement is correct.
    C. Only one of the statements is correct.

113. Which of the following statements for puts at expiration is *least accurate*? The:
    A. put buyer's maximum loss is the put option's premium.
    B. maximum loss to the writer of a put is the strike price less the premium.
    C. put holder will exercise the option whenever the stock's price is greater than the exercise price.

114. At initiation of a forward contract and a futures contract with identical terms, their prices are *most likely* to be different if:
    A. the spot price is highly volatile.
    B. the forward contract is marked to market daily.
    C. short-term interest rates are negatively correlated with futures prices.

115. Other things equal, a decrease in the value of a put option on a stock is *most likely* consistent with which of the following changes in the risk-free rate and stock return volatility?

	Risk-free rate	Volatility
A.	Increase	Decrease
B.	Decrease	Increase
C.	Decrease	Decrease

Questions 116 through 120 relate to Alternative Investments. (7.5 minutes)

116. Return and risk data on alternative investments may be affected by backfill bias if:
    A. data only include currently existing firms.
    B. the incorrect distribution is used to model volatility.
    C. previous performance data for firms added to a benchmark index is included.

©2014 Kaplan, Inc.

117. Which of the following strategies is *most likely* to be pursued by a private equity fund?
    A. Use debt financing to acquire control of a publicly traded firm.
    B. Buy convertible bonds and sell short the equity of the bond issuer.
    C. Influence a firm's policies by gaining a seat on its board of directors.

118. Which of the following is *least likely* a type of hedge fund strategy?
    A. Event-driven.
    B. Market-neutral.
    C. Exchange-traded.

119. Compared with purchasing commodities, long positions in commodity derivatives offer the benefit of:
    A. no storage costs.
    B. convenience yield.
    C. better correlation with spot prices.

120. Returns on which of the following alternative investments are *most likely* to include a liquidity premium?
    A. Private equity funds.
    B. Commodity-linked ETFs.
    C. Real estate investment trusts.

Exam 1
Afternoon Session

Calculating Your Score

Topic	Maximum Score	Your Score
Ethical and Professional Standards	18	
Quantitative Methods	14	
Economics	12	
Financial Reporting and Analysis	24	
Corporate Finance	9	
Portfolio Management	8	
Equity Investments	12	
Fixed Income	12	
Derivatives	6	
Alternative Investments	5	
Total	120	

The morning and afternoon exams are identically weighted over the topics and readings. You can therefore treat the morning and afternoon exams as independent exams.

If you took more than three hours (180 minutes) to complete this portion of the exam, you should adjust your score downward by one point for each minute you ran over.

Remember: the real exam *will be more difficult* than these practice exams. The main reason for this is the general anxiety and stress that you will be feeling on exam day, coupled with the time pressure you will be under. Many of the questions on this practice exam and the real exam are not individually difficult, so if you take extra time to answer the questions on this practice exam, your score will go up significantly. However, if you want an accurate measure of your potential performance on the exam, adhere to the 3-hour time limit.

After you have finished grading your practice exam, you may find it useful to use the exam questions and recommended solutions for review. Many of these questions were specifically written for your use as study tools. Once again, I feel I should remind you not to rely on memorizing these questions; you are not likely to see them on the actual exam. What you will see on the exam, though, are the concepts, terms, and procedures presented in these questions.

Your actual exam will most likely look different than what you see in this book. Please remember, no study provider knows the content of the actual exam. These practice exams are our best guess as to the structure, content, and difficulty of an actual exam.

Test Answers

1.	Ⓐ	Ⓑ	Ⓒ	41.	Ⓐ	Ⓑ	Ⓒ	81.	Ⓐ	Ⓑ	Ⓒ
2.	Ⓐ	Ⓑ	Ⓒ	42.	Ⓐ	Ⓑ	Ⓒ	82.	Ⓐ	Ⓑ	Ⓒ
3.	Ⓐ	Ⓑ	Ⓒ	43.	Ⓐ	Ⓑ	Ⓒ	83.	Ⓐ	Ⓑ	Ⓒ
4.	Ⓐ	Ⓑ	Ⓒ	44.	Ⓐ	Ⓑ	Ⓒ	84.	Ⓐ	Ⓑ	Ⓒ
5.	Ⓐ	Ⓑ	Ⓒ	45.	Ⓐ	Ⓑ	Ⓒ	85.	Ⓐ	Ⓑ	Ⓒ
6.	Ⓐ	Ⓑ	Ⓒ	46.	Ⓐ	Ⓑ	Ⓒ	86.	Ⓐ	Ⓑ	Ⓒ
7.	Ⓐ	Ⓑ	Ⓒ	47.	Ⓐ	Ⓑ	Ⓒ	87.	Ⓐ	Ⓑ	Ⓒ
8.	Ⓐ	Ⓑ	Ⓒ	48.	Ⓐ	Ⓑ	Ⓒ	88.	Ⓐ	Ⓑ	Ⓒ
9.	Ⓐ	Ⓑ	Ⓒ	49.	Ⓐ	Ⓑ	Ⓒ	89.	Ⓐ	Ⓑ	Ⓒ
10.	Ⓐ	Ⓑ	Ⓒ	50.	Ⓐ	Ⓑ	Ⓒ	90.	Ⓐ	Ⓑ	Ⓒ
11.	Ⓐ	Ⓑ	Ⓒ	51.	Ⓐ	Ⓑ	Ⓒ	91.	Ⓐ	Ⓑ	Ⓒ
12.	Ⓐ	Ⓑ	Ⓒ	52.	Ⓐ	Ⓑ	Ⓒ	92.	Ⓐ	Ⓑ	Ⓒ
13.	Ⓐ	Ⓑ	Ⓒ	53.	Ⓐ	Ⓑ	Ⓒ	93.	Ⓐ	Ⓑ	Ⓒ
14.	Ⓐ	Ⓑ	Ⓒ	54.	Ⓐ	Ⓑ	Ⓒ	94.	Ⓐ	Ⓑ	Ⓒ
15.	Ⓐ	Ⓑ	Ⓒ	55.	Ⓐ	Ⓑ	Ⓒ	95.	Ⓐ	Ⓑ	Ⓒ
16.	Ⓐ	Ⓑ	Ⓒ	56.	Ⓐ	Ⓑ	Ⓒ	96.	Ⓐ	Ⓑ	Ⓒ
17.	Ⓐ	Ⓑ	Ⓒ	57.	Ⓐ	Ⓑ	Ⓒ	97.	Ⓐ	Ⓑ	Ⓒ
18.	Ⓐ	Ⓑ	Ⓒ	58.	Ⓐ	Ⓑ	Ⓒ	98.	Ⓐ	Ⓑ	Ⓒ
19.	Ⓐ	Ⓑ	Ⓒ	59.	Ⓐ	Ⓑ	Ⓒ	99.	Ⓐ	Ⓑ	Ⓒ
20.	Ⓐ	Ⓑ	Ⓒ	60.	Ⓐ	Ⓑ	Ⓒ	100.	Ⓐ	Ⓑ	Ⓒ
21.	Ⓐ	Ⓑ	Ⓒ	61.	Ⓐ	Ⓑ	Ⓒ	101.	Ⓐ	Ⓑ	Ⓒ
22.	Ⓐ	Ⓑ	Ⓒ	62.	Ⓐ	Ⓑ	Ⓒ	102.	Ⓐ	Ⓑ	Ⓒ
23.	Ⓐ	Ⓑ	Ⓒ	63.	Ⓐ	Ⓑ	Ⓒ	103.	Ⓐ	Ⓑ	Ⓒ
24.	Ⓐ	Ⓑ	Ⓒ	64.	Ⓐ	Ⓑ	Ⓒ	104.	Ⓐ	Ⓑ	Ⓒ
25.	Ⓐ	Ⓑ	Ⓒ	65.	Ⓐ	Ⓑ	Ⓒ	105.	Ⓐ	Ⓑ	Ⓒ
26.	Ⓐ	Ⓑ	Ⓒ	66.	Ⓐ	Ⓑ	Ⓒ	106.	Ⓐ	Ⓑ	Ⓒ
27.	Ⓐ	Ⓑ	Ⓒ	67.	Ⓐ	Ⓑ	Ⓒ	107.	Ⓐ	Ⓑ	Ⓒ
28.	Ⓐ	Ⓑ	Ⓒ	68.	Ⓐ	Ⓑ	Ⓒ	108.	Ⓐ	Ⓑ	Ⓒ
29.	Ⓐ	Ⓑ	Ⓒ	69.	Ⓐ	Ⓑ	Ⓒ	109.	Ⓐ	Ⓑ	Ⓒ
30.	Ⓐ	Ⓑ	Ⓒ	70.	Ⓐ	Ⓑ	Ⓒ	110.	Ⓐ	Ⓑ	Ⓒ
31.	Ⓐ	Ⓑ	Ⓒ	71.	Ⓐ	Ⓑ	Ⓒ	111.	Ⓐ	Ⓑ	Ⓒ
32.	Ⓐ	Ⓑ	Ⓒ	72.	Ⓐ	Ⓑ	Ⓒ	112.	Ⓐ	Ⓑ	Ⓒ
33.	Ⓐ	Ⓑ	Ⓒ	73.	Ⓐ	Ⓑ	Ⓒ	113.	Ⓐ	Ⓑ	Ⓒ
34.	Ⓐ	Ⓑ	Ⓒ	74.	Ⓐ	Ⓑ	Ⓒ	114.	Ⓐ	Ⓑ	Ⓒ
35.	Ⓐ	Ⓑ	Ⓒ	75.	Ⓐ	Ⓑ	Ⓒ	115.	Ⓐ	Ⓑ	Ⓒ
36.	Ⓐ	Ⓑ	Ⓒ	76.	Ⓐ	Ⓑ	Ⓒ	116.	Ⓐ	Ⓑ	Ⓒ
37.	Ⓐ	Ⓑ	Ⓒ	77.	Ⓐ	Ⓑ	Ⓒ	117.	Ⓐ	Ⓑ	Ⓒ
38.	Ⓐ	Ⓑ	Ⓒ	78.	Ⓐ	Ⓑ	Ⓒ	118.	Ⓐ	Ⓑ	Ⓒ
39.	Ⓐ	Ⓑ	Ⓒ	79.	Ⓐ	Ⓑ	Ⓒ	119.	Ⓐ	Ⓑ	Ⓒ
40.	Ⓐ	Ⓑ	Ⓒ	80.	Ⓐ	Ⓑ	Ⓒ	120.	Ⓐ	Ⓑ	Ⓒ

Exam 1
Afternoon Session

Questions 1 through 18 relate to Ethical and Professional Standards.
(27 minutes)

1. Adam Schute, CFA, is on a conference call with the CFO of an investment banking client with his phone speaker on and his door open. As a result, salesmen and traders overhear the CFO describing problems with production target dates that have not been publicly disclosed. The salesmen relay this information to clients and the traders reduce their positions in the stock. With respect to the Standard on material nonpublic information, Schute has:
    A. not violated the Standard because he has not acted on the information, but the traders and salesmen have violated the Standard.
    B. violated the Standard because he should have taken steps to prevent the dissemination of the information.
    C. violated the Standard by not making the information public when he realized others had overheard the call.

2. Peter Wellington has changed his status in marketing materials to "Level III CFA candidate." Wellington passed the Level II CFA exam and just received his results. He intends to register for the next Level III CFA examination that is offered the following June. Wellington has:
    A. not violated the Standards of Professional Conduct.
    B. violated the Standard on conduct as participants in CFA Institute programs.
    C. violated the Standard on reference to the CFA Institute, the CFA Designation, and the CFA Program.

3. Which of the following statements relating to the Global Investment Performance Standards (GIPS®) is *least accurate*?
    A. Only investment management firms may claim compliance with GIPS.
    B. GIPS represent standards to which members of CFA Institute and CFA candidates must adhere.
    C. To claim GIPS compliance, a firm must present at least five years (or since its inception if less than five years) of annual investment performance that complies with GIPS.

4. When he assumed the job of compliance officer two years ago, Ed Michaels, CFA, issued written compliance procedures and made all covered employees aware of the procedures. A report by an external auditor found that on several occasions over the past two years, two different employees traded in recommended securities ahead of trades made in managed client accounts. Michaels fires both employees and recirculates the written compliance procedures that explain clearly which activities are prohibited. Michaels has violated the Standard concerning:
   A. Responsibilities of Supervisors by firing the employees instead of restricting their activities.
   B. Responsibilities of Supervisors by failing to implement reasonable procedures to detect violations.
   C. Misconduct because, as the compliance officer, he is associated with, and ultimately responsible for, the unethical activity.

5. Ralph Malone, CFA, has many clients, including a trust account that benefits three of his immediate family members. His firm changes its recommendation on a stock from "hold" to "buy" on a security that is suitable for many clients, including the trust. Which of the following would be considered a violation of the Standard concerning priority of transactions?
   A. Malone waits until after the firm purchases the security to buy it for the family trust account.
   B. Malone trades on the family account shortly after his firm's clients have been informed of the buy recommendation.
   C. The firm gives clients time to act on the new recommendation and then buys 100,000 shares for its own account prior to publicly disclosing the new recommendation.

6. Patricia Nelson, CFA, is informed by one of her clients that if she can get the performance of the client firm's pension portfolio above that of the Standard & Poor's average by year-end, the client will give her a free trip to Singapore to visit the firm's offices. If Nelson agrees to this arrangement, which of the following actions complies with CFA Institute Standards of Professional Conduct? Nelson:
   A. must inform her employer of this agreement but does not need consent.
   B. must inform her employer of this agreement and may accept it with verbal consent.
   C. may inform her employer by email of this agreement and must receive written consent.

©2014 Kaplan, Inc.

7. John Anderson, CFA, follows Radley Manufacturing for his employer, Atlas Brokers. Radley has announced a takeover bid for Palmer Industries, a company that Atlas does not follow. To get out a research note about the potential effects of the acquisition on Radley, Anderson purchases a report on Palmer from a research firm Atlas regularly uses. Anderson incorporates projections and analysis from the purchased report into his research note on what a post-acquisition Radley would look like but does not cite the source. Anderson has violated the Standard on:
    A. misrepresentation.
    B. independence and objectivity.
    C. diligence and reasonable basis.

8. Roger Smith, CFA, has been invited to join a group of analysts in touring the riverboats of River Casino Corp. For the tour, River Casino has arranged chartered flights from casino to casino since commercial flight schedules are not practical for the group's time schedule. River Casino has also arranged to pay for the analysts' lodging for the three nights of the tour. According to CFA Institute Standards of Professional Conduct, Smith:
    A. may accept the arrangements as they are.
    B. may accept the flight but is required to pay for his lodging.
    C. is required to pay for his flight and lodging.

9. Samuel Parkin, a principal of Argora Advisers, is in charge of preparing the firm's performance history in accordance with GIPS. At the end of each year, he assigns each portfolio to a single composite based on its holdings over the year. He uses the mean annual total return of portfolios assigned to a composite as the composite's return. With respect to GIPS compliance:
    A. both of these actions comply with GIPS.
    B. neither of these actions comply with GIPS.
    C. only one of these actions complies with GIPS.

10. Susan Smart, CFA, is about to change her "buy" recommendation on RollinsCo to "sell." RollinsCo had been growing rapidly over the past year, but Smart believes the growth potential is now gone. Smart sells the shares held in her discretionary client accounts and in her own personal account before issuing her report. According to the Standards that concern fair dealing and priority of transactions, Smart violated:
    A. both of these Standards.
    B. neither of these Standards.
    C. only one of these Standards.

11.   Matt Jacobs, CFA, recommended to a client that he buy shares in Timeco, which has subsequently underperformed the market. Timeco stock is thinly traded, and its price has decreased sharply over the past few weeks because two insiders have sold large blocks of shares. Jacobs believes this price decrease reflects an illiquid market. Because he still believes Timeco is a good long-term investment, he buys shares for his personal account in order to raise the price and help him convince his client to hold on to his investment in Timeco. Has Jacobs violated the Standards?
A. No, because the trade is for the benefit of his client.
B. Yes, because he intended to manipulate the market price of Timeco.
C. No, because he is providing liquidity to offset the effects of the recent large insider sales.

12.   William Rex, CFA, has a one-man firm that manages investment portfolios. In his marketing materials, Rex presents the asset-weighted returns for accounts he has managed over the last five years and does not disclose that the first two years of his performance history were achieved at a previous firm. He also includes simulated results of a stock selection model he employs and indicates that they are from a simulation. Has Rex violated any CFA Institute Standards of Professional Conduct?
A. No.
B. Yes, failing to disclose that two years of his performance results were with a previous employer is a violation, but including the simulated results is acceptable.
C. Yes, both by failing to disclose that two years of his performance results were with a previous employer and by including the simulated, rather than actual, performance results.

13.   Tony Roberts, CFA, is part of a team that manages equities accounts. He believes that a teammate, who is not a CFA Institute member or candidate, takes actions that, while not illegal under local law, violate CFA Institute Standards of Professional Conduct. According to the CFA Institute Standards of Professional Conduct, Roberts:
A. is required to dissociate from the team's activities if they continue.
B. is not required to act because the Code and Standards do not apply to non-members.
C. must report the suspected violations of the Code and Standards first to his supervisor and then to CFA Institute.

©2014 Kaplan, Inc.

14. Judy Blush is a CFA candidate and is recommending the purchase of a mutual fund that invests solely in long-term U.S. Treasury bonds (T-bonds) to one of her clients. She states that, "Since the U.S. government guarantees payment of both the bond's principal and interest, risk of loss with this investment is virtually zero." Blush's actions violated:
    A. the Standard on misrepresentation.
    B. the Standard on communication with clients and prospective clients.
    C. none of the CFA Institute Standards of Professional Conduct.

15. Which of the following actions is *least likely* a violation of the Standard concerning conduct as participants in CFA Institute programs?
    A. A member anonymously posts a disparaging comment about CFA Institute policies on an internet message board.
    B. A member fails to disclose a formal complaint from a client on her annual Professional Conduct Statement.
    C. A candidate discusses which topics were emphasized on the June Level I CFA exam with a candidate for the December exam.

16. According to the Standard concerning suitability, it is most likely that members and candidates in advisory relationships with clients should:
    A. document unsuccessful attempts to update client information.
    B. purchase only securities with low to medium risk for a client with moderate risk tolerance.
    C. decline to manage assets for clients who withhold important information about their financial circumstances and needs.

17. William Rogers, CFA, is a commercial insurance broker who sometimes recommends money managers to his high net worth clients. For those clients who hire the managers, the managers pay Rogers a percentage of the management fees on the account. Rogers tells prospects, "I receive referral fees from the money managers if you employ them." Rogers has:
    A. not violated the Standards.
    B. violated the Standard concerning referrals.
    C. violated the Standard on communications with clients and prospects.

18. Byron Bell, CFA, tells his assistant that Mary Mitchel, a client of his, confided to him that she is suffering from the early stages of Alzheimer's disease and that she is planning to leave almost all of her sizable estate to Prather House, a support facility for Alzheimer's patients. Bell directs his assistant to keep this information confidential. With respect to the Standard on preservation of confidentiality, Bell has:
    A. not violated the Standard.
    B. violated the Standard by sharing information about his client's health but not about planned bequest to Prather House.
    C. violated the Standard both by sharing the information about his client's health and about her planned bequest to Prather House.

Questions 19 through 32 relate to Quantitative Methods. (21 minutes)

19. A client plans to retire in 15 years and will need to withdraw $50,000 from his retirement account each year for 10 years, beginning on the day he retires. After that, he will need to withdraw $20,000 per year for 25 years. The account returns 4% annually. The amount he needs to have in the account on the day he retires is *closest* to:
    A. $580,000.
    B. $640,000.
    C. $655.000.

20. A company reports its past six years' earnings growth at 10%, 14%, 12%, 10%, –10%, and 12%. The company's average compound annual growth rate of earnings is *closest* to:
    A. 7.7%.
    B. 8.0%.
    C. 8.5%.

21. The following table summarizes the results of a poll (hypothetically) taken of CFA charterholders and CFA candidates regarding the importance of a continuing education requirement after the CFA designation is obtained:

Group	In Favor of a Continuing Education Requirement	Against a Continuing Education Requirement
CFA charterholders	235	765
CFA candidates	180	820

   Given the information that a member of the group is in favor of a continuing education requirement, what is the probability that she is a CFA candidate?
    A. 18%.
    B. 37%.
    C. 43%.

22. To test the hypothesis that actively managed international equities mutual funds outperformed an appropriate benchmark index, an analyst selects all of the current international equities funds that have been in existence for at least 10 years. His test results will most likely be subject to:
    A. look-ahead bias.
    B. time period bias.
    C. survivorship bias.

©2014 Kaplan, Inc.

23. Which of the following statements about common probability distributions is *least accurate*?
    A. A probability distribution specifies the probabilities of the possible outcomes of a random variable.
    B. In a binomial probability distribution, each observation has only two possible outcomes that are mutually exclusive.
    C. A normal distribution is a discrete symmetric probability distribution that is completely described by two parameters: its mean and variance.

24. For a binomial random variable with a 40% probability of success on each trial, the expected number of successes in 12 trials is *closest* to:
    A. 4.8.
    B. 5.6.
    C. 7.2.

25. Which of the following statements about the univariate, multivariate, and standard normal distributions is *least accurate*?
    A. A univariate distribution describes a single random variable.
    B. A multivariate distribution specifies the probabilities for a group of related random variables.
    C. The standard normal random variable, denoted Z, has mean equal to one and variance equal to one.

26. An investor is considering investing in one of the three following portfolios:

Statistical Measures	Portfolio X	Portfolio Y	Portfolio Z
Expected annual return	12%	17%	22%
Standard deviation of return	14%	20%	25%

If the investor's minimum acceptable return is 5%, the optimal portfolio using Roy's safety-first criterion is:
    A. Portfolio X.
    B. Portfolio Y.
    C. Portfolio Z.

27. An analyst is testing the hypothesis that the variance of monthly returns for Index L equals the variance of monthly returns for Index M based on samples of 50 monthly observations. The sample variance of Index L returns is 0.085, whereas the sample variance of Index M returns is 0.084. Assuming the samples are independent and the returns are normally distributed, which of the following represents the *most appropriate* test statistic?

   A. $\dfrac{\text{sample variance of Index L}}{\text{sample variance of Index M}}$.

   B. $\dfrac{\text{variance of Index L} - \text{variance of Index M}}{\text{standard error of squared differences}}$.

   C. $\dfrac{(\text{degrees of freedom}) \times (\text{Index L sample variance})}{\text{Index M sample variance}}$.

28. If the probability of event J multiplied by the probability of event K is not equal to the joint probability of events J and K, then events J and K are *most likely:*
   A. dependent events.
   B. independent events.
   C. mutually exclusive events.

29. Alan Barnes, CFA, is interested in the expected quarterly return on FTSE 100 stock index. He has data for the last five years and calculates the average return on the index over the last 20 quarters. This average return:
   A. is different from the statistic he is trying to estimate by the amount of the sampling error.
   B. overstates the return because he should divide by the square root of 20 when using a mean value.
   C. overstates the expected return because he should have used the geometric mean and not the simple average.

30. Which of the following statements regarding the significance level of a hypothesis test is *most accurate*?
   A. Given a significance level of 5%, a test will reject a true null hypothesis 5% of the time.
   B. If the significance level of a test is 5%, it will yield the correct decision about the null hypothesis 95% of the time.
   C. If the significance level of a test is 95%, it will yield the correct decision about the null hypothesis 95% of the time.

          ©2014 Kaplan, Inc.

31. A researcher needs to choose a probability distribution for the price of an asset that is quite volatile in order to simulate returns outcomes. She has a program that will generate random variables from any of a variety of distributions. The *most appropriate* distribution for her to select to generate the asset price distribution is a:
A. normal distribution.
B. lognormal distribution.
C. Student's *t*-distribution.

32. An investor is interested in the following piece of property:
- The property will cost $200,000 at time zero.
- It will provide cash flows of $50,000 in year 1, $60,000 in year 2, $70,000 in year 3, and $80,000 in year 4.
- A $20,000 investment will be required in year 5 as the property will have some environmental contamination and will have to be restored to its original condition.

What is the NPV of the project if the investor's required rate of return is 10%?
A. −$10,144.
B. $14,693.
C. $15,232.

Questions 33 through 44 relate to Economics. (18 minutes)

33. If investors' expected future incomes increase and the demand for financial capital increases, other things equal:
A. the equilibrium interest rate will rise.
B. the equilibrium interest rate will fall.
C. these two factors will have opposing effects on the equilibrium interest rate.

34. Assume that the required reserve ratio is 20%, and banks currently have no excess reserves. If the Federal Reserve then buys $100 million of Treasury bills from the banks, the money supply could potentially increase by:
A. $20 million.
B. $100 million.
C. $500 million.

35. If a minimum wage is set above the equilibrium wage in the labor market, what is the *most likely* effect?
A. The minimum wage will have no effect on the quantity of labor employed.
B. Firms will use less than the economically efficient amount of capital.
C. There will be excess supply of labor, and unemployment will increase.

36. The country of Hokah uses 30 units of labor to produce a unit of cheese and 35 units of labor to produce a unit of leather. The country of Ymer uses 25 units of labor to produce a unit of cheese and 20 units of labor to produce a unit of leather. Which of the following statements is *most accurate*?
    A. Ymer's opportunity cost of one unit of leather is 0.80 units of cheese.
    B. Hokah's opportunity cost of one unit of cheese is 1.167 units of leather.
    C. Ymer has an absolute and a comparative advantage in both cheese and leather.

37. As output quantities expand in an industry with a downward-sloping long-run industry supply curve, what is the *most likely* long-run effect on the equilibrium selling price per unit of the industry's output?
    A. Increase, because of upward pressure on input prices.
    B. Decrease, because of lower input costs per unit of output.
    C. No effect, because selling price is only affected in the short run.

38. If the government regulates a natural monopoly and enforces an average cost pricing, what are the effects on output quantity and price compared to an unregulated natural monopoly?
    A. Both are lower under average cost pricing.
    B. Both are higher under average cost pricing.
    C. One is higher and one is lower under average cost pricing.

39. Assume that one year ago, the exchange rate between the Japanese yen and the euro was 100 JPY/EUR, and the exchange rate between the Japanese yen and the U.S. dollar was 80 JPY/USD. Current exchange rates are 104.2 JPY/EUR and 76.6 JPY/USD. Which of the following statements is *most accurate*?
    A. The USD has depreciated relative to the EUR.
    B. The JPY has depreciated 4.2% relative to the EUR.
    C. The current U.S. dollar to euro exchange rate is approximately 1.25 USD/EUR.

40. Oligopolists have an incentive to cheat on collusive agreements in order to:
    A. avoid competitive practices.
    B. increase their individual share of the joint profit.
    C. restrict output and put upward pressure on price.

41. An increase in the supply of cars is *most likely* to be caused by a(n):
    A. increase in wages.
    B. decrease in price of steel.
    C. decrease in the price of cars.

©2014 Kaplan, Inc.

42. With respect to the IS-LM model, in an LM curve the real interest rate is:
    A. positively related to real income, holding the real money supply constant.
    B. held constant, resulting in excess savings being positively related to real income.
    C. negatively related to real income, holding the marginal propensity to save constant.

43. An individual sees her income rise from $80,000 to $88,000, and along with it, her consumption of Good X has decreased from eight dozen packages per year to six dozen packages per year. Good X should be classified as a(n):
    A. normal good.
    B. Veblen good.
    C. inferior good.

44. The Keynesian view suggests that the government can reduce aggregate demand by using:
    A. restrictive fiscal policy to shift the government budget toward a surplus (or smaller deficit).
    B. restrictive fiscal policy to shift the government budget toward a deficit (or a smaller surplus).
    C. expansionary fiscal policy to shift the government budget toward a surplus (or a smaller deficit).

Questions 45 through 68 relate to Financial Reporting and Analysis. (36 minutes)

45. Which of the following is *least likely* to be considered a barrier to developing one universally recognized set of reporting standards?
    A. Differences of opinion among various regulatory bodies.
    B. Reluctance of firms to adhere to a single set of reporting standards.
    C. Political pressure from stakeholders affected by reporting standards.

46. Which of the following items affects owners' equity but is not included as a component of net income?
    A. Depreciation.
    B. Dividends received on shares of another company classified as available for sale.
    C. Foreign currency translation gains and losses.

47. A company's financial statement data for the most recent year include the following:

• Net income	$100
• Depreciation expense	25
• Purchase of machine	50
• Sale of company trucks	30
• Sale of common stock	45
• Decrease in accounts receivable	10
• Increase in inventory	20
• Issuance of bonds	25
• Increase in accounts payable	15
• Increase in wages payable	10

Based only on these items, cash flow from financing activities is *closest* to:
A. $70.
B. $85.
C. $140.

48. A firm that rents DVDs to customers capitalizes the cost of newly released DVDs that it purchases and depreciates them over three years to a value of zero. Based on the underlying economics of the DVD rental business, the *most appropriate* method of depreciation for the firm to use on its financial statements is:
A. straight-line.
B. declining balance.
C. units-of-production.

49. The item "noncontrolling interest" included as a component of equity represents the portion of a subsidiary the parent company:
A. does not own.
B. owns, if less than 20% of the subsidiary's common stock.
C. owns, if less than 50% of the subsidiary's common stock.

50. An analyst gathered the following information about a company:

• Cash flow from operations	$800
• Purchase of plant and equipment	40
• Sale of land	30
• Interest expense	80
• Depreciation and amortization	100
• The company has a tax rate of 35% and prepares its financial statements under U.S. GAAP.	

The company's free cash flow to the firm (FCFF) is *closest* to:
A. $840.
B. $870.
C. $940.

©2014 Kaplan, Inc.

51. For which of the following balance sheet items is a change in market value *most likely* to affect net income?
    A. Debt securities issued by the firm.
    B. Debt securities that the firm intends to hold until maturity.
    C. Securities held with the intent to profit over the short term.

52. IFRS and U.S. GAAP are *most* similar in their requirements for:
    A. extraordinary items.
    B. discontinued operations.
    C. valuation of fixed assets.

53. A company using LIFO reports the following:
    - Cost of goods sold was $27,000.
    - Beginning inventory was $6,500, and ending inventory was $6,200.
    - The beginning LIFO reserve was $1,200.
    - The ending LIFO reserve was $1,400.

    The *best* estimate of the company's cost of goods sold on a FIFO basis would be:
    A. $21,300.
    B. $26,800.
    C. $27,500.

54. Which of the following items is *best* described as a listing of all the journal entries in order of their dates?
    A. Trial ledger.
    B. General ledger.
    C. General journal.

55. An analyst gathered the following data about a company:
    - 1,000,000 shares of common are outstanding at the beginning of the year.
    - 10,000 6% convertible bonds (conversion ratio is 20 to 1) were issued at par June 30 of this year.
    - The company has 100,000 warrants outstanding all year with an exercise price of $25 per share.
    - The average stock price for the period is $20, and the ending stock price is $30.

    If the convertible bonds are considered dilutive, the number of shares of common stock that the analyst should use to calculate diluted earnings per share is:
    A. 1,000,000.
    B. 1,100,000.
    C. 1,266,667.

56. During periods of rising prices:
    A. LIFO COGS > Weighted Average COGS > FIFO COGS.
    B. LIFO COGS > Weighted Average COGS < FIFO COGS.
    C. LIFO COGS < Weighted Average COGS < FIFO COGS.

57. Which of the following statements about calculating earnings per share (EPS) in simple versus complex capital structures is *least* accurate?
    A. If convertible bonds are dilutive, the numerator in the diluted EPS calculation is increased by the interest expense on the bonds.
    B. If convertible preferred stock is dilutive, the convertible preferred dividends must be added back to the numerator to calculate diluted EPS.
    C. The denominator in the basic EPS equation contains the number of shares of common stock issued, weighted by the days that the shares have been outstanding.

58. In the period when a firm makes an expenditure, capitalizing the expenditure instead of recognizing it as an expense will result in higher:
    A. debt-to-equity and debt-to-assets ratios.
    B. net income and have no effect on total cash flows.
    C. cash flow from investing and lower cash flow from operations.

59. Which of the following ratios is a component of the original (three-part) DuPont equation?
    A. Asset turnover.
    B. Gross profit margin.
    C. Debt-to-equity ratio.

60. Harding Corp. has a permanently impaired asset. The difference between its carrying value and the present value of its expected cash flows should be written down immediately and:
    A. reported as an operating loss.
    B. charged directly against retained earnings.
    C. reported as a non-operating loss in other comprehensive income.

61. If market interest rates have changed materially since a firm issued a bond, and the firm uses the effective interest rate method, how is a change in the market value of the firm's debt *most likely* to be reported in the firm's financial statements?
    A. The gain or loss in market value must be calculated and disclosed in the footnotes to the financial statements.
    B. Net income and equity are unaffected, but the change may be discussed in management's commentary.
    C. Net income is unaffected, but the change in market value is recorded in other comprehensive income.

©2014 Kaplan, Inc.

62. Which of the following statements regarding deferred taxes is *least* accurate?
    A. A permanent difference is a difference between taxable income and pretax income that will not reverse.
    B. A deferred tax asset is created when a temporary difference results in taxable income that exceeds pretax income.
    C. Deferred tax assets and liabilities are not adjusted for changes in tax rates.

63. A firm that reports its lease of a conveyer system as an operating lease must disclose:
    A. only the annual lease payment.
    B. minimum lease payments for each of the next five years and the sum of lease payments more than five years in the future.
    C. minimum lease payments for each of the next ten years and the sum of lease payments more than ten years in the future.

64. Meyer Company increases the promised payments for all employees in its defined benefit pension plan. Under which financial reporting standards would Meyer recognize past service costs in its income statement for the period?
    A. IFRS only.
    B. U.S. GAAP only.
    C. Both IFRS and U.S. GAAP.

65. Jordan Loney, CFA, issues a "sell" recommendation on Sullivan Company because she believes its financial reporting quality is low. Loney writes, "Rapid turnover of key employees in its information systems and accounting units have made Sullivan's internal monitoring controls ineffective." Which condition that may lead to low-quality financial reporting has Loney detected at Sullivan?
    A. Opportunity.
    B. Motivation.
    C. Rationalization.

66. Of the following methods of examining the uncertainty of financial outcomes around point estimates, which answers hypothetical questions about the effect of changes in a single variable and which uses assumed probability distributions for key variables?

	Hypothetical questions	Probability distributions
A.	Sensitivity analysis	Simulation
B.	Scenario analysis	Simulation
C.	Scenario analysis	Sensitivity analysis

67. At the beginning of the year, a firm securitizes half of its accounts receivable and uses the proceeds to pay down principal on a long-term bank loan. These transactions will:
A. increase the firm's current ratio.
B. decrease the firm's debt-to-equity ratio.
C. decrease the firm's interest coverage ratio.

68. A dealer of large earth movers that leases the machinery to its customers is *most likely* to treat the leases as:
A. operating leases, and account for inventory using last-in first-out.
B. sales-type leases, and account for inventory using specific identification.
C. direct financing leases, and account for inventory using weighted average cost.

Questions 69 through 77 relate to Corporate Finance. (13.5 minutes)

69. Business risk is *best* described as resulting from the combined effects of a firm's:
A. financial risk and sales risk.
B. sales risk and operating risk.
C. operating risk and financial risk.

70. To protect shareholders' long-term interests, the *most appropriate* characteristic for a board of directors is that:
A. the board meets regularly with management present.
B. the majority of board members are not firm executives.
C. board members represent firm suppliers, customers, or pension advisers.

71. The amount of a company's optimal capital budget is *most accurately* determined by the point on the company's investment opportunity schedule:
A. where the amount of new capital raised is at its minimum.
B. where it intersects the company's marginal cost of capital curve.
C. where the expected return on the next potential project is at its maximum.

72. A company is *most likely* faced with a drag on liquidity if its:
A. weighted average collection period increases from 42 days to 46 days.
B. largest vendor changes its invoice terms from "3/10 net 30" to "3/10 net 60."
C. inventory turnover was below the industry average last year and is above the industry average this year.

©2014 Kaplan, Inc.

73.   A firm with earnings per share of $2 decides to repurchase a portion of its shares at their market price of $25. The firm's after-tax cost of debt is 6% and the firm earns a 2% after-tax yield on its excess cash. When the firm repurchases shares, its earnings per share will:
A. increase if the firm funds the repurchase with debt or uses excess cash to repurchase the shares.
B. decrease if the firm funds the repurchase with debt or uses excess cash to repurchase the shares.
C. decrease if the firm funds the repurchase with debt, but increase if the firm uses excess cash to repurchase the shares.

74.   Faye Harlan, CFA, is estimating the cost of common equity for Cyrene Corporation. She prepares the following data for Cyrene:
*   Price per share = $50.
*   Expected dividend per share = $3.
*   Expected retention ratio = 30%.
*   Expected return on equity = 20%.
*   Beta = 0.89.
*   Yield to maturity on outstanding debt = 10%.
*   The expected market rate of return is 12% and the risk-free rate is 3%.

Based on these data, Harlan determines that Cyrene's cost of common equity is 14%. Harlan *most likely* arrived at this estimate by using the:
A. dividend discount model approach.
B. capital asset pricing model approach.
C. bond yield plus risk premium approach.

75.   Quixote Co. and Sisyphus Co., two similar-sized competitors, have had stable operating cycles of 180 days and cash conversion cycles of 140 days over the past several years. Sisyphus' operating and cash conversion cycles remained at these levels in the most recent year, but Quixote's cash conversion cycle contracted to 120 days while its operating cycle remained at 180 days. Relative to Sisyphus, Quixote has *most likely* begun:
A. taking more time to pay its suppliers.
B. operating with less inventory on hand.
C. offering easier credit terms to its customers.

76. A company prepares a chart with the net present value (NPV) profiles for two mutually exclusive projects with equal lives of five years. Project Jones and Project Smith have the same initial cash outflow and total undiscounted cash inflows, but 75% of the cash inflows for Project Jones occur in years 1 and 2, while 75% of the cash inflows for Project Smith occur in years 4 and 5. Which of the following statements is *most accurate* regarding these projects?
    A. Project Smith has a higher internal rate of return than Project Jones.
    B. There is a range of discount rates in which the optimal decision is to reject both projects.
    C. There is a range of discount rates in which the company should choose Project Jones and a range in which it should choose Project Smith.

77. Which of the following is a sign of a well-qualified board member?
    A. Major supplier to the firm.
    B. Has other board experience.
    C. Does not have a significant stock position.

Questions 78 through 85 relate to Portfolio Management. (12 minutes)

78. In the context of the capital asset pricing model, an active manager would be *most likely* to purchase a security that plots:
    A. on the security market line.
    B. below the security market line.
    C. above the security market line.

79. The investment needs of property and casualty insurers are characterized by a:
    A. short-term time horizon and low risk tolerance.
    B. long-term time horizon and high risk tolerance.
    C. short-term time horizon and high risk tolerance.

80. Using historical index returns for an equities market over a 20-year period, an analyst has calculated the average annual return as 5.60% and the holding period return as 170%. The compound annual index return over the period is *closest* to:
    A. 2.69%.
    B. 5.09%.
    C. 5.24%.

81. Which portion of an investment policy statement is *most likely* to state any restriction on portfolio leverage?
    A. Procedures.
    B. Investment guidelines.
    C. Duties and responsibilities.

©2014 Kaplan, Inc.

82.   Davis Samuel, CFA, is meeting with one of his portfolio management clients, Joseph Pope, to discuss Pope's investment constraints. Samuel has established that:
- Pope plans to retire from his job as a bond salesman in 17 years, after which this portfolio will be his primary source of income.
- Pope has sufficient cash available that he will not need this portfolio to generate cash outflows until he retires.
- Pope, as a registered securities representative, is required to have Samuel send a copy of his account statements to the compliance officer at Pope's employer.
- Pope opposes certain policies of the government of Lower Pannonia and does not wish to own any securities of companies that do business with its regime.

To complete his assessment of Pope's investment constraints, Samuel still needs to inquire about Pope's:
A. tax concerns.
B. liquidity needs.
C. unique needs and preferences.

83.   When a risk-free asset is combined with a portfolio of risky assets, which of the following is *least accurate*?
A. The standard deviation of the return for the newly created portfolio is the standard deviation of the returns of the risky asset portfolio multiplied by its portfolio weight.
B. The expected return for the newly created portfolio is the weighted average of the return on the risk-free asset and the expected return on the risky asset portfolio.
C. The variance of the resulting portfolio is a weighted average of the returns variances of the risk-free asset and of the portfolio of risky assets.

84.   If a stock's beta is equal to 1.2, its standard deviation of returns is 28%, and the standard deviation of the returns on the market portfolio is 14%, the covariance of the stock's returns with the returns on the market portfolio is *closest* to:
A. 0.168.
B. 0.024.
C. 0.600.

85.   For risk-averse investors, indifference curves in risk-return space (risk on the horizontal axis, expected return on the vertical axis) are:
A. linear and upward sloping.
B. nonlinear and upward sloping.
C. nonlinear and downward sloping.

Questions 86 through 97 relate to Equity Investments. (18 minutes)

86. An analyst classifies Mettler, Inc., an operator of retail grocery stores, in the same industry group as Powell Corporation, a manufacturer of industrial machinery. This analyst's classification system is *most likely* based on:
A. statistical methods.
B. products and services.
C. sensitivity to the business cycle.

87. To ensure the continuity of a value-weighted index when one of the stocks in the index is split:
A. no adjustment is necessary.
B. only the denominator must be adjusted for the split.
C. both the numerator and the denominator must be adjusted for the split.

88. Robert Higgins is estimating the price-earnings (P/E) ratio that will be appropriate for an index at the end of next year. He has estimated that:
  • Expected annual dividends will increase by 10% compared to this year.
  • Expected earnings per share will increase by 10% compared to this year.
  • The expected growth rate of dividends will be the same as the current estimate of 5%.
  • The required rate of return will rise from 8% to 11%.

Compared to the current P/E, the end-of-the-year P/E will be:
A. 50% lower.
B. 2% higher.
C. 10% higher.

89. An analyst gathered the following data about a stock:
  • The stock paid a $1 dividend last year.
  • Next year's dividend is projected to be 10% higher.
  • The stock is projected to sell for $25 at the end of the year.
  • The risk-free rate of interest is 8%.
  • The expected return on the market is 13%.
  • The stock's beta is 1.2.

The value of the stock today is *closest* to:
A. $19.45.
B. $22.89.
C. $26.74.

 ©2014 Kaplan, Inc.

90. A contract that requires one party to pay $100,000 each quarter to another company that will make a variable quarterly payment based on the market value of an equities portfolio is referred to as:
   A. a swap.
   B. an index option.
   C. portfolio insurance.

91. Visser, Inc. is an unprofitable fishing enterprise. Visser rents most of its boats and equipment but owns valuable transferable fishing quotas. If a competitor is interested in acquiring Visser, the *most appropriate* equity valuation model to use is a(n):
   A. asset-based valuation model.
   B. earnings multiplier model.
   C. Gordon growth model.

92. A firm has a constant growth rate of 7% and just paid a dividend of $6.25. If the required rate of return is 12%, what will the stock sell for two years from now based on the dividend discount model?
   A. $133.75.
   B. $149.80.
   C. $153.13.

93. In a transaction referred to as a management buyout (MBO):
   A. management sells its shares to an investor group attempting to gain control of a company.
   B. management buys a controlling interest in a public company to gain control of the board of directors.
   C. an investor group that includes management buys all the shares of a company and they no longer trade on an exchange.

94. Archer Products is in an industry that has experienced low levels of price competition but recently excess capacity has led to aggressive price cutting. An analyst would be *least likely* to describe Archer's industry as:
   A. concentrated and with high barriers to exit.
   B. in the shakeout stage with low concentration.
   C. in the maturity stage with high barriers to entry.

95. Assume the Wansch Corporation is expected to pay a dividend of $2.25 per share this year. Sales and profit for Wansch are forecasted to grow at a rate of 20% for two years after that, then grow at 5% per year forever. Dividend and sales growth are expected to be equal. If Wansch's shareholders require a 15% return, the per-share value of Wansch's common stock based on the dividend discount model is *closest* to:
   A. $22.75.
   B. $26.00.
   C. $28.50.

96. Under which of the following conditions are market values of securities *most likely* to be persistently greater than their intrinsic values?
    A. Short selling is restricted.
    B. Transactions costs are high.
    C. Arbitrage trading is restricted.

97. Moore Company stock is currently trading at $40 per share. An investor attempting to protect against losses of more than 10% on a short position in Moore should place a:
    A. stop buy order at $44.
    B. stop sell order at $36.
    C. limit buy order at $44.

Questions 98 through 109 relate to Fixed Income. (18 minutes)

98. An analyst collects the following spot rates, stated as annual BEYs:
    - 6-month spot rate = 6%.
    - 12-month spot rate = 6.5%.
    - 18-month spot rate = 7%.
    - 24-month spot rate = 7.5%.

    Given only this information, the price of a 2-year, semiannual-pay, 10% coupon bond with a face value of $1,000 is *closest* to:
    A. $918.30.
    B. $1,000.00.
    C. $1,046.77.

99. A bond has an effective duration of 7.5. If the bond yield changes by 100 basis points, the price of the bond will change by:
    A. exactly 0.75%.
    B. approximately 7.5%.
    C. approximately 0.75%.

100. Which of the following *best* describes the motivation for a corporation to issue securitized bonds? Securitization of specific assets by a corporation enables the corporation to:
    A. improve the recovery rate in the event of default.
    B. use the assets as collateral for additional borrowing.
    C. get a credit rating on the bonds that will result in a lower cost of borrowing.

101. Which of the following is a risk faced by issuers of commercial paper?
    A. Default risk.
    B. Rollover risk.
    C. Reinvestment risk.

©2014 Kaplan, Inc.

102. Other things equal, an increase in an option-free bond's yield to maturity will:
    A. increase its interest rate risk.
    B. decrease its interest rate risk.
    C. not change its interest rate risk.

103. An analyst collects the following information regarding spot rates:
    - 1-year rate = 4%.
    - 2-year rate = 5%.
    - 3-year rate = 6%.
    - 4-year rate = 7%.

    The 2-year forward rate two years from today is *closest* to:
    A. 7.02%.
    B. 8.03%.
    C. 9.04%.

104. A credit analyst determines the following selected financial ratios for three firms in an industry after making all appropriate adjustments:

	Johnson	*Knight*	*Lawrence*
EBIT / revenue	0.25	0.30	0.35
EBIT / interest	12.5	14.0	10.5
Debt / capital	0.55	0.70	0.35
Revenue / assets	0.20	0.15	0.10

    In evaluating the creditworthiness of these firms, the analyst should conclude that:
    A. Knight has the most favorable leverage and Johnson has the most favorable coverage.
    B. Lawrence has the most favorable leverage and Knight has the most favorable coverage.
    C. Johnson has the most favorable leverage and Lawrence has the most favorable coverage.

105. How should an analyst interpret a downward-sloping term structure of yield volatility? Short-term interest rates are:
    A. higher than long-term interest rates.
    B. more stable than long-term interest rates.
    C. more variable than long-term interest rates.

106.   Parsons Inc. is issuing an annual-pay bond that will pay no coupon for the first five years and then pay a 10% coupon for the remaining five years to maturity. The 10% coupon interest for the first five years will all be paid (without additional interest) at maturity. If the annual YTM on this bond is 10%, the price of the bond per $1,000 of face value is *closest to*:
   A. $778.
   B. $814.
   C. $856.

107.   For a five-year pure discount bond that is callable at par after two years, which of the following yield measures will be lowest?
   A. Current yield.
   B. Yield to first call.
   C. Yield to maturity.

108.   A floating-rate security is *most likely* to trade at a discount to its par value because the:
   A. next reset date is in three months.
   B. security's yield premium for credit risk decreases.
   C. floating rate includes a margin over LIBOR to compensate for the issue's liquidity risk.

109.   What is most likely to happen to the prepayment rate and the weighted average life of a typical pass-through security if mortgage rates decrease?
   A. Both will increase.
   B. Both will decrease.
   C. One will increase and one will decrease.

Questions 110 through 115 relate to Derivatives. (9 minutes)

110.   A programming error resulted in the issuance of a forward contract that ignored the convenience yield investors realize from holding the underlying asset. To gain an arbitrage profit from this error, an arbitrageur's position would *most likely* include a long position in the:
   A. forward contract.
   B. underlying asset.
   C. risk-free asset.

111.   Compared to an otherwise identical European put option, one that has a longer time to expiration:
   A. may be worth less than the put that is nearer to expiration.
   B. must be worth more than the put that is nearer to expiration.
   C. must be worth at least as much as the put that is nearer to expiration.

©2014 Kaplan, Inc.

112. For interest rate swaps, a replication process is used to determine:
    A. only the value.
    B. only the price.
    C. both the value and the price.

113. An investor has a call option on a stock that is currently selling for $35. The call option is in the money by $3. The call option's strike price is:
    A. $32.
    B. $35.
    C. $38.

114. Which of the following statements *most accurately* represents the positions of the parties to a derivatives contract?
    A. A call option imposes an obligation to buy the underlying security.
    B. A forward contract imposes an obligation on the seller but not the buyer.
    C. Both a put writer and a call writer have an obligation to exchange the underlying asset.

115. Given the put-call parity relationship, a synthetic underlying asset can be created by forming a portfolio of a:
    A. long call, long put, and short risk-free bond.
    B. long call, short put, and long risk-free bond.
    C. short call, long put, and long risk-free bond.

Questions 116 through 120 relate to Alternative Investments. (7.5 minutes)

116. Compared to traditional investment managers who invest in long-only stocks and bonds, alternative investment managers typically invest in assets that are:
    A. less regulated, less transparent, and less liquid.
    B. more transparent, less liquid, and less correlated with traditional investments.
    C. less transparent, more regulated, and less correlated with traditional investments.

117. Supplying capital to companies that are just moving into operation, but do not as yet have a product or service available to sell, is a description that *best* relates to which of the following stages of venture capital investing?
    A. Early stage.
    B. Mezzanine stage.
    C. Angel investing stage.

118. An equity hedge fund that uses technical analysis techniques to identify undervalued shares to buy and overvalued shares to sell short is *best* described as pursuing a(n):
    A. market neutral strategy.
    B. special situations strategy.
    C. quantitative directional strategy.

119. A hedge fund that requires incentive fees to be calculated only on the portion of returns above a benchmark return is said to have a:
    A. soft hurdle rate.
    B. hard hurdle rate.
    C. high water mark.

120. Compared to investing in commodities, investing in farmland is *most likely* to provide which of the following benefits?
    A. More liquidity.
    B. Higher income.
    C. Better inflation hedge.

©2014 Kaplan, Inc.

EXAM 2
MORNING SESSION

Calculating Your Score

Topic	Maximum Score	Your Score
Ethical and Professional Standards	18	
Quantitative Methods	14	
Economics	12	
Financial Reporting and Analysis	24	
Corporate Finance	8	
Portfolio Management	9	
Equity Investments	12	
Fixed Income	12	
Derivatives	6	
Alternative Investments	5	
Total	120	

The morning and afternoon exams are identically weighted over the topics and readings. You can therefore treat the morning and afternoon exams as independent exams.

If you took more than three hours (180 minutes) to complete this portion of the exam, you should adjust your score downward by one point for each minute you ran over.

Remember: the real exam *will be more difficult* than these practice exams. The main reason for this is the general anxiety and stress that you will be feeling on exam day, coupled with the time pressure you will be under. Many of the questions on this practice exam and the real exam are not individually difficult, so if you take extra time to answer the questions on this practice exam, your score will go up significantly. However, if you want an accurate measure of your potential performance on the exam, adhere to the 3-hour time limit.

After you have finished grading your practice exam, you may find it useful to use the exam questions and recommended solutions for review. Many of these questions were specifically written for your use as study tools. Once again, I feel I should remind you not to rely on memorizing these questions; you are not likely to see them on the actual exam. What you will see on the exam, though, are the concepts, terms, and procedures presented in these questions.

Your actual exam will most likely look different than what you see in this book. Please remember, no study provider knows the content of the actual exam. These practice exams are our best guess as to the structure, content, and difficulty of an actual exam.

Test Answers

1.	(A)	(B)	(C)	41.	(A)	(B)	(C)	81.	(A)	(B)	(C)
2.	(A)	(B)	(C)	42.	(A)	(B)	(C)	82.	(A)	(B)	(C)
3.	(A)	(B)	(C)	43.	(A)	(B)	(C)	83.	(A)	(B)	(C)
4.	(A)	(B)	(C)	44.	(A)	(B)	(C)	84.	(A)	(B)	(C)
5.	(A)	(B)	(C)	45.	(A)	(B)	(C)	85.	(A)	(B)	(C)
6.	(A)	(B)	(C)	46.	(A)	(B)	(C)	86.	(A)	(B)	(C)
7.	(A)	(B)	(C)	47.	(A)	(B)	(C)	87.	(A)	(B)	(C)
8.	(A)	(B)	(C)	48.	(A)	(B)	(C)	88.	(A)	(B)	(C)
9.	(A)	(B)	(C)	49.	(A)	(B)	(C)	89.	(A)	(B)	(C)
10.	(A)	(B)	(C)	50.	(A)	(B)	(C)	90.	(A)	(B)	(C)
11.	(A)	(B)	(C)	51.	(A)	(B)	(C)	91.	(A)	(B)	(C)
12.	(A)	(B)	(C)	52.	(A)	(B)	(C)	92.	(A)	(B)	(C)
13.	(A)	(B)	(C)	53.	(A)	(B)	(C)	93.	(A)	(B)	(C)
14.	(A)	(B)	(C)	54.	(A)	(B)	(C)	94.	(A)	(B)	(C)
15.	(A)	(B)	(C)	55.	(A)	(B)	(C)	95.	(A)	(B)	(C)
16.	(A)	(B)	(C)	56.	(A)	(B)	(C)	96.	(A)	(B)	(C)
17.	(A)	(B)	(C)	57.	(A)	(B)	(C)	97.	(A)	(B)	(C)
18.	(A)	(B)	(C)	58.	(A)	(B)	(C)	98.	(A)	(B)	(C)
19.	(A)	(B)	(C)	59.	(A)	(B)	(C)	99.	(A)	(B)	(C)
20.	(A)	(B)	(C)	60.	(A)	(B)	(C)	100.	(A)	(B)	(C)
21.	(A)	(B)	(C)	61.	(A)	(B)	(C)	101.	(A)	(B)	(C)
22.	(A)	(B)	(C)	62.	(A)	(B)	(C)	102.	(A)	(B)	(C)
23.	(A)	(B)	(C)	63.	(A)	(B)	(C)	103.	(A)	(B)	(C)
24.	(A)	(B)	(C)	64.	(A)	(B)	(C)	104.	(A)	(B)	(C)
25.	(A)	(B)	(C)	65.	(A)	(B)	(C)	105.	(A)	(B)	(C)
26.	(A)	(B)	(C)	66.	(A)	(B)	(C)	106.	(A)	(B)	(C)
27.	(A)	(B)	(C)	67.	(A)	(B)	(C)	107.	(A)	(B)	(C)
28.	(A)	(B)	(C)	68.	(A)	(B)	(C)	108.	(A)	(B)	(C)
29.	(A)	(B)	(C)	69.	(A)	(B)	(C)	109.	(A)	(B)	(C)
30.	(A)	(B)	(C)	70.	(A)	(B)	(C)	110.	(A)	(B)	(C)
31.	(A)	(B)	(C)	71.	(A)	(B)	(C)	111.	(A)	(B)	(C)
32.	(A)	(B)	(C)	72.	(A)	(B)	(C)	112.	(A)	(B)	(C)
33.	(A)	(B)	(C)	73.	(A)	(B)	(C)	113.	(A)	(B)	(C)
34.	(A)	(B)	(C)	74.	(A)	(B)	(C)	114.	(A)	(B)	(C)
35.	(A)	(B)	(C)	75.	(A)	(B)	(C)	115.	(A)	(B)	(C)
36.	(A)	(B)	(C)	76.	(A)	(B)	(C)	116.	(A)	(B)	(C)
37.	(A)	(B)	(C)	77.	(A)	(B)	(C)	117.	(A)	(B)	(C)
38.	(A)	(B)	(C)	78.	(A)	(B)	(C)	118.	(A)	(B)	(C)
39.	(A)	(B)	(C)	79.	(A)	(B)	(C)	119.	(A)	(B)	(C)
40.	(A)	(B)	(C)	80.	(A)	(B)	(C)	120.	(A)	(B)	(C)

Exam 2
Morning Session

Questions 1 through 18 relate to Ethical and Professional Standards. (27 minutes)

1. Which of the following statements about the CFA Institute's Professional Conduct Program (PCP) is *least accurate*?
    A. Possible sanctions include condemnation by a member's peers or suspension of a candidate's participation in the CFA Program.
    B. If the PCP staff determine that a sanction against a member is warranted, the member must either accept the sanction or lose the right to use the CFA designation.
    C. Members who cooperate with a PCP inquiry by providing confidential client information to PCP staff are not in violation of Standard III(E) Preservation of Confidentiality.

2. Robert Miguel, CFA, is a portfolio manager. On Saturday, one of his clients invited Miguel and his wife to be his guests at his luxury suite for a major league baseball playoff game, which they did. Miguel told his supervisor on Monday that they had attended the game with the client and that the suite was luxurious. Miguel has:
    A. not violated the Standards.
    B. violated the Standards because disclosure must be in writing.
    C. violated the Standards because he must disclose the gift prior to accepting.

3. At his golf club on Saturday morning, Paul Corwin, CFA, sees Frank Roberts, a friend and institutional client of his, who tells him that he is planning to sell his house on the 7th fairway. While golfing that day, Corwin tells Robert Lowe, a realtor, that Roberts is planning to sell his house and may need a realtor. He also tells Lowe that he manages an equities account for Roberts. If Corwin has not received permission from Roberts, he has violated the Standard on preservation of confidentiality:
    A. both by disclosing Roberts' plan to sell his home and that he is a client.
    B. by disclosing Roberts' plan to sell his home but not by mentioning that he was a client.
    C. by disclosing that Roberts is a client of his but not by mentioning Roberts' plan to sell his home.

4. Doug Watson, CFA, serves in a sales position at Sommerset Brokerage, a registered investment adviser. As part of his employment, he is expected to entertain clients. Frequently at these client outings, Watson drinks excessively. On one occasion, after dropping off a client, Watson was cited by local police for misdemeanor public intoxication. According to the Standard on knowledge of the law and the Standard on misconduct, Watson is in violation of:
    A. both of these Standards.
    B. neither of these Standards.
    C. only one of these Standards.

5. Reliable Wealth Managers wants to present a GIPS-compliant performance presentation and reference its GIPS compliance in marketing materials. Reliable is *least likely* required to:
    A. claim compliance with GIPS only if it has a compliant performance history of at least five years.
    B. apply GIPS compliance firmwide and not only to the specific asset classes mentioned in the marketing materials.
    C. include each discretionary fee-paying account in a composite based on its investment objectives and/or strategies.

6. Peter Taylor, a CFA charterholder and a food industry analyst for a large investment firm, has been invited by Sweet Pineapple Co. to visit the firm's processing plants in Hawaii. The Standard concerning independence and objectivity recommends that Taylor:
    A. use and pay for commercial transportation, if available.
    B. obtain written permission from his employer before he accepts this invitation.
    C. decline this invitation if he issues recommendations on the firm's securities.

7. Ruth Brett, a Level I CFA candidate, feels nervous and unprepared the night before the exam. Brett writes a few key notes on the bottom of her shoe. At the exam, Brett sees the large number of proctors present and decides not to risk getting caught and does not look at her shoe. According to the CFA Institute Code of Ethics and Standards of Professional Conduct, Brett is:
    A. not in violation of any Standard or the Code of Ethics because she did not use the notes.
    B. in violation of the Code of Ethics for bringing the notes into the examination room but is not in violation of any Standard because she did not use the notes.
    C. in violation of both the Code of Ethics and the Standard governing conduct as participants in CFA Institute programs for taking the notes into the examination room.

©2014 Kaplan, Inc.

8. Which of the following is *least likely* included in the CFA Code of Ethics? Members of CFA Institute must:
    A. place their clients' interests before their employer's interests.
    B. strive to maintain and improve the competence of others in the profession.
    C. use reasonable care and exercise independent professional judgment.

9. In formulating her report on GammaCorp's common stock, Barb Kramer, CFA, did a complex series of statistical tests on the company's past sales and earnings. Based on this statistical study, Kramer stated in her report that, "GammaCorp's earnings growth for the next five years will average 15% per year." Her conclusion was based in part on a regression analysis with a high level of statistical significance. Has Kramer violated the Standard on communication with clients and prospective clients?
    A. Yes, because she didn't give complete details of the statistical model used.
    B. Yes, because she failed to indicate that 15% growth is an estimate.
    C. No, because her projections are within the generally accepted bounds of statistical accuracy.

10. Alpha Advisors Inc. is an investment management firm with a client base that ranges from individuals to large foundations. Which of the following firm policies is *least appropriate* if Alpha adopts the Code and Standards? Alpha:
    A. monitors the personal trading activity of firm personnel and requires them to pre-clear personal trades.
    B. regularly calls larger accounts first after changes in investment recommendations have been faxed to all clients.
    C. excludes client accounts of family members of employees from participating in IPOs.

11. Dudley Thompson is a bond salesman for a small broker/dealer in London. His firm is the lead underwriter on a new junk bond issue for Ibex Corporation, and Thompson has sent details of the offering to clients. Thompson calls only his accounts over £1,000,000 for whom he thinks the issue is suitable. Thompson also posts his firm's optimistic projections for Ibex's performance in several Internet chat rooms. According to the Standards concerning market manipulation and fair dealing, Thompson is in violation of:
    A. both of these Standards.
    B. neither of these Standards.
    C. only one of these Standards.

12. Rob Elliott, CFA, is an analyst with a large asset management firm. His personal portfolio includes a large amount of common stock of Tech Inc., a semiconductor company, which his firm does not currently follow. The director of the research department has asked Elliott to analyze Tech and write a report about its investment potential. Based on the CFA Institute Standards of Professional Conduct, the *most appropriate* course of action for Elliot is to:

    A. decline to write the report.
    B. sell his shares of Tech before completing the report.
    C. disclose the ownership of the stock to his employer and in the report, if he writes it.

13. Antonio Mendoza, CFA, an investment manager operating as AM Investments, solicits new business by making brief presentations at which he makes available a single-page information sheet that summarizes his performance history for the past 10 years. On the sheet, Mendoza has his phone number for those who would like more information along with the statement, "AM Investments has prepared and presented this report in compliance with the Global Investment Performance Standards (GIPS®)." Mendoza's brief presentation and information sheet *most likely*:

    A. violate the Standard regarding performance presentation.
    B. comply with both GIPS and the Standard regarding performance presentation.
    C. do not comply with GIPS but comply with the Standard regarding performance presentation.

14. Anne Franklin, CFA, who covers technology stocks, joins a conference call for analysts presented by Cynthia Lucas, chief technology officer for LevelTech. Lucas tells the analysts that overseas shipments of the company's important new product are going to be delayed due to manufacturing defects, which is new information to the analysts. After the meeting Franklin changes her rating on LevelTech from "buy" to "hold" and sends a note to accounts recommending the sale of LevelTech. Franklin:

    A. did not violate the Standards.
    B. violated the Standard on nonpublic information by revising her rating on LevelTech.
    C. violated the Standard on fair dealing by rating the stock a "hold" but recommending sale of the shares to her accounts.

©2014 Kaplan, Inc.

15. According to the recommended procedures for complying with the Standard on suitability, which of the following statements regarding an investment policy statement (IPS) is *least accurate*?
    A. An IPS should describe the roles and responsibilities of both the adviser and the client.
    B. A member or candidate is not responsible for financial information withheld by the client.
    C. A client's IPS must be updated at least quarterly to reflect any changes in their investment profile.

16. Sue Johnson, CFA, has an elderly client with a very large asset base. The client intends to start divesting her fortune to various charities. Johnson is on the Board of a local charitable foundation. Johnson *most appropriately*:
    A. must not discuss anything regarding her client and her client's intentions with the charitable foundation without permission.
    B. can discuss her client's situation with the charitable foundation as long as she informs other local charities of her client's intentions.
    C. can make this known to the charitable foundation so that they can solicit the client, since it is the client's wish to divest assets to charities in the future.

17. According to the Standard related to loyalty, prudence, and care, which of the following statements regarding the voting of proxies on client holdings is *least accurate*?
    A. Proxies have economic value to a client.
    B. An investment management firm should vote all proxies on client holdings unless the client reserves that right.
    C. Members and candidates should explicitly disclose the firm's proxy voting policies to clients.

18. Alvin Gold, CFA, resides in Country T and does business as an investment advisor primarily in Country U. Country T allows trading on non-public information and does not require disclosure of referral fees. Country U prohibits trading on non-public information only if it is gained by illegal means and requires disclosure of referral fees of over $100 (U.S. equivalent). Gold accepts a referral fee of $75, and in the course of a meeting with two other analysts and the firm's CFO, Gold receives material non-public information. To comply with the Code and Standards, Gold:
    A. need not disclose the referral fee but cannot trade on the non-public information.
    B. must disclose the referral fee and cannot trade on the non-public information.
    C. must disclose the referral fee but may trade on the non-public information.

Questions 19 through 32 relate to Quantitative Methods. (21 minutes)

19. Three years from now, an investor will deposit the first of eight $1,000 payments into a special fund. The fund will earn interest at the rate of 5% per year until the third deposit is made. Thereafter, the fund will return a reduced interest rate of 4% compounded annually until the final deposit is made. How much money will the investor have in the fund at the end of ten years assuming no withdrawals are made?
    A. $8,872.93.
    B. $9,251.82.
    C. $9,549.11.

20. An investor places $5,000 in an account. The stated annual interest rate is 6% compounded monthly. The value of the account at the end of three years is *closest* to:
    A. $5,970.
    B. $5,978.
    C. $5,983.

21. Compared to a *t*-distribution with 10 degrees of freedom, and compared to a normal distribution, a *t*-distribution with 20 degrees of freedom and the same variance has:

Compared to df = 10	Compared to normal
A. thinner tails	fatter tails
B. fatter tails	thinner tails
C. fatter tails	fatter tails

22. The initial market value of a portfolio was $100,000. One year later the portfolio was valued at $90,000 and two years later at $99,000. The geometric mean annual return excluding any dividend income is *closest* to:
    A. –0.5%.
    B. –0.4%.
    C. 0.0%.

23. A college endowment fund has $150 million. The fund manager intends to withdraw $2 million from the fund for operations, and she has a minimum year-end acceptable level of $151 million. The fund has two choices for the portfolio. The endowment manager can choose Portfolio X, which has an expected return of 10% and a standard deviation of 14%, or Portfolio Y, which has an expected return of 12% and a standard deviation of 20%. Given this scenario, which of the following statements regarding Roy's safety-first criterion is *most accurate*?
    A. The fund should choose Portfolio Y.
    B. The fund should choose Portfolio X.
    C. Portfolios X and Y are both acceptable because their safety-first ratios fall in the acceptable range.

©2014 Kaplan, Inc.

24. An investor purchases 500 shares of Nevada Industries common stock for $22.00 per share today. At t = 1 year, this investor receives a $0.42 per share dividend (which is not reinvested) on the 500 shares and purchases an additional 500 shares for $24.75 per share. At t = 2 years, he receives another $0.42 (not reinvested) per share dividend on 1,000 shares and purchases 600 more shares for $31.25 per share. At t = 3 years, he sells 1,000 of the shares for $35.50 per share and the remaining 600 shares at $36.00 per share, but receives no dividends. Assuming no commissions or taxes, the money-weighted rate of return received on this investment is *closest* to:
   A. 14.3%.
   B. 17.6%.
   C. 18.5%.

25. The "up-move factor" in a binomial tree is *best* described as:
   A. the probability that the variable increases in any period.
   B. one minus the "down-move factor" for the binomial tree.
   C. one plus the percentage change in the variable when it increases.

26. Jane Acompora is calculating equivalent annualized yields based on the 1.3% holding period yield of a 90-day loan. The correct ordering of the annual money market yield (MMY), effective yield (EAY), and bond equivalent yield (BEY) is:
   A. MMY < EAY < BEY.
   B. MMY < BEY < EAY.
   C. BEY < EAY < MMY.

27.   An analyst develops the following probability distribution for the states of the economy and market returns.

	Unconditional Probability P(A)			Conditional Probability P(B × A)
Good economy	60%	Bull market		50%
		Normal market		30%
		Bear market		20%
Poor economy	40%	Bull market		20%
		Normal market		30%
		Bear market		50%

Which of the following statements about this probability distribution is *least accurate*?
A. The unconditional probability of a normal market is 0.30.
B. The joint probability of having a good economy and a bear market is 0.20.
C. Given that the economy is poor, the probability of a normal or a bull market is 0.50.

28.   An analyst estimates a stock has a 40% probability of earning a 10% return, a 40% probability of earning a 12.5% return, and a 20% probability of earning a 30% return. The stock's standard deviation of returns based on this returns model is *closest* to:
A. 3.74%.
B. 5.75%.
C. 7.58%.

29.   An investment manager has a pool of five security analysts he can choose from to cover three different industries. In how many different ways can the manager assign one analyst to each industry?
A. 15.
B. 60.
C. 125.

30.   Shortfall risk is *best* described as the probability:
A. of a credit rating downgrade due to possible earnings shortfalls.
B. of failing to make a contractually promised payment.
C. that portfolio value will fall below some minimum level at a future date.

    ©2014 Kaplan, Inc.

31.   If a two-tailed hypothesis test has a 5% probability of rejecting the null
        hypothesis when the null is true, it is *most likely* that the:
        A. power of the test is 95%.
        B. confidence level of the test is 95%.
        C. probability of a Type I error is 2.5%.

32.   Which of the following statements about hypothesis testing is *most
        accurate*?
        A. Rejecting a true null hypothesis is a Type I error.
        B. The power of a test is the probability of failing to reject the null
            hypothesis when it is false.
        C. For a one-tailed test involving X, the null hypothesis would be
            H_0: X = 0, and the alternative hypothesis would be H_A: X ≠ 0.

Questions 33 through 44 relate to Economics. (18 minutes)

33.   A business cycle theory developed by applying utility theory and
        budget constraints to macroeconomic models is *most closely* associated
        with which school of economic thought?
        A. Austrian.
        B. New Classical.
        C. New Keynesian.

34.   A loss of economic efficiency from price regulation is *least likely* to
        result from a:
        A. rent ceiling that effectively increases renters' search times for
            available units.
        B. minimum wage that is greater than the equilibrium wage for
            unskilled workers.
        C. maximum price for electricity set at a price level at which the
            quantity of electricity supplied is greater than the quantity
            demanded.

35.   Consider the following foreign exchange and interest rate information:
        •   Spot rate: 1.3382 USD/EUR.
        •   One year riskless USD rate = 2.5%.
        •   One year riskless EUR rate = 3.5%.

        The one-year arbitrage-free forward exchange rate is *closest* to:
        A. 1.2391 USD/EUR.
        B. 1.3253 USD/EUR.
        C. 1.3513 USD/EUR.

36. Monthly demand for gasoline at a particular location, as a function of the price of gasoline and the price of bus travel, is given (in hundreds of gallons) as $Q_D = 300 - 15\,P_{gas} + 2\,P_{bus}$. The slope of the demand curve for gasoline is *closest* to:
   A. −0.07.
   B. −0.13.
   C. −15.00.

37. Which of the following statements about monopolists is *most accurate*?
   A. Monopolists have imperfect information about demand.
   B. Without government intervention, monopolists will always earn economic profits.
   C. A monopolist maximizes total revenue where marginal revenue equals marginal cost.

38. A central bank's ability to achieve its policy goals is *most likely* to be limited by available resources when which of the following actual rates is below its target rate?
   A. Interest rate.
   B. Inflation rate.
   C. Exchange rate.

39. Which of the following statements regarding the money supply and determination of short-term interest rates is *least accurate*?
   A. On balance, growth in real GDP tends to increase the transactional demand for money.
   B. If the short-term interest rate is greater than the equilibrium rate, there will be excess supply of real money balances.
   C. An increase in the real money supply from an initial equilibrium situation will cause households and businesses to sell interest-bearing securities.

40. What are the *most likely* effects on aggregate demand in the current period of an increase in expected future incomes and of an increase in the money supply?
   A. Both increase aggregate demand.
   B. Both decrease aggregate demand.
   C. One increases aggregate demand and one decreases aggregate demand.

©2014 Kaplan, Inc.

41. Incorrect production decisions are *most likely* to occur when the inflation rate is:
     A. lower than expected only.
     B. higher than expected only.
     C. either higher or lower than expected.

42. The source of comparative advantage, according to the Heckscher-Ohlin model of international trade, is each country's:
     A. labor productivity.
     B. available natural resources.
     C. relative amounts of labor and capital.

43. Under which market structure is the profit maximizing strategy to produce the quantity of output for which the price is equal to marginal cost?
     A. Monopoly.
     B. Perfect competition.
     C. Monopolistic competition.

44. Which of the following statements about elasticity is *least accurate*?
     A. Both demand and supply are more elastic in the long run than in the short run.
     B. When demand is inelastic, an increase in price will cause a decrease in the total expenditure on a good.
     C. When the price of a product increases, consumers will reduce their consumption by a larger amount in the long run than in the short run.

Questions 45 through 68 relate to Financial Reporting and Analysis. (36 minutes)

45. Which of the following statements about nonrecurring items is *most accurate*?
     A. The correction of an accounting error is reported net of taxes below extraordinary items on the income statement.
     B. Discontinued operations are classified as unusual or infrequent and are reported as a component of net income from continuing operations.
     C. Uninsured losses from earthquakes and expropriations by foreign governments can be classified as extraordinary items under U.S. GAAP but not under IFRS.

46. On January 31, Dowling Inc. borrowed funds to purchase capital equipment for its business operations. On the same day, it also recorded the cost of salaries incurred to January 31, which will be paid on February 6. When these two transactions are recorded on January 31, the financial statement item that will increase the most is:
    A. assets.
    B. expenses.
    C. liabilities.

47. Under U.S. GAAP, which of the following statements about classifying cash flows is *most accurate*?
    A. Cash received from issuing long-term debt or stock is considered a financing cash flow.
    B. Income taxes paid are considered financing or investing cash flows if they arise from financing or investing activities.
    C. Dividend payments made are financing cash flows, while interest payments received are investing cash flows.

48. Kimberwick Technologies reported the following information for the year ending December 31.

Data	
Net sales	50,000
Cash expenses	3,250
Cash inputs	17,000
Cash taxes	7,000
Increase in receivables	500
Depreciation expense	1,000
Cash flow from investing	–5,000
Cash flow from financing	–4,250

If the cash balance increased $13,000 over the year, cash flow from operations (CFO) is *closest* to:
    A. $21,250.
    B. $21,750.
    C. $22,250.

49. A company has a cash conversion cycle of 80 days. If the company's average receivables turnover increases from 11 to 12, the company's cash conversion cycle:
    A. decreases by approximately 3 days.
    B. increases by approximately 3 days.
    C. decreases by approximately 1 day.

 ©2014 Kaplan, Inc.

50. Which of the following statements about a United States public corporation's annual reports, SEC filings, and press releases is *most accurate*?
A. Annual and quarterly SEC filings must be audited.
B. Interim SEC filings typically update the major financial statements and footnotes.
C. Annual reports to shareholders are typically the most factual and objective source of information about a company.

51. A company had the following changes in its stock:
- The company had 2 million shares outstanding on December 31, 20X6.
- On March 31, 20X7, the company paid a 10% stock dividend.
- On June 30, 20X7, the company sold $10 million face value of 7% convertible debentures, convertible into common at $5 per share.
- On September 30, 20X7, the company issued and sold 100,000 shares of common stock.

The company should compute its 20X7 basic earnings per share based on:
A. 2,225,000 shares.
B. 2,250,000 shares.
C. 3,225,000 shares.

52. Which of the following is *most likely* a motivation for a company's management to issue low-quality financial reports?
A. Management has provided optimistic earnings guidance.
B. Oversight provided by the board of directors is weak or inadequate.
C. Accounting principles permit a wide range of acceptable treatments and estimates.

53. Haltata Turf & Sod currently uses the first in, first out (FIFO) method to account for inventory. Due to significant tax-loss carryforwards, the company has an effective tax rate of zero. Prices are rising and inventory quantities are stable. If the company were to use last in, first out (LIFO) instead of FIFO:
A. net income would be lower and cash flow would be higher.
B. cash flow would remain the same and working capital would be lower.
C. gross margin would be higher and stockholder's equity would be lower.

54. Which of the following effects is *most likely* to occur when using ratio screens for high dividend yield stocks and low P/E stocks, respectively?

High dividend yield	Low P/E ratios
A. Include too many financial services firms	Exclude too many growth firms
B. Exclude too many financial services firms	Include too many growth firms
C. Include too many financial services firms	Include too many growth firms

55. The ratio of operating cash flow to net income is *least likely* to indicate low quality of earnings when it is:
    A. less than one.
    B. declining over time.
    C. highly variable.

56. A firm that reports under IFRS is producing under a long-term contract for which it cannot measure the outcome reliably. In the first year of the contract, the firm has spent €300,000 and collected €200,000 in cash. What amounts related to this contract should the firm recognize on its income statement for the year?
    A. Revenue of €300,000, expenses of €300,000, and no profit.
    B. No revenue, expenses, or profit until the contract is completed.
    C. Revenue of €200,000, expenses of €300,000, and a loss of €100,000.

57. Which of the following statements about the role of depreciable lives and salvage values in the computation of depreciation expenses for financial reporting is *most accurate*?
    A. The estimated useful life of the same depreciable asset should be the same regardless of which company owns the asset.
    B. Companies are specifically required to disclose data about estimated salvage values in the footnotes to the financial statements.
    C. Depreciable lives and salvage values are chosen by management and allow for the possibility of income manipulation.

58. A company's investments in marketable securities include a 3-year tax-exempt bond classified as held-to-maturity and a 5-year Treasury note classified as available-for-sale. On its income statement, the company should report the coupon interest received from:
    A. both of these securities.
    B. neither of these securities.
    C. only one of these securities.

©2014 Kaplan, Inc.

59. Acme Corp. purchased a new stamping machine for $100,000, paid $10,000 for shipping, and paid $5,000 to have it installed in their plant. Based on an estimated salvage value of $25,000 and an economic life of six years, the difference between straight-line depreciation and double-declining balance depreciation in the second year of the asset's life is *closest* to:
   A. $7,220.
   B. $10,556.
   C. $16,666.

60. How will a firm's operating cash flow be affected by a decrease in accounts receivable and by an increase in accounts payable?
   A. Both will increase operating cash flow.
   B. Both will decrease operating cash flow.
   C. One will increase operating cash flow and one will decrease operating cash flow.

61. From the point of view of a financial analyst, when evaluating companies that use different inventory cost assumptions, in a period of:
   A. stable prices, LIFO inventory is preferred to FIFO inventory.
   B. decreasing prices, FIFO inventory is preferred to LIFO inventory.
   C. increasing prices, FIFO cost of sales is preferred to LIFO cost of sales.

62. In general, as compared to companies with operating leases, companies with finance leases report:
   A. lower working capital and asset turnover.
   B. higher debt-to-equity ratios and return on equity in the early years.
   C. higher expenses in the early years and over the life of the lease.

63. Longboat, Inc. sold a luxury passenger boat from its inventory on December 31 for $2,000,000. It is estimated that Longboat will incur $100,000 in warranty expenses during its 5-year warranty period. Longboat's tax rate is 30%. To account for the tax implications of the warranty obligation prior to incurring warranty expenses, Longboat should:
   A. record a deferred tax asset of $30,000.
   B. record a deferred tax liability of $30,000.
   C. make no entry until actual warranty expenses are incurred.

64. During 20X3, Rory, Inc., reported net income of $15,000 and had 2,000 shares of common stock outstanding for the entire year. Rory also had 2,000 shares of 10%, $50 par value preferred stock outstanding during 20X3. During 20X1, Rory issued 100, $1,000 par, 6% bonds for $100,000. Each of these is convertible to 50 shares of common stock. Rory's tax rate is 40%. Assuming these bonds are dilutive, 20X3 diluted EPS for Rory is *closest* to:
   A. $0.71.
   B. $1.23.
   C. $2.50.

65. The category of items on the balance sheet that typically offers an analyst the best information on a non-financial firm's investing activities is:
   A. current assets.
   B. current liabilities.
   C. noncurrent assets.

66. A firm issues a 4-year semiannual-pay bond with a face value of $10 million and a coupon rate of 10%. The market interest rate is 11% when the bond is issued. The balance sheet liability at the end of the first semiannual period is *closest* to:
   A. $9,650,700.
   B. $9,683,250.
   C. $9,715,850.

67. The presentation format of balance sheet data that standardizes the first-year values to 1.0 and presents subsequent years' amounts relative to 1.0 is a(n):
   A. indexed balance sheet.
   B. vertical common-size balance sheet.
   C. horizontal common-size balance sheet.

68. For 20X1, Belcher Motors reported a decrease in its deferred tax liabilities, a decrease in its deferred tax assets, and an increase in its valuation allowance. To an analyst, this would *most likely* suggest that the company has:
   A. decreased its estimate of future profitability.
   B. increased the estimated useful life of some capitalized assets.
   C. increased its estimate of the period over which unearned revenue will be recognized.

©2014 Kaplan, Inc.

Questions 69 through 76 relate to Corporate Finance. (12 minutes)

69. At the beginning of the year, Breidel Company changes its inventory accounting method (for both financial and tax reporting) from first in first out to average cost. Assuming an environment of increasing prices, how will this accounting change affect Breidel's forecasts of its net cash position?
   A. No effect because this accounting change does not affect cash flows.
   B. Less net cash in both the short-term forecast and the long-term forecast.
   C. No effect on the short-term forecast but greater net cash in the long-term forecast.

70. A strong corporate code of ethics is *most likely* to permit:
   A. the company to award consulting contracts to board members.
   B. board members to simultaneously sit on the board of another firm.
   C. finder's fees for merger or acquisition targets to be paid to board members.

71. When using the CAPM to estimate the cost of common equity for a company in a developing country, an analyst should *most appropriately*:
   A. add a country risk premium to the market risk premium.
   B. add the sovereign yield spread to the CAPM cost of common equity.
   C. make no adjustments because country risk is reflected in the equity's beta.

72. The type of short-term financing for which the financing cost is *most closely* tied to the creditworthiness of a firm's customers is:
   A. factoring.
   B. issuing commercial paper.
   C. an uncommitted line of credit.

73. Smith Company's earnings per share are more sensitive to changes in operating income than are those of Jones Company. This implies that Smith Company has a higher degree of:
   A. total leverage.
   B. financial leverage.
   C. operating leverage.

74. If flotation costs are treated correctly in calculating the net present value of a project that will begin in the current period, the flotation costs are *most likely*:
   A. included in the initial outlay.
   B. reflected in the discount rate used for the project.
   C. included in the cost of the capital raised.

75. Thompson Products has seen its marginal tax rate increase from 28% to 34% over the last two years and believes the change is permanent. The effects of this change on Thompson's current WACC and on its financial leverage over time are *most likely* a(n):
    A. increase in both.
    B. decrease in both.
    C. increase in one and a decrease in the other.

76. The payment of a stock dividend will *most likely* decrease:
    A. a firm's net income and earnings per share.
    B. the value of a firm's equity and increase its return on equity.
    C. a firm's earnings per share but not affect the value of its equity.

Questions 77 through 85 relate to Portfolio Management. (13.5 minutes)

77. A portfolio manager and a client are developing an investment policy statement (IPS). The client works as an auditor for a public accounting firm that has a policy prohibiting its employees from investing in companies the firm audits. This restriction is *most appropriately*:
    A. not included in the IPS.
    B. listed in the IPS as a constraint.
    C. listed in an appendix to the IPS.

78. On average, which of the following types of investors has the shortest investment horizon?
    A. Endowment fund.
    B. Defined benefit plan.
    C. Property and casualty insurer.

79. In the market model, beta measures the sensitivity of an asset's rate of return to the market's:
    A. rate of return.
    B. excess return.
    C. risk-adjusted return.

80. A portfolio is invested 30% in Asset A with the remainder invested in Asset B. Asset A has an expected return of 6% and variance of returns of 0.031, while Asset B has an expected return of 7% and variance of returns of 0.045. The covariance between the returns of the two assets is 0.03735. The standard deviation of returns for the portfolio is *closest* to:
    A. 18%.
    B. 20%.
    C. 22%.

©2014 Kaplan, Inc.

81. Open-end mutual funds differ from closed-end funds in that:
    A. open-end funds stand ready to redeem their shares, while closed-end funds do not.
    B. closed-end funds require active management, while open-end funds do not.
    C. open-end funds issue shares that are then traded in secondary markets, while closed-end funds do not.

82. An analyst determines that four stocks have the following characteristics:

Stock	Beta	Estimated Return
X	1.0	10%
Y	1.6	16%
Z	2.0	16%

    If the risk-free rate is 4% and the expected return on the market is 10%, which of the following statements is *least accurate*?
    A. Stock X is properly valued.
    B. Stock Y is undervalued.
    C. Stock Z is overvalued.

83. According to the CAPM, a rational investor would be *least likely* to choose as his optimal portfolio:
    A. a 100% allocation to the risk-free asset.
    B. the global minimum variance portfolio.
    C. a 130% allocation to the market portfolio.

84. The risk-free rate is 5% and the expected market risk premium is 10%. A portfolio manager is projecting a return of 20% on a portfolio with a beta of 1.5. After adjusting for its systematic risk, this portfolio is expected to:
    A. equal the market's performance.
    B. outperform the market.
    C. underperform the market.

85. A researcher has collected a sample of annual total returns on an index portfolio for U.S. large capitalization equity securities over the past five years of 11%, 5%, –13%, 8%, and 9%. Based only on this information, the best estimate of the holding period return to be earned by investing in this index over the next two years is *closest to*:
    A. 7.3%.
    B. 8.0%.
    C. 8.2%.

Questions 86 through 97 relate to Equity Investments. (18 minutes)

86. An analyst determines that a company has a return on equity of 16% and pays 40% of its earnings in dividends. If the firm recently paid a $1.50 dividend and the stock is selling for $40, what is the required rate of return on the stock if it is priced according to the dividend discount model?
   A. 9.6%.
   B. 10.2%.
   C. 13.7%.

87. An investor buys a stock for $50. The initial margin requirement is 50%, and the maintenance margin requirement is 25%. The price below which the investor would receive a margin call would be:
   A. $25.00.
   B. $33.33.
   C. $37.50.

88. A securities market exhibits operational efficiency if it offers:
   A. low transaction costs.
   B. prices that respond rapidly to new information.
   C. rates of return that are proportional to risk on average.

89. A stock index consists of two stocks:
   • Company A has 50 shares outstanding valued at $2 each.
   • Company B has 10 shares outstanding valued at $10 each.
   • The price-weighted index is 6, and the value-weighted index is 100.

   In the next period, the price of Company A's stock increases to $4 per share, and Company B's stock splits two-for-one and is priced at $5. The value of the price-weighted index and the value-weighted index are:

	Price-weighted	Value-weighted
A.	7	150
B.	7	125
C.	4.5	150

90. Pam Robers, CFA, is performing a valuation analysis on the common stock of Allstare Inc. The stock's beta is 1.1, the risk-free rate is 5%, and the market risk premium is expected to be 8%. Allstare's ROE is expected to be constant at 18%, and its dividend payout ratio has been fairly constant over time at 40%. The forward-earnings multiplier that Robers should use to estimate the current value of the shares is *closest* to:
   A. 7.
   B. 13.
   C. 20.

©2014 Kaplan, Inc.

91. Pat McCoy, CFA, is analyzing a technology firm that has experienced annual earnings growth of 12%. McCoy does not expect the firm to begin paying dividends on its common shares in the foreseeable future. To estimate the value of this firm's common shares, McCoy should *most appropriately* use a:
   A. two-stage DDM.
   B. free cash flow model.
   C. Gordon growth model.

92. Over the past few years, the companies in an industry have experienced positive but decreasing profitability and growth rates. The companies have begun to compete intensely with each other and customers switch frequently among brands. This industry's life-cycle stage is *most accurately* described as:
   A. growth.
   B. maturity.
   C. shakeout.

93. An analyst gathered the following data about a company:
   - The historical earnings retention rate of 40% is projected to continue into the future.
   - The sustainable ROE is 12%.
   - The stock's beta is 1.2.
   - The nominal risk-free rate is 6%.
   - The expected market return is 11%.

   If the analyst believes next year's earnings will be $4 per share, what value should be placed on this stock?
   A. $22.24.
   B. $33.32.
   C. $45.45.

94. Which of the following classifications of firms is *least likely* to comprise cyclical firms?
   A. Housing.
   B. Technology.
   C. Telecommunications.

95. The assertion that investors, analysts, and portfolio managers exhibit psychological tendencies that cause them to make systematic errors is *most* consistent with:
   A. behavioral finance.
   B. weak-form market efficiency.
   C. fundamental analysis.

96. An investor purchases 1,000 shares of each of the stocks in a price-weighted index at their closing prices (ignore transactions costs). On a total return basis, if the index stocks remain the same, this portfolio will:
A. perform exactly like the index over time.
B. outperform the index over time.
C. underperform the index over time.

97. Among valuation models, the difficulty of estimating a required rate of return is *most likely* to be a disadvantage of using a(n):
A. Gordon growth model.
B. asset-based valuation model.
C. enterprise value multiplier model.

Questions 98 through 109 relate to Fixed Income. (18 minutes)

98. A 7.5% coupon, semiannual-pay, five-year bond has a yield to maturity of 6.80%. Over the next year, if the bond's yield to maturity remains unchanged, its price will:
A. increase.
B. decrease.
C. remain unchanged.

99. The type of credit risk that is most directly reflected in a bond's rating is:
A. default risk.
B. downgrade risk.
C. credit spread risk.

100. What effects will an increase in yield volatility have on the values of a putable bond and a callable bond?
A. Both bonds will increase in value.
B. Both bonds will decrease in value.
C. One bond will increase in value and the other will decrease.

101. Which of the following statements about debt securities is *least accurate*?
A. Commercial paper is a short-term vehicle for corporate borrowing.
B. A securitized bond is a security whose cash flows are linked to a pool of underlying loans or financial instruments.
C. A medium-term note (MTN) is a corporate bond with an original maturity of 2 to 10 years.

102. Portfolio duration *most accurately* approximates the sensitivity of the value of a bond portfolio to:
A. parallel shifts in the yield curve.
B. increases in the slope of the yield curve.
C. decreases in the slope of the yield curve.

©2014 Kaplan, Inc.

103. A firm is said to have a top-heavy capital structure if a high percentage of its total capital is:
    A. debt.
    B. short-term debt.
    C. secured bank debt.

104. An 8%, semiannual pay, option-free corporate bond that is selling at par has ten years to maturity. What is the approximate modified duration of the bond based on a 75 basis point change (up or down) in rates?
    A. 5.6.
    B. 6.8.
    C. 7.2.

105. The current 4-year spot rate is 4% and the current 5-year spot rate is 5.5%. What is the 1-year forward rate in four years?
    A. 9.58%.
    B. 10.14%.
    C. 11.72%.

106. A bond with nine years to maturity is quoted at an interpolated spread of +150 basis points. The benchmark yield for this bond is a:
    A. swap rate.
    B. matrix rate.
    C. government bond yield.

107. The face value of a $1,000,000 T-bill with 78 days to maturity is priced at $987,845. What is the bank discount yield (annualized) quote for the T-bill?
    A. 5.61%.
    B. 5.67%.
    C. 5.75%.

108. Bonds that are issued by a corporation, but paid from a pool of the corporation's assets that is legally bankruptcy-remote, are *best described* as:
    A. covered bonds.
    B. securitized bonds.
    C. collateralized bonds.

109. Extension in an agency residential mortgage-backed security is *most likely* to result from:
    A. a decrease in interest rates.
    B. exhaustion of a support tranche.
    C. slower-than-expected prepayments.

Questions 110 through 115 relate to Derivatives. (9 minutes)

110. When the underlying asset does not pay any cash flows, the value of an American call option is:
    A. equal to the value of an otherwise identical European call option.
    B. less than the value of an otherwise identical European call option.
    C. greater than the value of an otherwise identical European call option.

111. An investor writes a covered call with a strike price of $44 on a stock selling at $40 for a $3 premium. The range of possible payoffs to the writer of this covered call on the combined position is:
    A. −$40 to $47.
    B. −$37 to $7.
    C. $7 to infinity.

112. During the life of a European option, the amount by which its price is greater than its exercise value is *most accurately* described as its:
    A. time value.
    B. moneyness.
    C. intrinsic value.

113. Which of the following statements about plain vanilla interest rate swaps is *most accurate*? The swap counterparties:
    A. typically make a margin deposit with a clearinghouse.
    B. exchange fixed rate payments for variable rate payments.
    C. exchange the notional principal at initiation and termination.

114. The convenience yield associated with holding the underlying asset of a derivative is *most accurately* described as:
    A. the nonmonetary benefits of holding the asset.
    B. the monetary and nonmonetary benefits of holding the asset.
    C. the monetary and nonmonetary benefits of holding the asset, net of its holding costs.

115. Which of the following statements about futures margin is *least accurate*?
    A. The initial margin is set by the clearinghouse based on the volatility of the price of the underlying asset.
    B. If the balance of the margin account exceeds the initial margin requirement, the trader can remove the excess funds from the account.
    C. If the margin account balance falls below the maintenance margin level, the account balance must be brought back up to the maintenance level.

    ©2014 Kaplan, Inc.

Questions 116 through 120 relate to Alternative Investments. (7.5 minutes)

116. Josh Lacy, CFA, is analyzing a portfolio company held by his private equity firm to estimate its value in liquidation. Lacy should *most appropriately* use a(n):
    A. asset-based approach.
    B. comparables-based approach.
    C. discounted cash flow-based approach.

117. Which of the following statements with respect to hedge fund investing is *least accurate*?
    A. Hedge funds only publicly disclose performance information on a voluntary basis.
    B. Hedge funds are not typically registered with the SEC in the United States.
    C. Survivorship bias in hedge fund data causes risk to be overstated because funds that take on more risk tend to have higher returns.

118. An investor who wants to hedge against inflation by allocating a portion of a portfolio to alternative investments should *most appropriately* invest in:
    A. real estate and commodities.
    B. private equity and real estate.
    C. commodities and private equity.

119. A leveraged buyout firm that carries out a secondary sale has:
    A. offered additional shares to the public.
    B. exited an investment in a portfolio company.
    C. received new capital from its general or limited partners.

120. The notice period for a hedge fund is *best* described as the period following:
    A. the opening of the fund to investors, before the fund is closed to new investors.
    B. a request for redemption of shares, within which the fund must fulfill the request.
    C. an investment in the fund, during which the investor is not permitted to redeem shares.

EXAM 2
AFTERNOON SESSION

Calculating Your Score

Topic	Maximum Score	Your Score
Ethical and Professional Standards	18	
Quantitative Methods	14	
Economics	12	
Financial Reporting and Analysis	24	
Corporate Finance	9	
Portfolio Management	8	
Equity Investments	12	
Fixed Income	12	
Derivatives	6	
Alternative Investments	5	
Total	120	

The morning and afternoon exams are identically weighted over the topics and readings. You can therefore treat the morning and afternoon exams as independent exams.

If you took more than three hours (180 minutes) to complete this portion of the exam, you should adjust your score downward by one point for each minute you ran over.

Remember: the real exam *will be more difficult* than these practice exams. The main reason for this is the general anxiety and stress that you will be feeling on exam day, coupled with the time pressure you will be under. Many of the questions on this practice exam and the real exam are not individually difficult, so if you take extra time to answer the questions on this practice exam, your score will go up significantly. However, if you want an accurate measure of your potential performance on the exam, adhere to the 3-hour time limit.

After you have finished grading your practice exam, you may find it useful to use the exam questions and recommended solutions for review. Many of these questions were specifically written for your use as study tools. Once again, I feel I should remind you not to rely on memorizing these questions; you are not likely to see them on the actual exam. What you will see on the exam, though, are the concepts, terms, and procedures presented in these questions.

Your actual exam will most likely look different than what you see in this book. Please remember, no study provider knows the content of the actual exam. These practice exams are our best guess as to the structure, content, and difficulty of an actual exam.

Test Answers

1.	A	B	C
2.	A	B	C
3.	A	B	C
4.	A	B	C
5.	A	B	C
6.	A	B	C
7.	A	B	C
8.	A	B	C
9.	A	B	C
10.	A	B	C
11.	A	B	C
12.	A	B	C
13.	A	B	C
14.	A	B	C
15.	A	B	C
16.	A	B	C
17.	A	B	C
18.	A	B	C
19.	A	B	C
20.	A	B	C
21.	A	B	C
22.	A	B	C
23.	A	B	C
24.	A	B	C
25.	A	B	C
26.	A	B	C
27.	A	B	C
28.	A	B	C
29.	A	B	C
30.	A	B	C
31.	A	B	C
32.	A	B	C
33.	A	B	C
34.	A	B	C
35.	A	B	C
36.	A	B	C
37.	A	B	C
38.	A	B	C
39.	A	B	C
40.	A	B	C

41.	A	B	C
42.	A	B	C
43.	A	B	C
44.	A	B	C
45.	A	B	C
46.	A	B	C
47.	A	B	C
48.	A	B	C
49.	A	B	C
50.	A	B	C
51.	A	B	C
52.	A	B	C
53.	A	B	C
54.	A	B	C
55.	A	B	C
56.	A	B	C
57.	A	B	C
58.	A	B	C
59.	A	B	C
60.	A	B	C
61.	A	B	C
62.	A	B	C
63.	A	B	C
64.	A	B	C
65.	A	B	C
66.	A	B	C
67.	A	B	C
68.	A	B	C
69.	A	B	C
70.	A	B	C
71.	A	B	C
72.	A	B	C
73.	A	B	C
74.	A	B	C
75.	A	B	C
76.	A	B	C
77.	A	B	C
78.	A	B	C
79.	A	B	C
80.	A	B	C

81.	A	B	C
82.	A	B	C
83.	A	B	C
84.	A	B	C
85.	A	B	C
86.	A	B	C
87.	A	B	C
88.	A	B	C
89.	A	B	C
90.	A	B	C
91.	A	B	C
92.	A	B	C
93.	A	B	C
94.	A	B	C
95.	A	B	C
96.	A	B	C
97.	A	B	C
98.	A	B	C
99.	A	B	C
100.	A	B	C
101.	A	B	C
102.	A	B	C
103.	A	B	C
104.	A	B	C
105.	A	B	C
106.	A	B	C
107.	A	B	C
108.	A	B	C
109.	A	B	C
110.	A	B	C
111.	A	B	C
112.	A	B	C
113.	A	B	C
114.	A	B	C
115.	A	B	C
116.	A	B	C
117.	A	B	C
118.	A	B	C
119.	A	B	C
120.	A	B	C

Exam 2
Afternoon Session

Questions 1 through 18 relate to Ethical and Professional Standards.
(27 minutes)

1. Which of the following statements made in a marketing brochure is a violation of the Standards?
    A. "Roger Langley, Chartered Financial Analyst, has been a portfolio manager for ten years and passed all three levels of the CFA examinations on his first attempts."
    B. "Jennifer York has passed the Level II exam and will earn the right to use the CFA designation after completing the Level III exam this June."
    C. "Paul Yeng, CFA, has retired from the firm after 25 years of service. Much of the firm's past success can be attributed to Yeng's efforts as an analyst and portfolio manager."

2. Hedge Funds Unlimited, a global hedge fund, has publicly acknowledged in writing that it has adopted the CFA Institute Code and Standards as its policies. Which of the following is *least likely* a violation of the firm's policies?
    A. An analyst at the firm working overseas uses material nonpublic information as allowed by local law to make investment decisions for discretionary client accounts.
    B. A junior analyst at the firm uses a subscription to his local newspaper and the opinions of his friends and colleagues to make investment recommendations for discretionary client accounts.
    C. A CFA candidate at the firm, who is registered for the Level III exam, includes reference to participation in the CFA program and her status as a Level III candidate in her biographical background.

3. According to the Code and Standards, members and candidates who are involved in distributing an initial public offering (IPO) of equity shares and wish to participate in the IPO:
    A. may participate unless the IPO is oversubscribed.
    B. may not participate because this creates a conflict of interest.
    C. must obtain pre-clearance from a supervisor before participating.

4. Linda Bryant, CFA, is an employee of Roomkin Investment House, which underwrites equity and debt offerings. She has been approached by SimthCo to consult on a private debt placement. According to CFA Institute Standards of Professional Conduct, before Bryant agrees to accept this job, she is required to:
    A. obtain written consent from Roomkin after submitting details of the arrangement.
    B. talk to her immediate supervisor and get her approval to take this consulting job.
    C. inform SimthCo in writing that she will accept the job and provide details of the arrangement to Roomkin in writing.

5. To comply with the Code and Standards, analysts who send research recommendations to clients must:
    A. keep records of all the data and analysis that went into creating the report.
    B. send recommendations only to those clients for whom the investments are suitable.
    C. not send recommendations without including the underlying analysis and basic investment characteristics.

6. Amy Brooks, a CFA Level III candidate, has been given supervisory responsibilities. In carrying out her responsibilities, Brooks has discovered that the firm's compliance system is inadequate. She informed her supervisor, who is not supportive of Brooks's efforts to correct the situation. According to CFA Institute Standards of Professional Conduct, Brooks:
    A. has satisfied her obligation under the Code and Standards by informing her manager of the situation.
    B. must dissociate herself from the firm if the firm is not in compliance with the CFA Institute Standards.
    C. should decline in writing to accept supervisory responsibilities until an adequate compliance system is adopted.

7. Not including the results of terminated accounts when calculating historical performance is recommended by:
    A. both GIPS and the Standard concerning performance presentation.
    B. GIPS, but not by the Standard concerning performance presentation.
    C. neither GIPS nor the Standard concerning performance presentation.

©2014 Kaplan, Inc.

8. Ken Toma, CFA, has just completed an extensive analysis and concluded that the demand for vacation rentals in Hawaii will far exceed the supply for the foreseeable future. Toma writes a research report stating, "Based on the fact that the demand for Hawaiian beach vacations will exceed the supply of rooms for the foreseeable future, I recommend the purchase of shares of The Hawaiian REIT, a diversified portfolio of Hawaiian beachfront resorts." If Toma presents this report to his clients, he will *most likely* violate the CFA Institute Standards by:
   A. not distinguishing between fact and opinion.
   B. not considering the suitability of the investment for his clients.
   C. failing to have a reasonable and adequate basis for his recommendation.

9. Derek Stevens, CFA, manages the pension plan assets of Colors, Inc. When voting proxies for plan equities, Stevens owes a fiduciary duty to:
   A. the plan trustees who hired him.
   B. the plan participants and beneficiaries.
   C. the managers, stockholders, and bondholders of Colors, Inc. equally.

10. An analyst at Romer changes her rating on TelSky from "buy" to "hold" and sends an email explaining the change to all clients and firm brokers. Subsequently, Paul Stevens, CFA, a broker at Romer, receives a call from a client who wants to buy 15,000 shares of TelSky. Stevens must:
   A. advise his client of the change in recommendation before accepting the order.
   B. not accept the order until the customer has had time to receive and read the new report.
   C. accept the order without mentioning the ratings change because the order is unsolicited.

11. Which of the following is one of the nine major sections of the GIPS standards?
   A. Verification.
   B. Private equity.
   C. Sub-advisers.

12. Edie Pschorr, CFA, notices that a bond is priced at 98.0 in one market and 98.4 in another market. Pschorr places an order to buy a large number of these bonds in the first market and simultaneously places an order to sell the same number of bonds in the second market. The bond's price increases to 98.2 in the first market and decreases to 98.2 in the second market. Are Pschorr's trades a violation of the Code and Standards?
   A. No.
   B. Yes, because they violate the Standard concerning fair dealing.
   C. Yes, because they violate the Standard concerning market manipulation.

13. Greg Hoffman, CFA, has been hired by Hill Manufacturing, Inc. (HMI) to write a research report on their company. Hoffman writes a report on HMI with a "buy" recommendation and posts the report for purchase on his website but does not include the information that HMI paid for the research. According to the Standards that govern independence and objectivity and disclosure of conflicts, Hoffman has violated:
    A. both of these Standards.
    B. neither of these Standards.
    C. only one of these Standards.

14. Rhonda Morrow, CFA, is an analyst for Waller & Madison, a brokerage and investment banking firm. Waller & Madison is a market maker for CorpEast, and Tim Waller, a principal in Morrow's firm, sits on CorpEast's board. Morrow has been asked to write a research report on CorpEast. According to the Standard regarding disclosure of conflicts, Morrow:
    A. must not write the report.
    B. must disclose that Waller & Madison is a market maker in CorpEast shares but not that Waller is a board member.
    C. may write the report if she discloses both that Waller & Madison is a market maker in CorpEast shares and that Waller sits on the CorpEast board.

15. John Farr, CFA, has accumulated several pieces of nonmaterial nonpublic information about CattleCorp from his contacts with the company. From analysis based on this information, together with public information, Farr concludes that CattleCorp will have unexpectedly low earnings this year. Farr has contacted the company, but they will not confirm his conclusion. According to CFA Institute Standards of Professional Conduct, Farr:
    A. may trade or make recommendations based on his analysis.
    B. may not trade or make recommendations based on his analysis.
    C. may trade or make recommendations based on his analysis only if his company's compliance officer determines that the nonpublic information he used was not material.

16. According to the GIPS standards, which of the following statements is *most accurate*?
    A. Firms are required to obtain independent third-party verification for a claim of GIPS compliance.
    B. GIPS compliant firms are required to maintain written documentation of policies and procedures used to establish and maintain compliance with GIPS.
    C. To initially claim compliance with GIPS, a company must present a minimum of ten years (or since the firm's inception if less than ten years) of GIPS-compliant performance data.

 ©2014 Kaplan, Inc.

17. Shan Ang, CFA, is a portfolio manager at Huang Investments. Lian Jan, an old friend of Ang's, is an executive recruiter in the same city. Jan refers any high-level executives that she places locally to Ang. In return, Jan gives Ang one round of golf at her country club for each new client referred to her by Jan. According to the Standard concerning referral fees, Ang is required to disclose the referral arrangement:
   A. only to all prospective clients referred by Jan.
   B. to his employer and all prospective clients referred by Jan.
   C. to all prospective clients, current clients, and his employer.

18. Yvette Michaels, CFA, an analyst for Torborg Investments, inadvertently overhears a conversation between two executives of Collective Healthcare in which they mention an upcoming tender offer for Network, a stock she covers. Michaels has followed both companies extensively and feels their consolidation would be very beneficial for both companies. She tells her supervisor, a senior analyst, about the proposed tender offer. Michaels' actions are:
   A. in violation of the Standards.
   B. not in violation of the Standards because she told only her supervisor.
   C. not in violation of the Standards because she has not traded shares of Network or changed her report on the company.

Questions 19 through 32 relate to Quantitative Methods. (21 minutes)

19. The odds for an event occurring are calculated by dividing:
   A. one by the probability that the event occurs.
   B. the probability that the event does not occur by the probability that an event occurs.
   C. the probability that the event occurs by the probability that the event does not occur.

20. A successful investor has decided to set up a scholarship fund for deserving students at her alma mater. Her plan is for the fund to be capable of awarding $25,000 annually in perpetuity. The first scholarship is to be awarded and paid out exactly four years from today. The funds will be deposited into an account immediately and will grow at a rate of 4%, compounded semiannually, for the foreseeable future. How much money must the investor donate today to fund the scholarship?
   A. $528,150.
   B. $549,487.
   C. $574,253.

21. Which of the following statements about return distributions is *most accurate*?
    A. With positive skewness, the median is greater than the mean.
    B. If skewness is positive, the average magnitude of positive deviations from the mean is smaller than the average magnitude of negative deviations from the mean.
    C. If a return distribution has positive excess kurtosis and the analyst uses statistical models that do not account for the fatter tails, the analyst will underestimate the likelihood of extreme outcomes.

22. An analyst plans to use the following test statistic: $t_{n-1} = \dfrac{\bar{x} - \mu_0}{s / \sqrt{n}}$.

    This test statistic is appropriate for a hypothesis about the:
    A. mean difference of two normal populations.
    B. population mean of a normal distribution with unknown variance.
    C. the equality of two population means of two normally distributed populations based on independent samples.

23. Which of the following statements about covariance and the correlation coefficient is *least accurate*?
    A. Covariance is a measure of how the returns of two assets tend to move together over time.
    B. The correlation coefficient is computed by dividing the covariance of returns on two assets by the individual variances of returns for the two assets.
    C. The covariance of returns between two assets is equal to the correlation between the returns of the two assets, multiplied by the product of their standard deviations of returns.

24. Greg Goldman, research analyst in the fixed-income area of an investment bank, needs to determine the average duration of a sample of twenty 15-year fixed-coupon investment grade bonds. Goldman first categorizes the bonds by risk class and then randomly selects bonds from each class. After combining the bonds selected (bond ratings and other information taken as of March 31 of the current year), he calculates a sample mean duration of 10.5 years. Assuming that the actual population mean duration is 9.7 years, which of the following statements about Goldman's sampling process and sample is *least accurate*?
    A. Goldman is using time-series data.
    B. The sample mean is a random variable.
    C. The sampling error is 0.8 years.

25. The type of technical analysis chart *most likely* to be useful for intermarket analysis is a:
    A. candlestick chart.
    B. point and figure chart.
    C. relative strength chart.

 ©2014 Kaplan, Inc.

26. If Stock X has a standard deviation of returns of 18.9% and Stock Y has a standard deviation of returns equal to 14.73% and returns on the stocks are perfectly positively correlated, the standard deviation of an equally weighted portfolio of the two is:
    A. 10.25%.
    B. 14.67%.
    C. 16.82%.

27. Over a sample period, an investor gathers the following data about three mutual funds.

Mutual Fund	Risk-Free Rate	Portfolio Return	Portfolio Standard Deviation	Portfolio Beta
P	5%	13%	18%	1.2
Q	5%	15%	20%	1.4
R	5%	18%	24%	1.8

    Based solely on the Sharpe measure, an investor would prefer mutual fund:
    A. P.
    B. Q.
    C. R.

28. An investment manager wants to select three analysts from a group of six analysts to receive first-, second-, and third-place awards for outstanding performance. In how many ways can the investment manager make the three awards?
    A. 20 ways.
    B. 54 ways.
    C. 120 ways.

29. Which of the following statements about the central limit theorem is *least accurate*? The:
    A. standard deviation of the sample mean is called the standard error of the sample mean.
    B. standard error of the sample mean can be estimated by dividing the population standard deviation by $\sqrt{n-1}$.
    C. sample means for large sample sizes will have an approximately normal distribution regardless of the distribution of the underlying population.

30. An investment analyst takes a random sample of 100 aggressive equity
     funds and calculates the average beta as 1.7. The sample betas have a
     standard deviation of 0.4. Using a 95% confidence interval and a
     z-statistic, which of the following statements about the confidence interval
     and its interpretation is *most accurate*? The analyst can be confident at the
     95% level that the interval:
     A. 1.580 to 1.820 includes the mean of the population beta.
     B. 1.622 to 1.778 includes the mean of the population beta.
     C. 1.634 to 1.766 includes the mean of the population beta.

31. Which is the correct test statistic for a test of the null hypothesis that a
     population variance is equal to a chosen value?
     A. F-statistic.
     B. t-statistic.
     C. Chi-square statistic.

32. From a high of $180, a stock price decreases to a low of $100 and then
     begins increasing. A technical analyst states that she expects resistance
     levels to emerge at $140, $150, and $153.33. This analyst is *most likely*
     forecasting these resistance levels based on:
     A. Fibonacci numbers.
     B. an inverse head and shoulders pattern.
     C. moving average convergence/divergence lines.

Questions 33 through 44 relate to Economics. (18 minutes)

33. To benefit from price discrimination, a monopolist *least likely* needs to
     have:
     A. a higher-quality product at a premium price and a lower-quality
         alternative.
     B. a way to prevent reselling between types of consumers.
     C. two identifiable groups of consumers with different price
         elasticities of demand for the product.

34. Automatic stabilizers are government programs that require no legislation
     and tend to:
     A. automatically increase spending at the same growth rate as real GDP.
     B. reduce interest rates, thus stimulating aggregate demand.
     C. change the government budget deficit in an opposite direction to
         economic growth.

35. An economy is in full-employment equilibrium. If the government
     unexpectedly decreases the tax rate, in the short run the economy is
     most likely to experience:
     A. an increase in employment.
     B. a decrease in the price level.
     C. no change in employment and an increase in the price level.

©2014 Kaplan, Inc.

36. Notasled, Inc., a producer of cafeteria trays, operates in a perfectly competitive market. If the market price of a cafeteria tray is $3.25, Notasled will increase production so long as:
   A. marginal revenue is positive.
   B. marginal cost is less than $3.25.
   C. marginal revenue is greater than $3.25.

37. Three years ago, the U.S. dollar/euro exchange rate was 1.32 USD/EUR. Over the last three years, the price level in the United States has increased by 18%, and the price level in the eurozone has increased by 12%. If the current exchange rate is 1.40 USD/EUR, the real exchange rate over the period has:
   A. increased, and eurozone goods are now more expensive to U.S. consumers.
   B. decreased, and eurozone goods are now more expensive to U.S. consumers.
   C. increased, and U.S. goods are now more expensive to eurozone consumers.

38. Consider a market where quantity supplied = 1,500 − 3 × price, and quantity demanded = 2,000 − 5 × price. With respect to equilibrium price and quantity, there is:
   A. no market equilibrium.
   B. a stable market equilibrium.
   C. an unstable market equilibrium.

39. Which of the following is *most likely* a characteristic of monopolistic competition?
   A. Producer decisions are interdependent.
   B. Each producer offers a differentiated product.
   C. Producers face horizontal demand curves.

40. The Fisher effect describes the relationship among:
   A. savings, investment, the fiscal balance, and the trade balance.
   B. credit expansion, investor expectations, and the business cycle.
   C. nominal interest rates, real interest rates, and expected inflation.

41. Which of the following events is *most likely* to increase short-run aggregate supply (shift the curve to the right)?
   A. Inflation that results in an increase in goods prices.
   B. High unemployment puts downward pressure on money wages.
   C. An increase in government spending intended to increase real output.

42. An unexpected increase in businesses' inventory-to-sales ratios is *most likely* to occur as an economy:
   A. reaches a trough.
   B. enters a contraction phase.
   C. approaches the peak of an expansion.

43.   A government is auctioning 500 newly issued bonds and receives the
       following bids:

Bidder	Yield	Number of Bonds
Bidder 1	5.25%	200
Bidder 2	5.30%	100
Bidder 3	5.40%	300
Bidder 4	5.45%	400

Bidder 3 receives 200 bonds at a yield of 5.40%. This auction is *best*
described as a(n):
A. second price auction.
B. ascending price auction.
C. descending price auction.

44.   In the short run, the average product of labor:
A. is increasing when the total product of labor is increasing.
B. is at a maximum where it intersects the marginal product of labor
    curve.
C. is upward-sloping if the firm is experiencing diminishing marginal
    returns to labor.

**Questions 45 through 68 relate to Financial Reporting and Analysis.
(36 minutes)**

45.   When the Rivers Company filed its corporate tax returns for the first
       quarter of the current year, it owed a total of $6.7 million in corporate
       taxes. Rivers paid $4.4 million of the tax bill, but still owes $2.3 million. It
       also received $478,000 in the second quarter as a down payment towards
       $942,000 in custom-built products to be delivered in the third quarter. Its
       financial accounts for the second quarter *most likely* show the $2.3 million
       and the $478,000 as:

$2.3 million	$478,000
A. Income tax payable	Unearned revenue
B. Income tax payable	Accrued revenue
C. Deferred tax liability	Accrued revenue

46.   Which of the following statements about the appropriate revenue
       recognition method to use under U.S. GAAP is *most accurate*? Use the:
A. percentage-of-completion method if the firm cannot reliably estimate
    the outcome of the project.
B. completed contract method if ultimate payment is reasonably assured
    and revenue and costs can be reliably estimated.
C. installment method if collectability of payments for a sale cannot be
    reasonably estimated.

            ©2014 Kaplan, Inc.

47.   An analyst gathered the following data about a company:
- Collections from customers are $5,000.
- Depreciation is $800.
- Cash expenses (including taxes) are $2,000.
- Tax rate = 30%.
- Net cash increased by $1,000.

If inventory increases over the period by $800, cash flow from operations equals:
A. $1,600.
B. $2,400.
C. $3,000.

48.   Which of the following statements about the indirect method of calculating cash flow from operations is *least accurate*?
A. Depreciation is added back to net income because it is an expense not requiring cash.
B. No adjustment is needed to account for changes in accounts receivable because no cash is involved.
C. No adjustment is needed for the payment of taxes because the tax payment is already in net income.

49.   Assuming stable inventory quantities, in a period of:
A. rising prices, LIFO results in higher ending inventory and FIFO results in higher gross profit.
B. falling prices, LIFO results in higher gross profit and FIFO results in lower cost of goods sold.
C. rising prices, LIFO results in higher cost of goods sold and FIFO results in higher working capital.

50.   Compared to reporting in a country where life insurance payments on key employees are deductible for tax, a company that makes such payments and reports in a country in which they are not tax deductible would report a:
A. lower statutory tax rate.
B. higher effective tax rate.
C. greater deferred tax asset.

51.   Which of the following is *most likely* presented on a common-size balance sheet or common-size income statement?
A. Total asset turnover.
B. Operating profit margin.
C. Return on common equity.

52. An analyst gathers the following data about a company:
    - The company had 1 million shares of common stock outstanding for the entire year.
    - The company's beginning stock price was $50, its ending price was $70, and its average price was $60.
    - The company had 100,000 warrants outstanding for the entire year. Each warrant allows the holder to buy one share of common stock at $50 per share.

    How many shares of common stock should the company use in computing its diluted earnings per share?
    A. 1,100,000.
    B. 1,083,333.
    C. 1,016,667.

53. Under U.S. GAAP, land owned by the firm is *most likely* to be reported on the balance sheet at:
    A. historical cost.
    B. fair market value minus selling costs.
    C. historical cost less accumulated depreciation.

54. Which of the following items is *least likely* to contain details about various accruals, adjustments, balances, and management assumptions?
    A. Income statement.
    B. Supplementary schedules.
    C. Discussion and analysis by management.

55. A firm presents the following income statement, which complies with the standards under which it must report:

Sales	20,535
Cost of goods sold	14,525
Operating expenses	2,530
Operating income	3,480
Income taxes	1,220
Income from continuing operations	2,260
Extraordinary items, net of tax	(525)
Net income	1,735

    Based on the differences between U.S. GAAP and International Financial Reporting Standards, this firm:
    A. must report any dividends received as operating cash flows.
    B. is permitted to recognize upward revaluations of long-lived assets.
    C. cannot have used LIFO as its inventory cost assumption.

©2014 Kaplan, Inc.

56. A permanent difference between pretax and taxable income is *least likely* to arise when a firm:
    A. receives tax-exempt interest.
    B. uses the installment sales method for financial reporting.
    C. pays premiums on life insurance of key employees.

57. According to the IASB Conceptual Framework for Financial Reporting, what are the two fundamental qualitative characteristics of financial statements that make them useful to their users?
    A. Timeliness and comparability.
    B. Verifiability and understandability.
    C. Relevance and faithful representation.

58. A firm uses the first-in first-out (FIFO) cost flow assumption. Compared to gross profit with a periodic inventory system, the firm's gross profit with a perpetual inventory system would be:
    A. lower.
    B. higher.
    C. the same.

59. From the lessee's perspective, compared to an operating lease, a finance lease results in:
    A. higher asset turnover.
    B. a higher debt-to-equity ratio.
    C. lower operating cash flow.

60. Compared to a firm that appropriately expenses recurring maintenance costs, a firm that capitalizes these costs will have greater cash flow from:
    A. financing activities.
    B. investing activities.
    C. operating activities.

61. While motivation and opportunity both can lead to low quality of financial reporting, a third important contributing factor is:
    A. poor financial controls.
    B. rationalization of the actions.
    C. pressure to meet earnings expectations.

62. Which of the following firms is *most likely* to present a liquidity-based balance sheet rather than a classified balance sheet?
    A. Banking institution.
    B. Manufacturing firm.
    C. Chain of retail stores.

63. Lamar Athelston is comparing two firms in the same industry. After adjusting for dilutive securities and differences in financial reporting standards, Athelston calculates the following ratios:

	Earnings per Share	Operating Cash Flow per Share
Company Y	$3.00	$2.00
Company Z	$2.00	$3.00

Based only on this information, should Athelston conclude that Company Y exhibits better profitability than Company Z?
   A. Yes, because Company Y has higher earnings per share.
   B. No, because Company Z has higher operating cash flow per share.
   C. No, because these measures are not appropriate for comparing different companies.

64. Granite, Inc. owns a machine with a carrying value of $3.0 million and a salvage value of $2.0 million. The present value of the machine's future cash flows is $1.7 million. The asset is permanently impaired. Granite should:
   A. immediately write down the machine to its salvage value.
   B. immediately write down the machine to its recoverable amount.
   C. write down the machine to its recoverable amount as soon as it is depreciated down to salvage value.

65. Yamaska Mining issued a 5-year, $50 million face, 6% semiannual bond when market interest rates were 7%. The market yield of the bonds was 8% at the beginning of the next year. Using the effective interest rate method, what is the initial balance sheet liability, and what is the interest expense that the company should report for the first half of the second year of the bond's life (the third semiannual period)?

	Initial liability	Interest expense, first half of year 2
A.	$47,920,849	$1,689,853
B.	$47,920,849	$1,750,000
C.	$50,000,000	$1,500,000

66. Clement Company has revalued an intangible asset with an indefinite life upward by €25 million. In its financial statements, Clement will *most likely*:
   A. disclose how it determined the fair value of the intangible asset.
   B. report lower net income in subsequent periods because of increased amortization expense on the asset.
   C. report higher assets, net income, and shareholders' equity in the most recent period than it would have reported under the cost model.

67. As a result of a recent acquisition, Lombard, Inc. has placed the following items on their balance sheet as of the beginning of their fiscal year:

Goodwill	$30 million	
Patent	$10 million	Expires in 10 years.
Trademark	$15 million	Expires in 15 years, renewable at minimal cost.

If Lombard amortizes intangible assets using the straight line method, the amortization expense on these assets for the fiscal year will be:
A. $1 million.
B. $2 million.
C. $3 million.

68. A firm pays accrued wages with cash. Assuming a current ratio greater than one and a quick ratio that is less than one, what will be the impact on the current ratio and the quick ratio?
A. Both ratios will remain the same.
B. The current ratio will increase and the quick ratio will decrease.
C. The current ratio will decrease and the quick ratio will increase.

Questions 69 through 77 relate to Corporate Finance. (13.5 minutes)

69. Responsibilities of a board of directors' nominations committee are *least likely* to include:
A. recruiting qualified members to the board.
B. selecting an external auditor for the company.
C. preparing a succession plan for the company's executive management.

70. The following data applies to LeVeit Company:
- LeVeit has a target debt-to-equity ratio of 0.5.
- LeVeit's bonds are currently yielding 10%.
- LeVeit is a constant growth (5%) firm that just paid a dividend of $3.00.
- LeVeit's stock sells for $31.50 per share.
- The company's marginal tax rate is 40%.

The company's weighted after-tax cost of capital is *closest* to:
A. 10.5%.
B. 11.0%.
C. 12.0%.

71. Timely Taxis, Ltd. has signed a long-term lease for 20 underground parking spots at $150 each per month for its fleet of taxis. The firm currently has 18 taxis in operation and is performing an NPV analysis on the purchase of a 19th taxi. The cost of parking for the 19th taxi is *best* described as a(n):
    A. sunk cost.
    B. opportunity cost.
    C. incremental cost.

72. If a firm uses the weighted average cost of capital (WACC) to discount cash flows of higher than average risk projects, which one of the following will *most likely* occur?
    A. Project NPVs will be understated.
    B. The firm will reject profitable projects.
    C. The overall risk of the firm's investments will rise over time.

73. Michael Robe, CFA, is a junior analyst for a large financial institution and has been preparing an analysis of United Mines, a coal mining company located in the United States. As part of his research, he examines the company's proxy voting and rules and practices. Which of the following policies would be considered the *most* restrictive to shareholders?
    A. Shareholders of United Mines are allowed to cast confidential votes but must be present to do so.
    B. Corporate policy prohibits the use of share blocking prior to United Mines' annual meetings.
    C. United Mines requires shareowner attendance to vote but coordinates the timing of its annual meeting to be held on the same day as other companies in the region.

74. Wreathfield, Inc. is choosing between two mutually exclusive projects. The cash flows for the two projects are below. The firm has a cost of capital of 12%, and the risk of the projects is equivalent to the average risk of the firm.

	0	1	2	3	4	5	6
Project J:	−12,000	4,000	5,000	6,000			
Project K:	−20,000	3,000	3,000	3,000	5,000	8,000	8,000

    Wreathfield should accept:
    A. Project J.
    B. Project K.
    C. Neither project J nor project K.

 ©2014 Kaplan, Inc.

75. If firms Acme and Butler have the same amount of sales and equal quick ratios, but Acme's receivables turnover is higher, it is *most likely* that:
   A. Butler has better liquidity than Acme.
   B. Butler has a lower cash ratio than Acme.
   C. Acme's average days of receivables is higher than Butler's.

76. Daker Industries reports assets of £140 million and liabilities of £85 million. Daker decides to repurchase 5% of its 11 million outstanding shares through a tender offer at £5 per share when the market price is £4.75. If the tender offer is fully subscribed, the *most likely* effect on the book value of Daker's shares will be to:
   A. increase the book value of Daker shares by 5%.
   B. decrease the book value of Daker shares by 5%.
   C. have no effect on the book value of Daker shares.

77. A firm's optimal capital budget can be found by moving along its investment opportunity schedule until:
   A. it exhausts its capital budget.
   B. average project return is equal to average cost of capital.
   C. the next project's return is less than the marginal cost of capital.

Questions 78 through 85 relate to Portfolio Management. (12 minutes)

78. Which of the following types of institutions is *most likely* to have the lowest risk tolerance?
   A. Commercial bank.
   B. College endowment.
   C. Mutual fund company.

79. Under which type of pension plan are retirement benefit payments an obligation of the sponsoring firm?
   A. Defined benefit plan only.
   B. Defined contribution plan only.
   C. Both a defined benefit plan and a defined contribution plan.

80. When comparing portfolios that plot on the security market line (SML) to those that plot on the capital market line (CML), a financial analyst would *most accurately* state that portfolios that lie on the SML:
   A. have only systematic risk, while portfolios on the CML have both systematic and unsystematic risk.
   B. are not necessarily well diversified, while portfolios on the CML are well diversified.
   C. are not necessarily priced at their equilibrium values, while portfolios on the CML are priced at their equilibrium values.

81. Which of the following possible portfolios is *least likely* to lie on the efficient frontier?

Portfolio	Expected Return	Standard Deviation
X	9%	12%
Y	11%	10%
Z	13%	15%

  A. Portfolio X.
  B. Portfolio Y.
  C. Portfolio Z.

82. In extending the 3-factor model of Fama and French, the additional factor suggested by Carhart that is often used is:
  A. GDP growth.
  B. price momentum.
  C. market-to-book value.

83. Martin Dean, CFA, is a portfolio manager who is writing an investment policy statement (IPS) for Albert Francis, a new client. The *least likely* reason why Dean should prepare an IPS is to:
  A. set the target asset allocation for Francis's portfolio.
  B. comply with the Code and Standards with regard to suitability.
  C. specify a benchmark against which to measure Dean's performance.

84. An analyst gathered the following data about three stocks:

Stock	Beta	Estimated Return
A	1.5	18.1%
B	1.1	15.7%
C	0.6	12.5%

  If the risk-free rate is 8%, and the market risk premium is 7%, the analyst is *least likely* to recommend buying:
  A. Stock A.
  B. Stock B.
  C. Stock C.

85. Which of the following equity securities is *most likely* to have a beta greater than one?
  A. Utility stock.
  B. Health care stock.
  C. Homebuilder stock.

 ©2014 Kaplan, Inc.

Questions 86 through 97 relate to Equity Investments. (18 minutes)

86.   Martin Gomez holds 100 shares of each of the stocks in a price-weighted index and reinvests cash dividends in additional shares. Assuming there are no stock splits, stock dividends, or changes in the makeup of the index, how will Gomez's portfolio return compare with the price return of the index if the low-priced index stocks outperform the high-priced index stocks?
      A. Gomez's portfolio return will be higher.
      B. The price return of the index will be higher.
      C. Gomez's portfolio return will be equal to the price return of the index.

87.   Evelyn Stram, CFA, places a good-till-cancelled limit buy order at 86 for a stock. Stram's order specifies:
      A. clearing and validity instructions.
      B. validity and execution instructions.
      C. execution and clearing instructions.

88.   The type of equity security that gives its owners the right to vote the shares of, and receive dividends from, a foreign company is *best* described as a:
      A. global depository receipt.
      B. sponsored depository receipt.
      C. fully-owned depository receipt.

89.   Ron Egan, CFA, classifies firms in the transportation industry in peer groups that include airlines and bus operators. Egan learns that one of the airlines, Acme, derives half its revenue from its Acme Bus Lines subsidiary. Egan adds Acme to his peer group for bus operators while continuing to include Acme in his peer group for airlines. Is Egan's treatment of Acme appropriate?
      A. Yes.
      B. No, because each company should be included in only one peer group.
      C. No, because the bus operations are not the company's principal business activity.

90. An analyst gathered the following data about a company:
    - A historical earnings retention rate of 60% that is projected to continue into the future.
    - A sustainable return on equity of 10%.
    - A beta of 1.0.
    - The nominal risk-free rate is 5%.
    - The expected market return is 10%.

    If next year's EPS is $2 per share, what value should be estimated for this stock?
    A. $20.00.
    B. $30.50.
    C. $35.45.

91. The type of equity index *most likely* to require rebalancing is a(n):
    A. price-weighted index.
    B. equal-weighted index.
    C. market-capitalization index.

92. A high yield bond fund states that through active management, the fund's return has outperformed an index of Treasury securities by 4% on average over the past five years. As a performance benchmark for this fund, the index chosen is:
    A. appropriate.
    B. inappropriate, because the index return does not reflect active management.
    C. inappropriate, because the index does not reflect the actual bonds in which the fund invests.

93. The change in the intrinsic value of a firm's common stock resulting from an increase in ROE *most likely*:
    A. increases the stock's intrinsic value.
    B. decreases the stock's intrinsic value.
    C. depends on the reason for the increase in ROE.

94. Which of the following statements about short selling is *least accurate*?
    A. A short seller is required to set up a margin account.
    B. A short sale involves securities the investor does not own.
    C. A short seller loses if the price of the stock sold short decreases.

95. Compared to an index of 100 U.S. exchange-traded stocks, an index of 100 U.S. government and corporate bonds will *most likely*:
    A. reflect equally timely price data.
    B. be more difficult to build and maintain.
    C. have less turnover among the securities in the index.

 ©2014 Kaplan, Inc.

96. Beth Knight, CFA, and David Royal, CFA, are independently analyzing the value of Bishop, Inc. stock. Bishop paid a dividend of $1 last year. Knight expects the dividend to grow by 10% in each of the next three years, after which it will grow at a constant rate of 4% per year. Royal also expects a temporary growth rate of 10% followed by a constant growth rate of 4%, but he expects the supernormal growth to last for only two years. Knight estimates that the required return on Bishop stock is 9%, but Royal believes the required return is 10%. Royal's valuation of Bishop stock is approximately:
    A. equal to Knight's valuation.
    B. $5 less than Knight's valuation.
    C. $5 greater than Knight's valuation.

97. An industry in the growth phase of the industry life cycle is *most likely* to experience:
    A. increasing prices.
    B. increasing profitability.
    C. intense competition among competitors.

Questions 98 through 109 relate to Fixed Income. (18 minutes)

98. Consider the following Treasury spot rates expressed as bond equivalent yields:

Maturity	Spot Rate
6 months	3.0%
1 year	3.5%
1.5 years	4.0%
2 years	4.5%

    If a Treasury note with two years remaining to maturity has a 5% semiannual coupon and is priced at $1,008, the note is:
    A. overpriced.
    B. underpriced.
    C. correctly priced.

99. Which of the following is an advantage of a callable bond (compared to an identical option-free bond) to an investor?
    A. Less reinvestment risk.
    B. Higher yield.
    C. More convexity.

100. An investor is considering the purchase of Security X, which matures in ten years and has a par value of $1,000. During the first five years, X has a 6% coupon with quarterly payments. During the remaining five years, X has an 8% coupon with quarterly payments. The face value is paid at maturity. A second 10-year security, Security Z, has a 6% semiannual coupon and is selling at par. Assuming that X has the same bond equivalent yield as Z, the price of Security X is *closest* to:
   A. $943.
   B. $1,036.
   C. $1,067.

101. The yield spreads between corporate bonds and government bonds are *most likely* to decrease if:
   A. liquidity decreases in the market for the corporate bonds.
   B. a credit rating downgrade on the corporate bonds becomes more likely.
   C. investors increase their estimates of the recovery rate on the corporate bonds.

102. The full price of a bond:
   A. includes accrued interest.
   B. includes commissions and taxes.
   C. is also known as the "clean" price.

103. Which of the following is a disadvantage to bondholders if a bond has a sinking fund provision?
   A. Lower credit quality.
   B. Unfavorable tax status.
   C. Greater reinvestment risk.

104. A debt covenant designates one of a holding company's subsidiaries as restricted. Which of the following credit-related considerations does this covenant address?
   A. Credit migration risk.
   B. Structural subordination.
   C. Payments to equity holders.

105. Consider a collateralized mortgage obligation (CMO) structure with one planned amortization class (PAC) class and one support tranche outstanding. If the prepayment speed is higher than the upper collar on the PAC, the:
   A. life of the PAC tranche will increase.
   B. PAC tranche has no risk of prepayments.
   C. life of the support tranche will decrease.

©2014 Kaplan, Inc.

106. For a bond currently priced at $1,018 with an effective duration of 7.48, if the market yield moved down 75 basis points, the new price would be approximately:
    A. $961.
    B. $1,075.
    C. $1,094.

107. A public offering of bonds issued over a period of time is *most accurately* described as a:
    A. serial structure.
    B. shelf registration.
    C. waterfall structure.

108. The minimum data required to calculate the implied forward rate for three years beginning three years from now is:
    A. the 3-year and 6-year spot rates.
    B. the 4-year, 5-year, and 6-year spot rates.
    C. spot rates at 1-year intervals for the 6-year period.

109. A 3-year, 6% coupon, semiannual-pay note has a yield to maturity of 5.5%. If an investor holds this note to maturity and earns a 4.5% return on reinvested coupon income, his realized yield on the note is *closest* to:
    A. 5.46%.
    B. 5.57%.
    C. 5.68%.

Questions 110 through 115 relate to Derivatives. (9 minutes)

110. Ed Verdi has a long position in a European put option on a stock. At expiration, the stock price is greater than the exercise price. The value of the put option to Verdi on its expiration date is:
    A. zero.
    B. positive.
    C. negative.

111. Janet Powers writes a covered call on a stock she owns, Billings, Inc. The current price of the stock is $45, and Powers writes the call at a strike price of $50. The call option premium is $3.50. Which of the following statements regarding Powers's covered call strategy is *most accurate*?
    A. Powers is trading the stock's upside potential in exchange for current income.
    B. The price of the stock must rise to at least $48.50 before Powers will lose money.
    C. Powers is eliminating downside risk at the same time she is increasing her current income with the covered call strategy.

112. Which of the following is *most likely* to be an impediment to arbitrage?
    A. The law of one price.
    B. Short-sale restrictions.
    C. Investors' risk aversion.

113. The put-call-forward parity relationship is similar to the standard put-call parity relationship with a forward price substituted for:
    A. the risk-free bond.
    B. the underlying asset.
    C. either the call or put option.

114. Over-the-counter derivatives are:
    A. standardized and backed by a clearinghouse.
    B. not standardized but are backed by a clearinghouse.
    C. neither standardized nor backed by a clearinghouse.

115. The time value of an option is *most accurately* described as:
    A. increasing as the option approaches its expiration date.
    B. equal to the entire premium for an out-of-the-money option.
    C. the amount by which the intrinsic value exceeds the option premium.

Questions 116 through 120 relate to Alternative Investments. (7.5 minutes)

116. Over time, compared to traditional stock and bond investments, the commodities asset class has exhibited:
    A. lower returns and lower price volatility.
    B. lower returns and higher price volatility.
    C. higher returns and lower price volatility.

117. A hedge fund uses derivative positions to take a long position in the Japanese yen and a short position in the euro. The classification of this hedge fund is *most likely* a(n):
    A. event-driven fund.
    B. macro strategy fund.
    C. quantitative directional fund.

118. Chip Jergen, CFA, is an asset manager who wishes to allocate a percentage of his portfolio to alternative investments. Jergen invests in a security that represents a proportional claim to cash flows from a pool of loans. In which category of alternative investments has Jergen *most likely* invested?
    A. Real estate.
    B. Commodities.
    C. Private equity.

©2014 Kaplan, Inc.

119. Compared to its net asset value (NAV) calculated in accordance with accounting standards, a hedge fund's trading NAV:
    A. will be lower because of adjustments for illiquid positions.
    B. is likely to be higher because of upward bias in model-based security values.
    C. may be higher or lower, reflecting gains or losses on securities designated for short-term trading.

120. The mezzanine financing portion of a leveraged buyout (LBO) is *most likely* to:
    A. represent committed capital.
    B. be convertible to equity or include warrants.
    C. have seniority over other bonds issued to finance the LBO.

EXAM 3
MORNING SESSION

Calculating Your Score

Topic	Maximum Score	Your Score
Ethical and Professional Standards	18	
Quantitative Methods	14	
Economics	12	
Financial Reporting and Analysis	24	
Corporate Finance	8	
Portfolio Management	9	
Equity Investments	12	
Fixed Income	12	
Derivatives	6	
Alternative Investments	5	
Total	120	

The morning and afternoon exams are identically weighted over the topics and readings. You can therefore treat the morning and afternoon exams as independent exams.

If you took more than three hours (180 minutes) to complete this portion of the exam, you should adjust your score downward by one point for each minute you ran over.

Remember: the real exam *will be more difficult* than these practice exams. The main reason for this is the general anxiety and stress that you will be feeling on exam day, coupled with the time pressure you will be under. Many of the questions on this practice exam and the real exam are not individually difficult, so if you take extra time to answer the questions on this practice exam, your score will go up significantly. However, if you want an accurate measure of your potential performance on the exam, adhere to the 3-hour time limit.

After you have finished grading your practice exam, you may find it useful to use the exam questions and recommended solutions for review. Many of these questions were specifically written for your use as study tools. Once again, I feel I should remind you not to rely on memorizing these questions; you are not likely to see them on the actual exam. What you will see on the exam, though, are the concepts, terms, and procedures presented in these questions.

Your actual exam will most likely look different than what you see in this book. Please remember, no study provider knows the content of the actual exam. These practice exams are our best guess as to the structure, content, and difficulty of an actual exam.

Test Answers

1.	(A)	(B)	(C)
2.	(A)	(B)	(C)
3.	(A)	(B)	(C)
4.	(A)	(B)	(C)
5.	(A)	(B)	(C)
6.	(A)	(B)	(C)
7.	(A)	(B)	(C)
8.	(A)	(B)	(C)
9.	(A)	(B)	(C)
10.	(A)	(B)	(C)
11.	(A)	(B)	(C)
12.	(A)	(B)	(C)
13.	(A)	(B)	(C)
14.	(A)	(B)	(C)
15.	(A)	(B)	(C)
16.	(A)	(B)	(C)
17.	(A)	(B)	(C)
18.	(A)	(B)	(C)
19.	(A)	(B)	(C)
20.	(A)	(B)	(C)
21.	(A)	(B)	(C)
22.	(A)	(B)	(C)
23.	(A)	(B)	(C)
24.	(A)	(B)	(C)
25.	(A)	(B)	(C)
26.	(A)	(B)	(C)
27.	(A)	(B)	(C)
28.	(A)	(B)	(C)
29.	(A)	(B)	(C)
30.	(A)	(B)	(C)
31.	(A)	(B)	(C)
32.	(A)	(B)	(C)
33.	(A)	(B)	(C)
34.	(A)	(B)	(C)
35.	(A)	(B)	(C)
36.	(A)	(B)	(C)
37.	(A)	(B)	(C)
38.	(A)	(B)	(C)
39.	(A)	(B)	(C)
40.	(A)	(B)	(C)
41.	(A)	(B)	(C)
42.	(A)	(B)	(C)
43.	(A)	(B)	(C)
44.	(A)	(B)	(C)
45.	(A)	(B)	(C)
46.	(A)	(B)	(C)
47.	(A)	(B)	(C)
48.	(A)	(B)	(C)
49.	(A)	(B)	(C)
50.	(A)	(B)	(C)
51.	(A)	(B)	(C)
52.	(A)	(B)	(C)
53.	(A)	(B)	(C)
54.	(A)	(B)	(C)
55.	(A)	(B)	(C)
56.	(A)	(B)	(C)
57.	(A)	(B)	(C)
58.	(A)	(B)	(C)
59.	(A)	(B)	(C)
60.	(A)	(B)	(C)
61.	(A)	(B)	(C)
62.	(A)	(B)	(C)
63.	(A)	(B)	(C)
64.	(A)	(B)	(C)
65.	(A)	(B)	(C)
66.	(A)	(B)	(C)
67.	(A)	(B)	(C)
68.	(A)	(B)	(C)
69.	(A)	(B)	(C)
70.	(A)	(B)	(C)
71.	(A)	(B)	(C)
72.	(A)	(B)	(C)
73.	(A)	(B)	(C)
74.	(A)	(B)	(C)
75.	(A)	(B)	(C)
76.	(A)	(B)	(C)
77.	(A)	(B)	(C)
78.	(A)	(B)	(C)
79.	(A)	(B)	(C)
80.	(A)	(B)	(C)
81.	(A)	(B)	(C)
82.	(A)	(B)	(C)
83.	(A)	(B)	(C)
84.	(A)	(B)	(C)
85.	(A)	(B)	(C)
86.	(A)	(B)	(C)
87.	(A)	(B)	(C)
88.	(A)	(B)	(C)
89.	(A)	(B)	(C)
90.	(A)	(B)	(C)
91.	(A)	(B)	(C)
92.	(A)	(B)	(C)
93.	(A)	(B)	(C)
94.	(A)	(B)	(C)
95.	(A)	(B)	(C)
96.	(A)	(B)	(C)
97.	(A)	(B)	(C)
98.	(A)	(B)	(C)
99.	(A)	(B)	(C)
100.	(A)	(B)	(C)
101.	(A)	(B)	(C)
102.	(A)	(B)	(C)
103.	(A)	(B)	(C)
104.	(A)	(B)	(C)
105.	(A)	(B)	(C)
106.	(A)	(B)	(C)
107.	(A)	(B)	(C)
108.	(A)	(B)	(C)
109.	(A)	(B)	(C)
110.	(A)	(B)	(C)
111.	(A)	(B)	(C)
112.	(A)	(B)	(C)
113.	(A)	(B)	(C)
114.	(A)	(B)	(C)
115.	(A)	(B)	(C)
116.	(A)	(B)	(C)
117.	(A)	(B)	(C)
118.	(A)	(B)	(C)
119.	(A)	(B)	(C)
120.	(A)	(B)	(C)

EXAM 3
MORNING SESSION

**Questions 1 through 18 relate to Ethical and Professional Standards.
(27 minutes)**

1. Courtney Johnson, CFA, manages equity accounts and recommends
    Reliable Management to clients who ask about fixed-income
    investments. Reliable, in turn, provides Johnson with equity research.
    Johnson has not informed her equity clients, who are always very
    happy with Reliable's performance, of the arrangement with Reliable.
    Johnson has violated:
    A. none of the Standards.
    B. the Standard concerning client referrals.
    C. the Standard concerning soft dollar arrangements.

2. Russell Finley, CFA, is a managing director at Wilson Brothers and
    is responsible for the supervision of all trading and sales operations.
    Finley receives information indicating that a sales assistant made
    personal trades on a restricted security. According to the Standard
    regarding responsibilities of supervisors, the *least appropriate* action
    for Finley to take is to:
    A. begin an investigation to determine the extent of the wrongdoing.
    B. restrict and increase the monitoring of the employee's activities at the
       firm.
    C. speak directly to the employee and attain assurance that the violation
       will not be repeated.

3. Charlotte Stein, a CFA candidate, received a copy of a stock selection
    model designed by a Wall Street analyst friend, who told her she
    was free to use it. After reviewing the program and making some
    adjustments, Stein shows the new model to her supervisor. Her
    supervisor says she did a great job and tells Stein to incorporate the
    new model in her next industry review. Stein has:
    A. violated the Standard concerning misrepresentation.
    B. violated the Standard concerning conflicts of interest.
    C. not violated CFA Institute Standards of Professional Conduct.

4. Justin Matthews, CFA, is chief financial officer of a bank and serves on the bank's investment committee. The majority of the committee has voted to invest in medium-term euro debt. Matthews feels very strongly that this is a poor strategy and that trends in both the exchange rate and in euro interest rates over the next year will result in large losses on the position. According to the Code and Standards, Matthews should *most appropriately*:
   A. document his difference of opinion with the committee.
   B. express his concerns to the bank's chief executive officer directly.
   C. dissociate from the recommendation by asking that his name not be included.

5. Howard Klein, CFA, supervises a group of research analysts, none of whom is a CFA charterholder or CFA candidate. He has attempted on several occasions to get his firm to adopt a compliance system to ensure that applicable laws and regulations are followed. The firm's principals, however, have never adopted his recommendations. According to CFA Institute Standards of Professional Conduct, Klein at this point:
   A. should decline in writing to accept supervisory responsibility until his firm adopts reasonable compliance procedures.
   B. needs to take no action because the employees are not CFA charterholders or CFA candidates.
   C. must resign from the company and document in writing his reasons for doing so.

6. Lisa Crocker, CFA, manages several pension accounts and directs most of her trades to Zeta Brokers, which provides excellent trade execution as well as equities research. Regional Brokers, which also has excellent trading services, has offered to execute trades for Crocker at half of what she pays Zeta, but Regional does not supply equities research. If Crocker declines to switch her business from Zeta to Regional, has she violated any CFA Institute Standards of Professional Conduct?
   A. Yes, because she has not obtained explicit permission from her clients to use Zeta.
   B. No, if the higher commissions are justified by the value of the research services she receives.
   C. Yes, because the Standard concerning loyalty, prudence, and care states that she must minimize trading costs for her accounts.

©2014 Kaplan, Inc.

7. Katrina Anderson, CFA, left her job as an account manager at RTJ Capital Management and joined Parnell Associates. Anderson did not sign a noncompete agreement at RTJ and took no RTJ property with her when she left. According to CFA Institute Standards of Professional Conduct, Anderson:

A. must not harm RTJ by soliciting her previous clients.
B. is free to contact her previous clients at RTJ after her employment there ends.
C. must seek permission from RTJ before contacting her previous clients there.

8. Scott Houser, CFA, is a widely known equity analyst whose recommendations often influence share prices. Houser changes his recommendation to "Sell" on Drywall Company and distributes this recommendation only to his clients, many of whom act on the recommendation before it becomes known to the public. Has Houser violated the Code and Standards?

A. No.
B. Yes, he has violated the Standard concerning communications with clients.
C. Yes, he has violated the Standard concerning material nonpublic information.

9. Isabelle Burns, CFA, is an investment advisor and holds shares of Torex in her personal account because she thinks it is undervalued. According to the CFA Institute Standards of Professional Conduct, Burns may:

A. recommend Torex to clients but must disclose her investment in Torex.
B. not recommend Torex to clients while she has a personal investment in the stock.
C. recommend Torex to clients for whom it is suitable without disclosing her investment in Torex.

10. Christopher Kim, CFA, is a banker with Batts Brothers, an investment banking firm. Kim follows the energy industry and has frequent contact with industry executives. Kim is contacted by the CEO of a large oil and gas corporation who wants Batts Brothers to underwrite a secondary offering of the company's stock. The CEO offers Kim the opportunity to fly on his private jet to his ranch in Texas for an exotic game hunting expedition if Kim's firm can complete the underwriting within 90 days. According to CFA Institute Standards of Conduct, Kim:

A. may accept the offer as long as he discloses the offer to Batts Brothers.
B. may not accept the offer because it is considered lavish entertainment.
C. must obtain written consent from Batts Brothers before accepting the offer.

11. When GIPS and local laws conflict, in order to be in compliance with GIPS, the investment firm must:
    A. follow local law but disclose the conflict with GIPS.
    B. follow local law, and no additional disclosure is required.
    C. follow GIPS but disclose that this is in conflict with local laws.

12. Kim Vance, CFA, tells a prospective client, "Over the three years I have been in the business, my equity-oriented accounts have had a mean return of more than 20% a year." The statement is accurate, but the mean return was influenced by the account of one client realizing a large gain on a position in a small-cap company he took based on his own research. Without this account, the average gain would have been 18% per year. Has Vance violated CFA Institute Standards of Professional Conduct?
    A. Yes, because the statement misrepresents Vance's performance.
    B. Yes, because returns for an equities composite must be asset-weighted.
    C. No, because it is accurate and Vance has not guaranteed such returns in the future.

13. Joseph Drake, CFA, an investment advisor at Best Wealth Managers, has identified a growth stock that he believes has the potential to provide excellent returns over the next five years. He includes this stock on a "recommended list" that he sends to all of his clients. Drake includes recent earnings, his estimates of future earnings, and a note that more information is available on request. Drake has:
    A. not violated the Standards.
    B. violated the Standard on suitability.
    C. violated the Standard on client communications.

14. Brian Farley, CFA, is an investment manager with one client, a $75 million university endowment fund. A representative of the endowment fund calls Farley and places a "sell" order on a portfolio holding whose management has just reduced its earnings guidance for the coming year. Farley also owns the security and, because the new guidance is public information, places simultaneous "sell" orders for both the client account and his personal account. According to the Standards on fair dealing and priority of transactions, Farley is in violation of:
    A. both of these Standards.
    B. neither of these Standards.
    C. only one of these Standards.

©2014 Kaplan, Inc.

15. Paul White, CFA, works as an analyst at an investment banking firm that also manages equity-only accounts for clients. White has agreed independently to manage a portfolio of fixed-income securities for an endowment fund but has not received permission from his employer. Additionally, White's supervisor has asked him to work this weekend on a proposal for a large IPO that must be delivered on Monday morning, but White declines as he would prefer to spend the weekend with his family. White has *most likely*:
    A. not violated the Standards.
    B. violated the Standard on loyalty.
    C. violated the Standard on additional compensation arrangements.

16. Art Dodd, CFA, is a registered representative with Owens Securities. He is currently in a dispute with one client, Madge Phillips, about a limit order for her account that she feels was entered incorrectly, resulting in a loss (in her opinion) of $500. Dodd has 1,000 shares of an oversubscribed new issue to allocate to clients. He suggests to Phillips that he will give her 250 shares of this allocation to make up for the supposed trade error. Further, he offers to buy her dinner at a nice restaurant. According to the Standards of Practice, Dodd has *most likely* violated the Standard concerning:
    A. misconduct.
    B. fair dealing.
    C. additional compensation.

17. Which of the following is *least likely* one of the nine major topics of the CFA Institute Global Investment Performance Standards (GIPS)?
    A. Real Estate.
    B. Private Equity.
    C. Venture Capital.

18. Graham Carson, CFA, is an investment advisor to Ron Grayson, a client with moderate risk tolerance and an investment horizon of 15 years. Grayson calls Carson to complain about two stocks in his account that have performed poorly. He feels that one stock was too risky for him as it paid no dividend and had a beta of 1.4. The other stock had a beta of 0.9 and paid a dividend of 3%, but financial regulators have indicated that the firm's reported earnings were incorrectly stated. Based on this information, Carson has *most likely*:
    A. not violated the Standards.
    B. violated only the Standard on suitability.
    C. violated both the Standard on suitability and the Standard on diligence and reasonable basis.

Questions 19 through 32 relate to Quantitative Methods. (21 minutes)

19.   Five years ago, an investor borrowed $5,000 from a financial institution that charged a 6% annual interest rate, and he immediately took his family to live in Nepal. He made no payments during the time he was away. When he returned, he agreed to repay the original loan plus the accrued interest by making five end-of-year payments starting one year after he returned. If the interest rate on the loan is held constant at 6% per year, what annual payment must the investor make in order to retire the loan?
    A. $1,338.23.
    B. $1,588.45.
    C. $1,638.23.

20.   If an investment of $4,000 will grow to $6,520 in four years with monthly compounding, the effective annual interest rate will be *closest* to:
    A. 11.2%.
    B. 12.3%.
    C. 13.0%.

21.   An analyst constructs a histogram and frequency polygon of monthly returns for aggressive equity funds over a 20-year period. Which of the following statements about these displays is *most accurate*?
    A. The height of each bar in a frequency polygon represents the absolute frequency for each return interval.
    B. Both a histogram and a frequency polygon provide a graphical display of data found in a frequency distribution.
    C. To construct a histogram, the analyst would plot the midpoint of the return intervals on the x-axis and the absolute frequency for that interval on the y-axis, connecting neighboring points with a straight line.

22.   An investor holds a portfolio consisting of one share of each of the following stocks:

Stock	Price at the Beginning of the Year	Price at the End of the Year	Cash Dividend During the Year
X	$20	$10	$0
Y	$40	$50	$2
Z	$100	$105	$4

For the 1-year holding period, the portfolio return is *closest* to:
    A. 6.9%.
    B. 9.1%.
    C. 13.1%.

23. An analyst takes a sample of yearly returns of aggressive growth funds resulting in the following data set: 25, 15, 35, 45, and 55. The mean absolute deviation (MAD) of the data set is *closest* to:
    A. 12.
    B. 16.
    C. 20.

24. A security has annual returns of 5%, 10%, and 15%. The coefficient of variation of the security (using the population standard deviation) is *closest* to:
    A. 0.3.
    B. 0.4.
    C. 0.5.

25. If an analyst concludes that the distribution of a large sample of returns is positively skewed, which of the following relationships involving the mean, median, and mode is *most likely*?
    A. Mean > median > mode.
    B. Mean < median < mode.
    C. Mean > median < mode.

26. An analyst has been hired to evaluate a high-risk project. The analyst estimates the probability that the project will fail in the first year as well as the conditional probability of failure for each of the remaining four years of the project, as follows:

Year	1	2	3	4	5
Failure probability	0.25	0.20	0.20	0.15	0.10

    The project will have no payoff if it fails, but it will have a payoff of $20,000 at the end of the fifth year if it succeeds. Because of its high risk, the required rate of return for an investment in this project is 25%. Based on this information, the expected present value of the project is *closest* to:
    A. $2,400.
    B. $3,010.
    C. $5,900.

27. An investor opens an account by purchasing 1,000 shares of stock at $42 per share. One year later, these shares are trading at $55 per share, and the investor purchases 1,000 more shares. At the end of the second year, the shares are trading at $54. The time-weighted rate of return on the account is *closest* to:
    A. 7.7%.
    B. 13.4%.
    C. 16.4%.

28. Which of the following distributions is *most likely* a discrete distribution?
    A. A normal distribution.
    B. A univariate distribution.
    C. A binomial distribution.

29. An investment has a mean return of 15% and a standard deviation of returns equal to 10%. If the distribution of returns is approximately normal, which of the following statements is *least accurate*? The probability of obtaining a return:
    A. less than 5% is about 16%.
    B. greater than 35% is about 2.5%.
    C. between 5% and 25% is about 95%.

30. Which of the following statements about the central limit theorem is *least accurate*?
    A. The central limit theorem has limited usefulness for skewed distributions.
    B. The mean of the population and the mean of all possible sample means are equal.
    C. When the sample size is large, the sampling distribution of the sample means is approximately normal.

31. An analyst takes a random sample of the returns on 225 stocks from a population with a known variance of returns of 100. The standard error of the sample mean return is *closest* to:
    A. 0.44.
    B. 0.67.
    C. 2.26.

32. Which of the following statements about hypothesis testing involving a *z*-statistic is *least accurate*?
    A. The *p*-value is the smallest significance level at which the null hypothesis can be rejected.
    B. A *z*-test is theoretically acceptable in place of a *t*-test for tests concerning a mean when sample size is small.
    C. If the confidence level is set at 95%, the chance of rejecting the null hypothesis when in fact it is true is 5%.

Questions 33 through 44 relate to Economics. (18 minutes)

33. According to the crowding-out effect, the sale of government bonds used to finance excess government spending is *least likely* to:
    A. increase the real interest rate.
    B. reduce private investment spending.
    C. increase the profitability of corporate investment projects.

 ©2014 Kaplan, Inc.

34. Which of the following statements on the economic implications of trade restrictions is *most accurate*?
    A. Quota rents are the amounts received by the domestic government when it charges for import licenses.
    B. In the importing country, import quotas, tariffs, and voluntary export restraints all decrease producer surplus.
    C. In the case of a quota, if the domestic government collects the full value of the import licenses, the result is the same as that of a tariff.

35. In a demand function, if the price of a complement to Good J decreases, the quantity demanded of Good J:
    A. increases.
    B. decreases.
    C. may increase or decrease.

36. Based on her forecast for the economy, a portfolio manager increases her investments in high-quality bonds and decreases her investments in commodities. The portfolio manager *most likely* expects the economy to experience:
    A. stagflation.
    B. a recessionary gap.
    C. an inflationary gap.

37. The long-run production decision differs from the short-run production decision in that:
    A. fixed costs can be changed in the long run but not the short run.
    B. variable costs can be changed in the long run but not the short run.
    C. variable costs can be changed in the short run but not the long run.

38. Demand for gasoline (in hundreds of liters) at a particular station, as a function of the price of gasoline and the price of bus travel, is $Q_D = 300 - 14 P_{gas} + 2 P_{bus}$. If the price of gasoline per liter (P_{gas}) is 1.50 euros, and the price of a standardized unit of bus travel (P_{bus}) is 12 euros, the cross price elasticity of gasoline demand with respect to the price of bus travel is *closest* to:
    A. 0.01.
    B. 0.08.
    C. 2.00.

39. Which of the following statements about a monopolist is *least accurate*?
    A. The monopolist faces a downward sloping demand curve.
    B. Unlike an oligopolist, a monopolist will always be able to earn economic profit.
    C. A profit-maximizing monopolist will expand output until marginal revenue equals marginal cost.

40. A market has the following characteristics: a large number of independent sellers, each producing a differentiated product; low barriers to entry; producers facing downward sloping demand curves; and demand that is highly elastic. This description *most* closely describes:
   A. an oligopoly.
   B. pure competition.
   C. monopolistic competition.

41. One year ago, the currency of Xyland (XYZ) was at a three-month forward premium to the currency of Piqua (PQR). Today, the XYZ is at a three-month forward discount to the PQR. Assuming the interest rate parity relationship holds, this change implies that:
   A. the XYZ has depreciated relative to the PQR.
   B. today the XYZ three-month interest rate is higher than the PQR three-month interest rate.
   C. one year ago the XYZ three-month interest rate was higher than the PQR three-month interest rate.

42. Accounting profit is often an unsatisfactory performance measure from an economic point of view because it:
   A. does not consider depreciation.
   B. considers marginal costs rather than average costs.
   C. does not consider the opportunity costs of equity capital.

43. Depreciation of a country's currency will be more effective in reducing its trade deficit if its:
   A. imports do not have good substitutes.
   B. exports are primarily luxury goods.
   C. exports represent a small portion of foreign consumer expenditures.

44. The *most likely* effects of the imposition of an effective increase in the minimum wage include:
   A. an increase in the real wage, gains in efficiency, and a decrease in inflation.
   B. increased unemployment, an excess supply of labor at the new wage rate, and a decrease in economic efficiency.
   C. a reduction in non-monetary labor benefits, excess demand for labor, and a shortage of highly skilled workers.

Questions 45 through 68 relate to Financial Reporting and Analysis. (36 minutes)

45. Normal Corp. has a current ratio above 1 and a quick ratio less than 1. Which of the following actions will increase the current ratio and decrease the quick ratio? Normal Corp.:
   A. buys fixed assets on credit.
   B. uses cash to purchase inventory.
   C. pays off accounts payable from cash.

 ©2014 Kaplan, Inc.

46. A company has a cash conversion cycle of 70 days. If the company's payables turnover decreases from 11 to 10 and days of sales outstanding increase by 5, the company's cash conversion cycle will:
    A. decrease by approximately 8 days.
    B. decrease by approximately 3 days.
    C. increase by approximately 2 days.

47. A manager whose compensation is tied to improving the firm's inventory turnover *most likely* has an incentive to:
    A. overstate assets.
    B. understate earnings.
    C. overstate working capital.

48. Which of the following is *least likely* to be considered an objective of financial market regulation according to the International Organization of Securities Commissions (IOSCO)?
    A. Reduce systemic risk.
    B. Ensure the fairness, efficiency, and transparency of markets.
    C. Develop individual financial regulatory standards for each country to reflect the unique needs of each market.

49. Napa Corp. sells 1-year memberships to its Fine Wine Club for $180. Wine Club members each receive a bottle of white wine and a bottle of red wine, selected by the club director, four times each year at the beginning of each quarter. To properly account for sales of Wine Club memberships, Napa will record:
    A. an asset for prepaid sales.
    B. a liability for accrued expenses.
    C. a liability for unearned revenue.

50. An analyst gathered the following data about a company:
    - Net sales $4,000
    - Dividends declared   170
    - Cost of goods sold   2,000
    - Inventory increased by   100
    - Accounts payable increased by   300
    - Cash expenses for other inputs   500
    - Long-term debt principal repayment   250
    - Cash tax payments   200
    - Purchase of new equipment   300

    The company's cash flow from operations, based on these data only, is:
    A. $1,200.
    B. $1,500.
    C. $1,575.

51. Jennifer Frye, CFA, is comparing the financial performance of a firm that presents its results under IFRS to that of a firm that complies with U.S. GAAP. The U.S. firm uses the LIFO method for inventory accounting, and the other firm uses the FIFO method. If Frye performs the appropriate adjustments to make the U.S. firm's financial statements comparable to the firm that reports under IFRS, her adjustments are *least likely* to change the firm's:
    A. quick ratio.
    B. debt-to-equity ratio.
    C. cash conversion cycle.

52. A reconciliation of beginning and ending carrying values for long-lived tangible assets is required for firms reporting under:
    A. IFRS.
    B. U.S. GAAP.
    C. both U.S. GAAP and IFRS.

53. The following data pertains to a company's common-size financial statements.
    - Current assets   40%
    - Total debt   40%
    - Net income   16%
    - Total assets $2,000
    - Sales $1,500
    - Total asset turnover ratio   0.75
    - The firm has no preferred stock in its capital structure.

    The company's after-tax return on common equity is *closest* to:
    A. 15%.
    B. 20%.
    C. 25%.

54. Which of the following statements about the calculation of earnings per share (EPS) is *least accurate*?
    A. Shares issued after a stock split must be adjusted for the split.
    B. Options outstanding may have no effect on diluted EPS.
    C. Reacquired shares are excluded from the computation from the date of reacquisition.

©2014 Kaplan, Inc.

55. A company has 1,000,000 warrants outstanding at the beginning of the year, each convertible into one share of stock with an exercise price of $50. No new warrants were issued during the year. The average stock price during the period was $60, and the year-end stock price was $45. What adjustment for these warrants should be made, under the treasury stock method, to the number of shares used to calculate diluted earnings per share (EPS)?
   A. 0.
   B. 166,667.
   C. 200,000.

56. Which of the following statements about financial ratios is *most accurate*?
   A. A company with a high debt-to-equity ratio will have a return on asssets that is greater than its return on equity.
   B. Any firm with a high net profit margin will have a high gross profit margin and vice versa.
   C. A company that has an inventory turnover of 6 times, a receivables turnover of 9 times, and a payables turnover of 12 times will have a cash conversion cycle of approximately 71 days.

57. In accounting for a defined benefit pension plan, the amount reported as "prior service cost" refers to the:
   A. total value of benefits already paid to retirees who are still receiving pension payments.
   B. present value of the pension benefits due to employees based on their employment up to the date of the statement.
   C. present value of the increase in future pension benefits from a change in the terms of the pension plan.

58. During an accounting period, a company has the following sequence of transactions with a beginning inventory of zero:

Purchases	Sales
100 units at $210	80 units at $240
90 units at $225	90 units at $250

The company's cost of goods sold (COGS) using FIFO for inventory accounting, and its ending inventory using LIFO, are *closest* to:

	FIFO COGS	LIFO ending inventory
A.	$36,750	$4,200
B.	$37,050	$4,200
C.	$37,050	$4,500

59. On January 2, a company acquires some state-of-the-art production equipment at a net cost of $14 million. For financial reporting purposes, the firm will depreciate the equipment over a 7-year life using straight-line depreciation and a zero salvage value; for tax reporting purposes, however, the firm will use 3-year accelerated depreciation. Given a tax rate of 35% and a first-year accelerated depreciation factor of 0.333, by how much will the company's deferred tax liability increase in the first year of the equipment's life?
    A. $931,700.
    B. $1,064,800.
    C. $1,730,300.

60. When comparing two firms, an analyst should *most* appropriately adjust the financial statements when they include significant:
    A. acquisition goodwill, if one of the firms reports under IFRS and the other under U.S. GAAP.
    B. property, plant, and equipment, if one of the firms uses accelerated depreciation and the other uses straight-line depreciation.
    C. unrealized losses from securities held for trading, if one of the firms uses fair value reporting for securities investments and the other does not.

61. A software company holds a number of marketable securities as investments. For the most recent period, the company reports that the market value of its securities held for trading decreased by $2 million and the market value of its securities available for sale increased in value by $3 million. Together, these changes in value will:
    A. reduce net income and shareholders' equity by $2 million.
    B. increase shareholders' equity by $1 million and have no effect on net income.
    C. reduce net income by $2 million and increase shareholders' equity by $1 million.

62. Maritza Inc. is involved in an exchange of debt for equity. In which of the following sections of the cash flow statement would Maritza record this transaction?
    A. Investing activities section.
    B. Financing activities section.
    C. Footnotes to the cash flow statement.

 ©2014 Kaplan, Inc.

63. An analyst calculates the following ratios for Lebicke Company:

	20X6	20X5	20X4
Debt-to-capital ratio	56.3%	56.4%	56.2%
Fixed charge coverage ratio	3.3×	3.4×	3.5×
Interest coverage ratio	4.0×	3.9×	3.8×

These ratios *most likely* suggest that during the period shown, Lebicke's:
A. use of operating leases increased.
B. interest obligations increased faster than earnings.
C. capital structure became more reliant on equity financing.

64. Analysts reviewing Amber, Inc.'s and Bold, Inc.'s long-term contracting activities observe that Amber's contracts are being accounted for under the percentage-of-completion method while Bold's are being accounted for under the completed contract method. This difference is *least likely* to affect the two companies':
A. income statements.
B. statements of cash flows.
C. assets on the balance sheets.

65. Which of the following statements regarding an audit and a standard auditor's opinion is *most accurate*?
A. The objective of an audit is to enable the auditor to provide an opinion on the numerical accuracy of the financial statements.
B. To provide an independent review of a company's financial statements, an independent certified public accounting firm is appointed by the company's management.
C. The absence of an explanatory paragraph in the audit report relating to the going concern assumption suggests that there are no serious problems that require a close examination of that assumption by the analyst.

66. Two growing firms are identical except that Alfred Company capitalizes costs for some long-lived assets that Canute Company expenses. For these two firms, which of the following financial statement effects is *most likely*? Alfred will show higher:
A. net income than Canute.
B. working capital than Canute.
C. investing cash flow than Canute.

67. A company fails to record accrued wages for a reporting period. What effect will this error have on the company's financial statements?
A. Assets and liabilities are understated.
B. Assets and owners' equity are overstated.
C. Liabilities are understated and owners' equity is overstated.

68. Which of the following statements about the treatment of leases on the lessor's financial statements is *least accurate*?
   A. If the present value of the payments on a finance lease is greater than the carrying value of the asset, the lease is a sales-type lease on the books of the lessor.
   B. In a direct financing lease, the lessor recognizes gross profit at the lease inception, while in a sales-type lease it does not.
   C. To be a finance lease for the lessor, collectibility must be reasonably certain and the lessor must have substantially completed performance.

Questions 69 through 76 relate to Corporate Finance. (12 minutes)

69. Rodgers, Inc. has fixed operating expenses of $2 million and will break even with sales of $5 million. For sales of $7 million, an analyst would estimate the firm's operating income as:
   A. $800,000.
   B. $1,200,000.
   C. $2,000,000.

70. Weights to be used in calculating a company's weighted average cost of capital are *least appropriately* based on:
   A. information from the company about its target capital structure.
   B. the average capital structure weights for companies of a similar size.
   C. the average capital structure weights for companies in the same industry.

71. An accounts receivable aging schedule is *best* used to:
   A. determine how the receivables turnover ratio has changed over time.
   B. identify trends in how well the firm is doing at collecting receivables and converting them to cash.
   C. compare a company's receivables management to those of the average for its industry or for a group of peer companies.

72. A company has 35 million shares outstanding with a current market price of $49.75 per share. The company has maintained a $1.00 per share quarterly dividend for several years, but for the next quarter, management is considering whether to implement a $35 million share repurchase in place of the regular quarterly dividend. Assuming the tax treatments and information effects of either alternative are the same, the net impact of the share repurchase, compared to the payment of a cash dividend, is to:
   A. decrease shareholder wealth.
   B. have no effect on shareholder wealth.
   C. increase shareholder wealth.

©2014 Kaplan, Inc.

73. Ron's Organic Markets has limited access to borrowed funds and must choose among ten independent projects with returns greater than their cost of capital. All the projects under consideration have the same required investment of $2 million, and Ron's has $10 million available for capital investments this year. Which of the following selection criteria is *least likely* to identify the five projects that will produce the greatest expected increase in the value of the firm? Choose the five projects with:
    A. the highest IRRs.
    B. the greatest total NPV.
    C. the largest sum of profitability indexes.

74. Which of the following is *least* relevant in determining project cash flow for a capital investment?
    A. Sunk costs.
    B. Tax impacts.
    C. Opportunity costs.

75. From a liquidity management perspective, an increase in the number of days of payables is *best* described as:
    A. liquidity neutral.
    B. a drag on liquidity.
    C. a source of liquidity.

76. Which of the following characteristics is *least likely* required to ensure that a company's Board of Directors Audit Committee is adequately representing shareowner interests?
    A. Any conflicts between the external auditor and the firm are resolved in a manner that favors shareholders.
    B. The shareholders vote on whether to approve of the Board's selection of the external auditor.
    C. The committee regularly reviews the performance, independence, skills, and experience of existing board members.

Questions 77 through 85 relate to Portfolio Management. (13.5 minutes)

77. A security's systematic risk is *best* estimated by the slope of the:
    A. capital market line.
    B. security market line.
    C. security's characteristic line.

78. The creation and redemption of shares by authorized participants, which keeps the price of fund shares close to their net asset value, is a feature unique to which of the following types of pooled investments?
    A. Hedge funds.
    B. Closed-end funds.
    C. Exchange-traded funds (ETFs).

79. In choosing asset classes for establishing strategic portfolio allocation across assets, the manager would *most* prefer that:
    A. asset classes are only those with tradable liquid assets.
    B. the asset classes span the broadest universe of investable assets.
    C. correlations of asset returns within an asset class are significantly greater than correlations of asset class returns.

80. Which of the following is *least likely* among the usual investment constraints that should be considered?
    A. Legal and regulatory factors.
    B. Unique needs and preferences.
    C. Adherence to the Standards of Practice.

81. Given the following correlation matrix, a risk-averse investor would *least* prefer which of the following 2-stock portfolios (all else equal)?

Stock	W	X	Y	Z
W	+1			
X	−0.2	+1		
Y	+0.6	−0.1	+1	
Z	+0.8	−0.3	+0.5	+1

    A. W and Y.
    B. X and Y.
    C. X and Z.

82. Which type of risk is positively related to expected excess returns according to the CAPM?
    A. Unique.
    B. Systematic.
    C. Diversifiable.

83. Which of the following statements about the security market line (SML) and capital market line (CML) is *most accurate*?
    A. The SML involves the concept of a risk-free asset, but the CML does not.
    B. The SML uses beta, but the CML uses standard deviation as the risk measure.
    C. Both the SML and CML can be used to explain a stock's expected return.

©2014 Kaplan, Inc.

84. Becky Scott and Sid Fiona have the same expectations about the risk and return of the market portfolio; however, Scott selects a portfolio with 30% T-bills and 70% invested in the market portfolio, while Fiona holds a leveraged portfolio, having borrowed to invest 130% of his portfolio equity value in the market portfolio. Regarding their preferences between risk and return and their indifference curves, it is *most likely* that:
   A. Scott is risk averse but Fiona is not.
   B. Fiona's indifference curves are flatter than Scott's.
   C. Scott is willing to take on more risk to increase her expected portfolio return than Fiona is.

85. A portfolio manager who is comparing portfolios based on their total risk should most appropriately use:
   A. Jenson's alpha.
   B. the Sharpe ratio.
   C. the Treynor measure.

Questions 86 through 97 relate to Equity Investments. (18 minutes)

86. An index is composed of three stocks. Their performance in a recent period is as follows:

Stock	Number of Shares Outstanding (Thousands)	Beginning Price	Ending Price	Percent Change
X	100	160	136	−15%
Y	100	80	100	+25%
Z	1,000	60	66	+10%

   None of the stocks split during the period. This index will have the smallest percentage increase for the period if it is a(n):
   A. value-weighted index.
   B. price-weighted index.
   C. equal-weighted index using the geometric mean.

87. A company is *most likely* to earn economic profits if it is operating in an industry characterized by:
   A. high industry concentration, high barriers to entry, and low industry capacity.
   B. low industry concentration, low barriers to entry, and low industry capacity.
   C. low industry concentration, high barriers to entry, and high industry capacity.

88.   Among the types of factors that influence industry growth and profitability, the one that is *most likely* to affect consumer discretionary goods producers more than consumer staples producers is:
        A. social factors.
        B. demographic factors.
        C. macroeconomic factors.

89.   Which form of the efficient markets hypothesis (EMH) implies that an investor can achieve positive abnormal returns on average by using technical analysis?
        A. None.
        B. Weak form.
        C. Weak form or semistrong form.

90.   A stock has a steady 5% growth rate in dividends. The required rate of return for stocks of this risk class is 15%. The stock is expected to pay a $1 dividend this coming year. The expected value of the stock at the end of the fourth year is:
        A. $12.16.
        B. $14.21.
        C. $16.32.

91.   An investor has long exposure to the risk of the asset underlying an option when taking a:
        A. short position in a put option.
        B. short position in a call option.
        C. long position in a put option.

92.   If all other factors remain unchanged, which of the following would *most likely* reduce a company's price/earnings ratio?
        A. The dividend payout ratio increases, and the dividend growth rate increases.
        B. The dividend growth rate increases, and the required rate of return decreases.
        C. The required rate of return increases, and the dividend payout ratio decreases.

93.   Porter, Inc. sells 200,000 newly issued shares to two institutions without registering the shares with its country's securities regulators. This transaction is *best* described as being:
        A. illegal.
        B. in the primary market.
        C. in the secondary market.

                                      ©2014 Kaplan, Inc.

94. Callable shares *most likely*:
    A. are less risky than noncallable shares.
    B. pay a higher dividend than noncallable shares.
    C. give the investor the right to sell the shares back to the issuer at a specified price.

95. An asset-based valuation model would *most likely* provide a reliable estimate of market value for a:
    A. pure-play online news site.
    B. multinational freight distribution firm.
    C. privately held metal fabrication company.

96. Beachballs, Inc., expects abnormally high earnings for the next three years due to the forecast of unusually hot summers. After the 3-year period, their growth will level off to its normal rate of 6%. Dividends and earnings are expected to grow at 20% for years 1 and 2 and 15% in year 3. The last dividend paid was $1.00. If an investor requires a 10% return on Beachballs, the price she is willing to pay for the stock is *closest* to:
    A. $26.00.
    B. $36.50.
    C. $50.00.

97. If stock markets are semistrong-form efficient, a portfolio manager is *least likely* to create value for investors by:
    A. monitoring clients' needs and circumstances.
    B. allocating invested funds among asset classes.
    C. analyzing financial statements to select undervalued stocks.

Questions 98 through 109 relate to Fixed Income. (18 minutes)

98. Compared to corporate bonds, secondary market trading in government bonds is *most likely* to feature:
    A. brokered markets.
    B. earlier trade settlement.
    C. narrower bid-ask spreads.

99. An investor buys an option-free bond that has a Macaulay duration of 15.0 and a modified duration of 14.5. If the rate of return on reinvested coupon income is 4.0% and the bond is sold after three years, the investor's annualized holding period return is *most likely* to be:
    A. equal to the bond's yield to maturity at the time of purchase.
    B. less than the bond's yield to maturity at the time of purchase.
    C. greater than the bond's yield to maturity at the time of purchase.

100. A 10%, 10-year bond is sold to yield 8%. One year passes, and the yield remains unchanged at 8%. Holding all other factors constant, the bond's price during this period will have:
A. increased.
B. decreased.
C. remained constant.

101. An analyst is considering a bond for purchase. The bond has a coupon that resets semiannually and is determined by the following formula:

$$coupon = 12\% - (3.0 \times \text{6-month Treasury bill rate})$$

This bond is *most* accurately described as a(n):
A. step-up note.
B. inverse floater.
C. inflation protected security.

102. Exactly one year ago, an investor purchased a $1,000 face value, zero-coupon bond with 11 years remaining to maturity. The YTM (semiannual) was 8.0%. Now, one year later, with market rates unchanged, an investor purchases an annuity that pays $40 every six months for 10 years. The combined value of the two investments based on the 8% semiannual yield is *approximately*:
A. $966.
B. $1,000.
C. $1,456.

103. A five-year corporate bond and its benchmark government bond had the following yields over a one-month period:

	Beginning of Month	End of Month
Corporate bond yield	6.75%	7.00%
Government bond yield	4.25%	4.75%

Over this month, the price of the corporate bond *most likely* experienced:
A. unfavorable macroeconomic and microeconomic factors.
B. favorable macroeconomic factors and unfavorable microeconomic factors.
C. unfavorable macroeconomic factors and favorable microeconomic factors.

104. An investor most concerned with reinvestment risk would be *least likely* to:
A. prefer a noncallable bond to a callable bond.
B. prefer a lower coupon bond to a higher coupon bond.
C. eliminate reinvestment risk by holding a coupon bond until maturity.

©2014 Kaplan, Inc.

105. For an asset-backed security (ABS), a special purpose vehicle:
   A. sells an asset to the issuing corporation, which then proceeds to issue the ABS.
   B. is a legal entity used to separate assets used as collateral from those of the company seeking financing through an ABS.
   C. acts as an intermediary that purchases an asset from the company issuing an ABS and then resells it to obtain sufficient liquid funds to provide collateral for the ABS.

106. The following interest rate information is observed:

	Spot Rates
1 year	10%
2 years	11%
3 years	12%

   Based on this data, the 2-year forward rate one year from now is *closest* to:
   A. 12%.
   B. 13%.
   C. 14%.

107. A fixed-income portfolio manager is estimating portfolio duration based on the weighted average of the durations of each bond in the portfolio. The manager should calculate duration using:
   A. parallel shifts of the benchmark yield curve.
   B. equal-sized increases and decreases in a benchmark bond's yield.
   C. equal-sized increases and decreases in the portfolio's cash flow yield.

108. Bert Reed owns a junior secured bond of a firm that has entered bankruptcy proceedings. Mia Tano owns a senior unsecured bond of the same firm. As a result of the bankruptcy, Reed and Tano each recover 80% of the interest and principal owed on their bonds. This outcome is *least likely* the result of:
   A. an order of the bankruptcy court.
   B. the pari passu ranking of these creditors.
   C. a negotiated settlement among the firm's creditors.

109. A repurchase agreement is *most accurately* described as a(n):
   A. embedded option held by a bondholder.
   B. form of credit enhancement in a bond issue.
   C. source of short-term funding for a bondholder.

Questions 110 through 115 relate to Derivatives. (9 minutes)

110. How does the cost of holding the underlying asset affect option values?
    A. Decreases both call and put values.
    B. Decreases call values and increases put values.
    C. Increases call values and decreases put values.

111. Open interest in a futures market is *most accurately* described as the total number of:
    A. contracts outstanding.
    B. contracts that change hands in a given period.
    C. buyers and sellers currently holding outstanding positions.

112. The payoff diagram of a protective put option has the same shape as the payoff diagram for:
    A. writing a put option.
    B. buying a call option.
    C. writing a call option.

113. Under which of the following conditions does a forward contract have a positive value to the short party at expiration?
    A. The forward price is less than the value of the forward contract.
    B. The spot price of the underlying asset is less than the forward price.
    C. The value of the forward contract is less than the spot price of the underlying asset.

114. At expiration, exercise value is equal to time value for an:
    A. in-the-money call or an out-of-the-money put.
    B. out-of-the-money call or an in-the-money put.
    C. out-of-the-money call or an out-of-the-money put.

115. A put on a stock with a strike price of $50 is priced at $4 per share, while a call with a strike price of $50 is priced at $6. What is the maximum per share loss to the writer of the put?
    A. $46.
    B. $50.
    C. Unlimited.

Questions 116 through 120 relate to Alternative Investments. (7.5 minutes)

116. A portfolio manager is *most likely* to expect higher returns from allocating a portion of assets to the alternative investments asset class because alternative investments:
    A. provide liquidity.
    B. often employ leverage.
    C. are more efficiently priced than traditional assets.

 ©2014 Kaplan, Inc.

117. The component of the yield on a long-only commodity futures position that is independent of whether the contract is in contango or backwardation is the:
    A. roll yield.
    B. collateral yield.
    C. convenience yield.

118. With respect to venture capital, the term "mezzanine-stage financing" is used to describe the financing:
    A. to prepare for an initial public offering.
    B. to initiate commercial manufacturing.
    C. that supports product development and market research.

119. Cathy Werner, CFA, is considering adding exposure to hedge funds to her portfolio of traditional investments. Based on historical mean and standard deviation of hedge fund index returns and their correlation with traditional investment returns, Werner estimates the diversification benefits from allocating 5% of portfolio assets to hedge funds. Assuming her calculations are correct, Werner is *most likely* to:
    A. overestimate the potential diversification benefits to the portfolio.
    B. underestimate the potential diversification benefits to the portfolio.
    C. accurately estimate the potential diversification benefits to the portfolio.

120. A private equity firm that wants to receive money from a portfolio company without giving up control of the portfolio company is *most likely* to engage in a:
    A. trade sale.
    B. secondary sale.
    C. recapitalization.

Exam 3
Afternoon Session

Calculating Your Score

Topic	Maximum Score	Your Score
Ethical and Professional Standards	18	
Quantitative Methods	14	
Economics	12	
Financial Reporting and Analysis	24	
Corporate Finance	9	
Portfolio Management	8	
Equity Investments	12	
Fixed Income	12	
Derivatives	6	
Alternative Investments	5	
Total	120	

The morning and afternoon exams are identically weighted over the topics and readings. You can therefore treat the morning and afternoon exams as independent exams.

If you took more than three hours (180 minutes) to complete this portion of the exam, you should adjust your score downward by one point for each minute you ran over.

Remember: the real exam *will be more difficult* than these practice exams. The main reason for this is the general anxiety and stress that you will be feeling on exam day, coupled with the time pressure you will be under. Many of the questions on this practice exam and the real exam are not individually difficult, so if you take extra time to answer the questions on this practice exam, your score will go up significantly. However, if you want an accurate measure of your potential performance on the exam, adhere to the 3-hour time limit.

After you have finished grading your practice exam, you may find it useful to use the exam questions and recommended solutions for review. Many of these questions were specifically written for your use as study tools. Once again, I feel I should remind you not to rely on memorizing these questions; you are not likely to see them on the actual exam. What you will see on the exam, though, are the concepts, terms, and procedures presented in these questions.

Your actual exam will most likely look different than what you see in this book. Please remember, no study provider knows the content of the actual exam. These practice exams are our best guess as to the structure, content, and difficulty of an actual exam.

Test Answers

1. (A) (B) (C)	41. (A) (B) (C)	81. (A) (B) (C)
2. (A) (B) (C)	42. (A) (B) (C)	82. (A) (B) (C)
3. (A) (B) (C)	43. (A) (B) (C)	83. (A) (B) (C)
4. (A) (B) (C)	44. (A) (B) (C)	84. (A) (B) (C)
5. (A) (B) (C)	45. (A) (B) (C)	85. (A) (B) (C)
6. (A) (B) (C)	46. (A) (B) (C)	86. (A) (B) (C)
7. (A) (B) (C)	47. (A) (B) (C)	87. (A) (B) (C)
8. (A) (B) (C)	48. (A) (B) (C)	88. (A) (B) (C)
9. (A) (B) (C)	49. (A) (B) (C)	89. (A) (B) (C)
10. (A) (B) (C)	50. (A) (B) (C)	90. (A) (B) (C)
11. (A) (B) (C)	51. (A) (B) (C)	91. (A) (B) (C)
12. (A) (B) (C)	52. (A) (B) (C)	92. (A) (B) (C)
13. (A) (B) (C)	53. (A) (B) (C)	93. (A) (B) (C)
14. (A) (B) (C)	54. (A) (B) (C)	94. (A) (B) (C)
15. (A) (B) (C)	55. (A) (B) (C)	95. (A) (B) (C)
16. (A) (B) (C)	56. (A) (B) (C)	96. (A) (B) (C)
17. (A) (B) (C)	57. (A) (B) (C)	97. (A) (B) (C)
18. (A) (B) (C)	58. (A) (B) (C)	98. (A) (B) (C)
19. (A) (B) (C)	59. (A) (B) (C)	99. (A) (B) (C)
20. (A) (B) (C)	60. (A) (B) (C)	100. (A) (B) (C)
21. (A) (B) (C)	61. (A) (B) (C)	101. (A) (B) (C)
22. (A) (B) (C)	62. (A) (B) (C)	102. (A) (B) (C)
23. (A) (B) (C)	63. (A) (B) (C)	103. (A) (B) (C)
24. (A) (B) (C)	64. (A) (B) (C)	104. (A) (B) (C)
25. (A) (B) (C)	65. (A) (B) (C)	105. (A) (B) (C)
26. (A) (B) (C)	66. (A) (B) (C)	106. (A) (B) (C)
27. (A) (B) (C)	67. (A) (B) (C)	107. (A) (B) (C)
28. (A) (B) (C)	68. (A) (B) (C)	108. (A) (B) (C)
29. (A) (B) (C)	69. (A) (B) (C)	109. (A) (B) (C)
30. (A) (B) (C)	70. (A) (B) (C)	110. (A) (B) (C)
31. (A) (B) (C)	71. (A) (B) (C)	111. (A) (B) (C)
32. (A) (B) (C)	72. (A) (B) (C)	112. (A) (B) (C)
33. (A) (B) (C)	73. (A) (B) (C)	113. (A) (B) (C)
34. (A) (B) (C)	74. (A) (B) (C)	114. (A) (B) (C)
35. (A) (B) (C)	75. (A) (B) (C)	115. (A) (B) (C)
36. (A) (B) (C)	76. (A) (B) (C)	116. (A) (B) (C)
37. (A) (B) (C)	77. (A) (B) (C)	117. (A) (B) (C)
38. (A) (B) (C)	78. (A) (B) (C)	118. (A) (B) (C)
39. (A) (B) (C)	79. (A) (B) (C)	119. (A) (B) (C)
40. (A) (B) (C)	80. (A) (B) (C)	120. (A) (B) (C)

EXAM 3
AFTERNOON SESSION

Questions 1 through 18 relate to Ethical and Professional Standards.
(27 minutes)

1. Gabe Klein, CFA, an analyst for HB Investments, is responsible for the valuation model for an IPO. Without his knowledge, others at HB adjusted the inputs to the model to increase the estimated value of the shares, and the offering is oversubscribed. Complying with local securities laws, Klein purchases shares of the IPO for his personal account and allocates the remaining shares to client accounts on a pro rata basis. With regard to the Standard on knowledge of the law, the analyst:
    A. did not violate the Standard.
    B. violated the Standard by purchasing the shares of the IPO but not by allowing the IPO valuation to be published.
    C. violated the Standard by allowing the IPO valuation to be published and by purchasing the shares of the IPO.

2. Green Investments utilizes the CFA Institute Standards of Professional Conduct as their standards for ethical practice. For purposes of compliance, which of the following is *least likely* a violation of Green Investments' policies?
    A. One of Green Investments' marketing brochures states that several of the firm's portfolio managers passed all three levels of the CFA exam on their first attempts.
    B. At a meeting with potential clients, Green's chief investment officer states that he is among a group of the most qualified investment professionals because he holds the CFA charter.
    C. In interviewing a prospective employee, a portfolio manager at the firm says that the position could be financially rewarding because CFA charterholders are known to achieve superior performance results.

3. Charmaine Townsend, CFA, has been managing equity portfolios for clients using a model that identifies growth companies selling at reasonable multiples. With economic growth slowing for the foreseeable future, she has decided to change to a securities selection model that emphasizes dividend income and low valuation. To comply with the Code and Standards, Townsend should *most appropriately*:
   A. promptly notify her clients of the change.
   B. get written permission from her clients prior to the change.
   C. get written acknowledgment of the change from her clients within a reasonable period of time after the change is made.

4. Emily Wells, CFA, receives an unsolicited trade request from a client that Wells believes is unsuitable based on the client's investment policy statement (IPS). Wells wishes to discuss this request with the client before executing the trade. The focus of Wells's discussion with the client should *most appropriately*:
   A. be on updating the IPS to reflect a change in the client's objectives and constraints.
   B. depend on whether the requested trade has a material impact on the client's portfolio.
   C. be on educating the client about the way in which the requested trade deviates from the IPS.

5. With respect to the Standard on material nonpublic information, materiality is *least likely* to be affected by:
   A. the source of the information.
   B. liquidity of the subject security.
   C. ambiguity about the price effect of the information.

6. Alberto Cosini is the top-rated, sell-side analyst in the biotechnology industry. His recommendations significantly affect prices of industry stocks regularly. Yesterday Cosini changed his rating on Biopharm from "hold" to "buy," and Cosini's firm emailed the change to its clients although no public disclosure has yet been made. If Peter Allen, CFA, who heard about Cosini's rating change for Biopharm from his brother, purchases Biopharm in his personal account, Allen will *most likely*:
   A. not violate the Standards.
   B. violate the Standard concerning diligence and reasonable basis.
   C. violate the Standard concerning material nonpublic information.

7. Judy Dudley, CFA, is an analyst and plans to visit a company that she is analyzing in order to prepare a research report. The Standard related to independence and objectivity:
   A. requires Dudley to pay for her own transportation costs and not to accept any gifts or compensation for writing the report, but allows her to accept accommodations and meals that are not lavish.
   B. requires Dudley not to accept any compensation for writing a research report, but allows her to accept company paid transportation, lodging, and meals.
   C. allows Dudley to accept transportation, lodging, expenses, and compensation for writing a research report, but requires that she disclose such an arrangement in her report.

8. Campbell Hill, CFA, has recently accepted the position of Chief Compliance Officer at an investment management firm. Hill distributes a memo stating that effective immediately (1) material supporting all company research reports will be kept in the company database in electronic form for 10 years, and hard copies of the same material will be maintained for one year only, and (2) hard copy records of all trade confirmations sent to clients must be kept on file for five years, the period mandated by local regulations. With respect to record retention:
   A. neither of Hill's policies violates the Standards.
   B. Hill's policies regarding both research reports and trade confirmations violate the Standards.
   C. Hill's policy regarding research reports does not violate the Standards, but the policy regarding trade confirmations does.

9. In calculating total firm assets for a GIPS-compliant performance statement, Allen Bund, CFA, finds that there is a mix of fee-paying and non-fee-paying accounts, some of which are discretionary and some of which are non-discretionary accounts. Should Bund include non-discretionary accounts and non-fee-paying accounts in the calculation of total firm assets?

	Non-discretionary accounts	Non-fee-paying accounts
A.	Yes	Yes
B.	No	Yes
C.	No	No

10. Dawn Shepard, CFA, is a broker for a regional brokerage firm. Her company's research department recently changed its recommendation on the common stock of Orlando (ORL) from "buy" to "sell" and sent the change to all firm clients who own ORL. The next day, a client places a "buy" order for ORL. According to the Standards, under these circumstances, Shepard:
   A. must advise the customer of the change in recommendation before accepting the order.
   B. has complied with the fair dealing Standard and may accept the order because it is unsolicited.
   C. may accept the order only if the customer acknowledges in writing that she was notified of the change in the recommendation.

11. Paul James, CFA, a retail stock broker, notices that one client in particular, Chet Young, Ph.D., is especially adept at picking stocks. James decides to replicate Young's trades in his own account after he enters them. By doing so, James:
   A. is not in violation of any Standards.
   B. is in violation of the Standard on priority of transactions because he is front running the client's account.
   C. is in violation of the Standard on misconduct because he has misappropriated confidential client information.

12. Nicholas Hart, CFA, is a portfolio manager for individuals. Last year, Hart's wife was hospitalized for several months. Despite his best efforts to pay her bills, Hart was forced to declare personal bankruptcy but did not disclose this to his clients. According to the CFA Institute Standards of Professional Conduct, Hart:
   A. is not in violation of any Standard.
   B. is in violation of the Standard on communication with clients for not disclosing his bankruptcy to his clients.
   C. is in violation of the Standard on misconduct for personal conduct that reflects adversely on his professional reputation.

13. Marie Marshall, CFA, charges clients a management fee and commissions on securities transactions. Marshall receives an annual bonus based on the overall success of the firm and a quarterly bonus based on the trading volume in her clients' accounts. If Marshall does not tell clients about her compensation package, she is violating the Standard concerning:
   A. disclosure of conflicts.
   B. communication with clients.
   C. additional compensation arrangements.

©2014 Kaplan, Inc.

14. Lunar Wealth, a subsidiary of Galaxy Financial, has prepared GIPS-compliant performance data and asks Galaxy's president about his interest in presenting GIPS-compliant performance data, but he does not believe it is a priority. Lunar may:
    A. claim partial compliance with GIPS if Lunar's performance presentations are in compliance.
    B. not claim compliance with GIPS because compliance must be made on a company-wide basis.
    C. claim compliance with GIPS as long as Lunar is presented to the public as a distinct business entity.

15. Fred Reilly, CFA, is an investment advisor. Roger Harrison, a long-term client of Reilly, decides to move his accounts to a new firm. In his review of Harrison's account history, Reilly discovers some transfers of funds from the account of Harrison's company that Reilly suspects were illegal. Which of the following actions is *most appropriate* for Reilly to take under the Standards?
    A. Discuss his suspicions with outside counsel.
    B. Inform Harrison's company of the suspected illegal activities because Harrison is no longer a client.
    C. Do nothing because he must maintain the confidentiality of client information even after the client has left the firm.

16. Fred Dean, CFA, has just taken a job as trader for LPC. One of his first assignments is to execute the purchase of a block of East Street Industries. While working with East Street on an assignment for his previous employer, he learned that East Street's sales have weakened and will likely be significantly below the LPC analyst's estimate, but no public announcement of this has been made. Which of the following actions would be the *most appropriate* for Dean to take according to the Standards?
    A. Contact East Street's management and urge them to make the information public and make the trade if they refuse.
    B. Request that the firm place East Street's stock on a restricted list and decline to make any trades of the company's stock.
    C. Post the information about the drop in sales on an internet bulletin board to achieve public dissemination and inform his supervisor of the posting.

17. When members and candidates report performance data, according to the Code and Standards, it is:
    A. permissible to leave details out in a brief presentation.
    B. recommended that a minimum of five years performance history be included.
    C. a requirement to present composite performance rather than individual account performance.

18.   Bob Sampson is the head portfolio manager for Global Equities, which has been in existence for eight years. Beginning this year, the firm has decided to present performance information in compliance with GIPS. To claim GIPS compliance, the firm must present at least:
          A. eight years of GIPS-compliant performance information.
          B. five years of GIPS-compliant performance information with no additional disclosure required for prior years.
          C. five years of GIPS-compliant performance information and may include noncompliant performance information for the prior three years in the "Disclosures" section.

Questions 19 through 32 relate to Quantitative Methods. (21 minutes)

19.   An investor wants to receive $10,000 annually for ten years with the first payment five years from today. If the investor can earn a 14% annual return, the amount that she will have to invest today is *closest* to:
          A. $27,091.
          B. $30,884.
          C. $52,161.

20.   Which of the following statements about the frequency distribution shown below is *least accurate*?

Return Interval	Frequency
0% to 5%	10
> 5% to 10%	20
> 10% to 15%	30
> 15% to 20%	20

          A. The return intervals are mutually exclusive.
          B. The cumulative absolute frequency of the fourth interval is 20.
          C. The relative frequency of the second return interval is 25%.

21.   A contrarian technical analyst is *most likely* to be bullish based on a:
          A. low put-call ratio.
          B. high volatility index.
          C. low mutual fund cash position.

©2014 Kaplan, Inc.

22. An investor in a mutual fund earns a 25% return the first year, loses 25% in the second year, gains 30% in the third year, and then loses 30% in the fourth year. The average annual compound growth rate of this investment is *closest* to:
    A. −3.9%.
    B. 0.0%.
    C. 5.6%.

23. An analyst obtains the following annual returns for a group of stocks: 10%, 8%, 7%, 9%, 10%, 12%, 11%, 10%, 30%, and 13%. This distribution:
    A. has a median greater than its mode.
    B. is skewed to the right, and the mean is less than the median.
    C. is skewed to the right, and the mean is greater than the mode.

24. An analyst gathers the following data about the mean monthly returns of three securities:

Security	Mean Monthly Return	Standard Deviation
X	0.9	0.7
Y	1.2	4.7
Z	1.5	5.2

    Which security has the highest level of relative risk as measured by the coefficient of variation?
    A. X.
    B. Y.
    C. Z.

25. The median of a distribution is *least likely* equal to the:
    A. second quartile.
    B. third quintile.
    C. fifth decile.

26. Which of the following statements about probability concepts is *most accurate*?
    A. Subjective probability is a probability that is based on personal judgment.
    B. A conditional probability is the probability that two or more events happen concurrently.
    C. An empirical probability is one based on logical analysis rather than on observation or personal judgment.

27.   Which of the following is *least likely* an underlying assumption of technical analysis?
A. Supply and demand are governed solely by rational behavior.
B. Actual shifts in supply and demand can be observed in market price behavior.
C. Prices for individual securities and the market tend to move in trends that persist for long periods of time.

28.   Alex White, CFA, is examining a portfolio that contains 100 stocks that are either value or growth stocks. Of these 100 stocks, 40% are value stocks. The previous portfolio manager had selected 70% of the value stocks and 80% of the growth stocks. What is the probability of selecting a stock at random that is either a value stock or was selected by the previous portfolio manager?
A. 28%.
B. 76%.
C. 88%.

29.   Which of the following statements about the normal distribution is *least accurate*? The normal distribution:
A. has a mean of zero and a standard deviation of one.
B. is completely described by its mean and standard deviation.
C. is bell-shaped, with tails extending without limit to the left and to the right.

30.   A manager forecasts a bond portfolio return of 10% and estimates a standard deviation of annual returns of 4%. Assuming a normal returns distribution and that the manager is correct, there is a:
A. 90% probability that the portfolio return will be between 3.2% and 17.2%.
B. 95% probability that the portfolio return will be between 2.16% and 17.84%.
C. 32% probability that the portfolio return will be between 6% and 14%.

31.   An investment has an expected return of 10% with a standard deviation of 5%. If the returns are normally distributed, the chance of losing money is *closest* to:
A. 2.5%.
B. 5.0%.
C. 16.0%.

©2014 Kaplan, Inc.

32.   Which of the following statements about sampling and estimation is *least accurate*?
       A. Sampling error is the difference between the observed value of a statistic and the value it is intended to estimate.
       B. A simple random sample is a sample obtained in such a way that each element of the population has an equal probability of being selected.
       C. The central limit theorem states that the sample mean for a large sample size will have a distribution that is the same as the distribution of the underlying population.

Questions 33 through 44 relate to Economics. (18 minutes)

33.   The crowding-out effect suggests that:
       A. government borrowing will lead to an increase in private savings.
       B. as government spending increases, so will incomes and taxes, and the higher taxes will reduce both aggregate demand and output.
       C. greater government deficits will drive up interest rates, thereby reducing private investment.

34.   Consider two currencies, the WSC and the BDR. The spot WSC/BDR exchange rate is 2.875, the 180-day riskless WSC rate is 1.5%, and the 180-day riskless BDR rate is 3.0%. The 180-day forward exchange rate that will prevent arbitrage profits is *closest* to:
       A. 2.833 WSC/BDR.
       B. 2.854 WSC/BDR.
       C. 2.918 WSC/BDR.

35.   At the equilibrium levels of output and price in a competitive industry without taxes:
       A. consumer and producer surplus are equal.
       B. both consumer and producer surplus are maximized.
       C. the sum of producer and consumer surplus is maximized.

36.   Which of the following does the U.S. central bank *most often* use to change the money supply?
       A. The discount rate.
       B. Open market operations.
       C. The required reserve ratio.

37.   The price of milk in a country increases from €1.00 per liter to €1.10 per liter, and the quantity supplied does not change. This suggests the elasticity of the short-run supply of milk in this country is equal to:
       A. infinity, and supply is perfectly elastic.
       B. zero, and supply is perfectly inelastic.
       C. infinity, and supply is perfectly inelastic.

38. In the short run, will an increase in the money supply increase the price level and real output?
   A. Both will increase in the short run.
   B. Neither will increase in the short run.
   C. Only one will increase in the short run.

39. The law of diminishing marginal returns explains:
   A. the shape of the long-run average cost curve.
   B. the upward sloping portion of the short-run marginal cost curve.
   C. the upward sloping portion of the long-run marginal cost curve.

40. A firm in a perfectly competitive market will tend to expand its output as long as:
   A. its marginal revenue is positive.
   B. the market price is greater than the marginal cost.
   C. its marginal revenue is greater than the market price.

41. Unlike members of free trade areas, customs union members:
   A. adopt a single currency.
   B. remove barriers to trade with all members.
   C. adopt uniform trade restrictions with non-members.

42. In utility analysis, a consumer's optimal bundle of goods lies on an indifference curve that is:
   A. most preferred by the consumer.
   B. tangent to the consumer's budget line.
   C. contained within the consumer's opportunity set.

43. Reasons why the unemployment rate is a lagging indicator of the business cycle *least likely* include:
   A. discouraged workers who begin seeking work.
   B. action lag in the implementation of unemployment insurance.
   C. high costs to employers of frequently hiring or firing employees.

44. A natural monopoly is *most likely* to exist when:
   A. economies of scale are great.
   B. average total cost increases as output increases.
   C. a single firm owns essentially all of a productive resource.

 ©2014 Kaplan, Inc.

Questions 45 through 68 relate to Financial Reporting and Analysis.
(36 minutes)

45. Which of the following statements about types of nonrecurring items
     under U.S. GAAP is *least accurate*?
     A. Unusual or infrequent items are included in income from continuing
         operations.
     B. Extraordinary items are unusual and infrequent items that are reported
         net of taxes and included in nonrecurring income from continuing
         operations.
     C. Discontinued operations are reported net of taxes below income from
         continuing operations.

46. A company has the following sequence of events regarding its stock:
     • The company had 1,000,000 shares outstanding at the beginning of
        the year.
     • On June 30, the company declared and issued a 10% stock
        dividend.
     • On September 30, the company sold 400,000 shares of common
        stock at par.

     The number of shares that should be used to compute basic earnings per
     share at year end is:
     A. 1,000,000.
     B. 1,100,000.
     C. 1,200,000.

47. Snow Blower Industries operates in an increasing price environment and
     uses the FIFO method for inventory reporting. Compared to the weighted
     average cost method, Snow Blower's use of the FIFO method will *most
     likely* decrease:
     A. net income.
     B. ending inventory.
     C. cost of goods sold.

48. Time-series analysis of a firm's common-size balance sheets reveals the following data:

	20X3	20X4	20X5
Current assets	20%	22%	25%
Inventory	8%	9%	11%
Short-term debt	10%	11%	12%
Long-term debt	24%	21%	18%

Based only on the data provided, an analyst can conclude that the firm's:
A. debt ratio is decreasing.
B. quick ratio is decreasing.
C. inventory/sales ratio is increasing.

49. Which of the following statements about the analysis of cash flows is *least accurate*?
A. Interest payments on debt are not a financing cash flow under U.S. GAAP.
B. Both the direct and indirect methods involve adding back noncash items such as depreciation and amortization.
C. When using the indirect method, an analyst should add any losses on the sales of fixed assets to net income.

50. A company that reports under U.S. GAAP and changes its inventory cost assumption from weighted average cost to last-in first-out is required to apply this change in accounting principle:
A. retrospectively, and disclose the new cost flow method being used.
B. prospectively, and explain the reasons for the change in the financial statement disclosures.
C. retrospectively, and explain the reasons for the change in the financial statement disclosures.

 ©2014 Kaplan, Inc.

51.   An analyst gathered the following data about a company:

	20X6	20X7
EBIT margin (EBIT / revenue)	0.15	0.10
Asset turnover (revenue / assets)	1.5	1.8
Leverage multiplier (assets / equity)	1.5	1.6
Tax burden (net income / EBT)	0.7	0.7
Interest burden (EBT / EBIT)	0.85	0.85

The company's return on equity:
A. decreased because the company's profit margin decreased.
B. increased because the company's asset turnover and leverage increased.
C. remained constant because the company's decreased profit margin was just offset by increases in asset turnover and leverage.

52.   For which of the following investments in securities is a firm *most likely* to report unrealized gains or losses on its income statement?
A. Preferred stock, which the firm classifies as available-for-sale.
B. Five-year bonds, which the firm purchased in a private placement.
C. Listed call options, which the firm intends to exercise at expiration.

53.   Bentlom Company's common-size financial statements show the following information:
- Earnings after taxes   15%
- Current liabilities   20%
- Equity   45%
- Sales $800
- Cash   10%
- Total assets $2,000
- Accounts receivable   15%
- Inventory   20%

Bentlom's long-term debt-to-equity ratio and current ratio are *closest* to:

Long-term debt-to-equity ratio	Current ratio
A. 78%	2.25
B. 88%	2.50
C. 98%	2.75

54. Consider a manufacturing company and a financial services company. Interest expense is *most likely* classified as a non-operating component of income for:
   A. both of these companies.
   B. neither of these companies.
   C. only one of these companies.

55. The two primary assumptions in preparing financial statements under IFRS are:
   A. accrual and going concern.
   B. reasonable accuracy and accrual.
   C. going concern and reasonable accuracy.

56. Compared to an operating lease, a capital lease will have what effects on operating income (earnings before interest and taxes) and net income in the first year?
   A. Both will be lower.
   B. Both will be higher.
   C. One will be lower and one will be higher.

57. An analyst gathered the following data about a company:
   - 1,000 common shares are outstanding (no change during the year).
   - Net income is $5,000.
   - The company paid $500 in preferred dividends.
   - The company paid $600 in common dividends.
   - The average market price of their common stock is $60 for the year.
   - The company had 100 warrants (for one share each) outstanding for the entire year, exercisable at $50.

   The company's diluted earnings per share is *closest* to:
   A. $4.42.
   B. $4.55.
   C. $4.83.

58. Which of the following sources of information should an analyst consider the *least* reliable?
   A. Form 10-Q.
   B. Proxy statement.
   C. Corporate press release.

59. A company takes a $10 million impairment charge on a depreciable asset in 20X3. The *most likely* effect will be to:
   A. increase reported net income in 20X4.
   B. decrease net income and taxes payable in 20X3.
   C. increase return on equity and operating cash flow in 20X4.

©2014 Kaplan, Inc.

60. Xanos Corporation faced a 50% marginal tax rate last year and showed the following financial and tax reporting information:
    - Deferred tax asset of $1,000.
    - Deferred tax liability of $5,000.

    Based only on this information and the news that the tax rate will decline to 40%, Xanos Corporation's:
    A. deferred tax asset will be reduced by $400 and deferred tax liability will be reduced by $2,000.
    B. deferred tax liability will be reduced by $1,000 and income tax expense will be reduced by $800.
    C. deferred tax asset will be reduced by $200 and income tax expense will be reduced by $1,000.

61. For the year in which a firm increases its promised pension benefits per year of service for existing employees, net income will be:
    A. higher under IFRS than U.S. GAAP.
    B. higher under U.S. GAAP than IFRS.
    C. the same under IFRS and U.S. GAAP.

62. A company that capitalizes costs instead of expensing them will have:
    A. higher income variability and higher cash flows from operations.
    B. lower cash flows from investing and lower income variability.
    C. lower cash flows from operations and higher profitability in early years.

63. Under accrual accounting, the payment of $15,000 at the end of fiscal year 20X8 for a special advertising campaign that will run for the first three months of 20X9 would affect the 20X8 financial statements by decreasing cash by $15,000 and generating a $15,000 increase in:
    A. advertising expense.
    B. a prepaid asset account.
    C. a prepaid liability account.

64. Al Pike, CFA, is analyzing Red Company by projecting pro forma financial statements. Pike expects Red to generate sales of $3 billion and a return on equity of 15% in the next year. Pike forecasts that Red's total assets will be $5 billion and that the company will maintain its financial leverage ratio of 2.5. Based on these forecasts, Pike should project Red's net income to be:
    A. $100 million.
    B. $300 million.
    C. $500 million.

65. A company issues $10 million in 8% annual-pay, 5-year bonds, when the market rate is 8.25%. The initial balance sheet liability and liability one year from the date of issue are *closest* to:

Initial liability	Liability one year later
A. $9,900,837	$9,917,656
B. $10,000,000	$9,975,000
C. $10,099,163	$10,082,344

66. Which of the following items would affect owners' equity and also appear on the income statement?
   A. Dividends paid to shareholders.
   B. Unrealized gains and losses on trading securities.
   C. Unrealized gains and losses on available-for-sale securities.

67. Copper, Inc., had $4 million in bonds outstanding that were convertible into common stock at a conversion rate of 100 shares per $1,000 bond. In 20X1, all of the outstanding bonds were converted into common stock. Copper's average share price for 20X1 was $15. Copper's statement of cash flows for the year ended December 31, 20X1, should *most likely* include:
   A. a footnote describing the conversion of the bonds into common stock.
   B. cash flows from financing of +$4 million from issuance of common stock and –$4 million from retirement of bonds.
   C. cash flows from financing of +$6 million from issuance of common stock and –$4 million from retirement of bonds and cash flows from investing of –$2 million for a loss on retirement of bonds.

68. During a period of falling costs of manufacturing, which of the following inventory cost formulas would result in the greatest reported net income?
   A. LIFO.
   B. FIFO.
   C. Average cost.

Questions 69 through 77 relate to Corporate Finance. (13.5 minutes)

69. An analyst identifies the following cash flows for an average-risk project:
   - Year 0   –$5,000
   - Years 1–2 $1,900
   - Year 3 $2,500
   - Year 4 $2,000

   If the company's cost of capital is 12%, the project's discounted payback period is *closest* to:
   A. 2.5 years.
   B. 3.0 years.
   C. 3.9 years.

©2014 Kaplan, Inc.

70. Mary Miller, CFA, manages the short-term cash position for Young Company. Miller can invest in one of three securities that will mature in 180 days: a Treasury bill priced at 97.5% of par, commercial paper with a bond-equivalent yield of 5.10%, and a 6-month certificate of deposit that will return 2.5% over the 180-day holding period. Miller should purchase the:
    A. Treasury bill.
    B. commercial paper.
    C. certificate of deposit.

71. Which of the following is the *least appropriate* method for estimating a firm's before-tax cost of debt capital?
    A. Use the market yield on bonds with a rating and maturity similar to the firm's existing debt.
    B. Assume the firm's cost of debt capital is equal to the yield to maturity on its publicly traded debt.
    C. Use the coupon rate on the firm's most recently issued debt.

72. Paul Dufray, CFA, is estimating the asset beta for a new project based on a firm that primarily makes and sells a similar product. In addition to the beta of that firm, Dufray will need to estimate the firm's:
    A. sales risk and financial risk.
    B. debt-to-equity ratio and tax rate.
    C. operating leverage and financial leverage.

73. Sarah Evens has been studying the effects of takeover defenses on shareholder value. Evens is evaluating various uses of golden parachutes, poison pills, and greenmail, all of which can affect share value. Good corporate governance requires a careful review of a firm's takeover defenses. When conducting this review, Evens should *most likely* consider which of the following a negative factor?
    A. In a hostile bidder situation, the board would be willing to pay cash to such a bidder to preserve the company's independence.
    B. Shareholders have voted down an amendment to the bylaws that would have provided a poison pill.
    C. A change of control issue would not trigger the interest of a local government.

74. The committee charged with recommending a compensation package for members of a firm's board of directors has recommended that in addition to compensation of $10,000 for each board meeting attended, board members (1) will be able to use one of the firm's corporate jets up to twice each year and (2) will receive a finder's fee of 0.1% if they identify an acquisition target that the firm acquires while the member is still on the board. Are these policies consistent with good corporate governance practices?
   A. Both policies are consistent with good corporate governance.
   B. Neither policy is consistent with good corporate governance.
   C. Only one of these policies is consistent with good corporate governance.

75. Which of the following is *least likely* a problem associated with the internal rate of return (IRR) method of choosing investment projects?
   A. Using IRR to rank mutually exclusive projects assumes reinvestment of cash flows at the IRR.
   B. For independent projects, the IRR and NPV can lead to different investment decisions.
   C. If the project has an unconventional cash flow pattern, the result can be multiple IRRs.

76. Break points in a firm's marginal cost of capital schedule are *best* interpreted as representing the:
   A. maximum amounts of debt, preferred stock, and common stock the firm can issue.
   B. amounts of new securities a firm would need to issue to take advantage of flotation cost discounts.
   C. amounts of capital expenditure at which the company's weighted average cost of capital increases.

77. A financial advisor makes the following statements about dividends: (1) With respect to dividends, an investor should be indifferent between purchasing a stock before or after the payment date because on the payment date the value of the shares will fall by approximately the amount of the dividend; (2) The holder-of-record date occurs two business days before the ex-dividend date. Are the advisor's statements accurate?
   A. Both of these statements are accurate.
   B. Neither of these statements is accurate.
   C. Only one of these statements is accurate.

©2014 Kaplan, Inc.

Questions 78 through 85 relate to Portfolio Management. (12 minutes)

78. Which of the following portfolios will have the lowest diversification ratio? A portfolio of:
    A. 30 equally-weighted stocks with companies from the same industry.
    B. 20 equally-weighted stocks with companies from different industries.
    C. 30 equally-weighted stocks with companies from different industries.

79. In a case where a client's capacity to bear risk is significantly less than the client's expressed willingness to bear risk, the *most appropriate* action for a financial advisor is to:
    A. counsel the client and attempt to change his attitude towards risk.
    B. base the assessment of risk tolerance in the IPS on client's ability to bear risk.
    C. attempt to educate the client about investment risk and correct any misconceptions.

80. Which of the following statements about risk is *most accurate*?
    A. The capital market line plots expected return against market risk.
    B. The efficient frontier plots expected return against unsystematic risk.
    C. The security market line plots expected return against systematic risk.

81. A portfolio manager is constructing a new equity portfolio consisting of a large number of randomly chosen domestic stocks. As the number of stocks in the portfolio increases, what happens to the expected levels of systematic and unsystematic risk?

Systematic risk	Unsystematic risk
A. Increases	Remains the same
B. Decreases	Increases
C. Remains the same	Decreases

82. The risk-free rate is 5% and the expected market return is 15%. A portfolio manager is estimating a return of 20% on a stock with a beta of 1.5. Based on the SML and the analyst's estimate, this stock is:
    A. properly valued.
    B. overvalued.
    C. undervalued.

83. Refusing to invest in companies that sell tobacco products, alcohol, or products that are harmful to the environment would constitute a set of investment restrictions that *best* illustrates which of the following investment constraints?
    A. Regulatory factors.
    B. Unique needs and preferences.
    C. Legal restrictions.

84.   Rolly Parker, CFA, has managed the retirement account funds for Misto Inc. for the last two years. Contributions and withdrawals from the account are decided by Misto's CFO. The account history is as follows, with account values calculated before same-date deposits and withdrawals:

Jan 1, 20X1	Beginning portfolio value	$10 million
Jul 1, 20X1	Account value	$11.2 million
Jul 1, 20X1	Deposit of cash	$1.2 million
Jan 1, 20X2	Account value	$12.5 million
Jan 1, 20X2	Withdrawal of cash	$0.6 million
Dec 31, 20X2	Account value	$15 million

The appropriate annual return to use in evaluating the manager's performance is *closest* to:
A. 9%.
B. 19%.
C. 22%.

85.   Which of the following pooled investment shares is *least likely* to trade at a price different from its NAV?
A. Exchange-traded fund shares.
B. Open-end mutual fund shares.
C. Closed-end mutual fund shares.

Questions 86 through 97 relate to Equity Investments. (18 minutes)

86.   Which of the following statements about types of orders is *least accurate*?
A. Market orders are orders to buy or sell at the best price available.
B. Limit orders are orders to buy or sell at or away from the market price.
C. A stop buy order is typically used to protect a short position in a security and is placed below the current market price.

87.   A stock has the following data associated with it:
- A required rate of return of 14%.
- A return on equity of 15%.
- An earnings retention rate of 40%.

The stock's justified price-to-earnings ratio is *closest* to:
A. 5.0.
B. 6.7.
C. 7.5.

88.   The required rate of return used in the dividend discount model is *least likely* to be affected by a change in the:
A. expected rate of inflation.
B. real risk-free rate of return.
C. growth rate of earnings and dividends.

                    ©2014 Kaplan, Inc.

89. High return on invested capital and high pricing power are *most likely* to be associated with an industry that has:
   A. high capacity.
   B. low barriers to entry.
   C. high concentration.

90. With regard to the implications of stock market efficiency for technical analysis and fundamental analysis, if market prices are:
   A. weak-form efficient, technical analysis that depends only on past trading data should be of limited or no value.
   B. semistrong-form efficient, fundamental analysis using the top-down approach should yield consistently superior returns.
   C. semistrong-form efficient, fundamental analysis using only publicly available market information should generate abnormal returns after considering risk and transaction costs.

91. The following data pertains to a firm's common stock:
   - The stock will pay no dividends for two years.
   - The dividend three years from now is expected to be $1.
   - Dividends are expected to grow at a 7% rate from that point onward.

   If an investor requires a 17% return on this investment, how much will the investor be willing to pay for this stock now?
   A. $6.24.
   B. $7.31.
   C. $8.26.

92. A stock's price currently is $100. An analyst forecasts the following for the stock:
   - The normalized trailing price earnings (P/E) ratio will be 12×.
   - The stock is expected to pay a $5 dividend this coming year on projected earnings of $10 per share.

   If the analyst were to buy and hold the stock for the year, the projected rate of return based on these forecasts is *closest* to:
   A. 15%.
   B. 20%.
   C. 25%.

93. Which of the following statements about short sales is *least accurate*?
   A. Proceeds from short sales cannot be withdrawn from the account.
   B. The short seller must pay the lender of the stock any dividends paid by the company.
   C. The short seller is required to replace the borrowed securities within six months of a short sale.

94. Which of the following firms' earnings are likely to exhibit the greatest degree of sensitivity to the business cycle?
   A. Furniture producer with high fixed costs as a proportion of total costs.
   B. Entertainment producer with high variable costs as a proportion of total costs.
   C. Food and beverage producer with high fixed costs as a proportion of total costs.

95. The type of share voting *most likely* to result in significant minority shareholders having an approximately proportional representation on the board of directors is:
   A. statutory voting.
   B. weighted voting.
   C. cumulative voting.

96. Which of the following indexes is *most likely* to be rebalanced on a regular basis?
   A. Price-weighted index.
   B. Equal-weighted index.
   C. Market-capitalization weighted index.

97. Over the most recent period, Ladden Materials has seen slow growth, increased competition, and declining profitability in its industry. The phase of the industry life cycle for Ladden's industry is *most likely*:
   A. mature.
   B. decline.
   C. shakeout.

Questions 98 through 109 relate to Fixed Income. (18 minutes)

98. Which of the following is *least likely* a reason that floating rate bonds may trade at prices different from their par values?
   A. A time lag exists between the rate change in the market and the time when the coupon rate is reset.
   B. The fixed quoted margin on the floating rate security may differ from the margin required by the market.
   C. Resetting interest rates makes floating rate bonds more susceptible to the price risk that results from changing interest rates.

99. Compared to a bond's Macaulay duration, its modified duration:
   A. is lower.
   B. is higher.
   C. may be lower or higher.

©2014 Kaplan, Inc.

100. An analyst obtains a market quote for the two-year forward rate two years from now. To derive the next point on a theoretical annual forward rate curve, the analyst can use the:
    A. two-year and five-year spot rates.
    B. three-year and four-year spot rates.
    C. three-year and five-year spot rates.

101. The credit rating agency practice of "notching" is *best* described as:
    A. assigning different ratings to different debt issues from the same issuer.
    B. downgrading or upgrading the rating of a debt issue or issuer by one increment.
    C. adding a plus or minus sign to a rating to indicate a positive or negative outlook.

102. A bond priced at par ($1,000) has a modified duration of 8 and a convexity of 100. If interest rates fall 50 basis points, the new price will be *closest* to:
    A. $1,041.25.
    B. $958.75.
    C. $875.00.

103. An analyst needs to estimate the value of an illiquid 7% BB+ rated bond that has eight years to maturity. Using matrix pricing, the analyst should *most appropriately* base an estimate for this bond on yields of:
    A. on-the-run eight-year government bonds.
    B. more frequently traded bonds rated BB+.
    C. other BB+ rated bonds with similar liquidity to this bond.

104. Acme Holdings operates in an industry for which three-year average financial ratios by credit rating are as follows:

Ratio	AAA	AA	A	BBB	BB	B	CCC
FCF/debt	32.0%	25.9%	21.8%	18.7%	12.3%	7.0%	3.1%
Debt/EBITDA	0.9×	1.3×	1.5×	1.9×	2.3×	3.5×	5.0×

    If Acme has a three-year average debt-to-EBITDA ratio of 2.4 and a free cash flow to debt ratio of 7.1, its credit rating is most likely to be:
    A. investment grade.
    B. below investment grade.
    C. borderline investment grade.

105. Commercial mortgage-backed securities (CMBS) loans typically have greater call protection than agency MBS loans because:
    A. commercial mortgages may have yield maintenance charges.
    B. smaller-sized mortgages typically are not refinanced if interest rates fall.
    C. CMBS typically receive higher credit ratings from credit agencies than residential MBS.

106. A non-amortizing fixed income security is *most accurately* described as a:
    A. bullet bond.
    B. balloon bond.
    C. mortgage bond.

107. For a domestic investor purchasing foreign bonds:
    A. appreciation of both the asset and the foreign currency benefits the domestic investor.
    B. depreciation of both the asset and the foreign currency benefits the domestic investor.
    C. appreciation of the asset and depreciation of the foreign currency benefit the domestic investor.

108. Reinvestment risk is *least likely*:
    A. minimized with zero-coupon bond issues.
    B. more problematic for those investors with longer time horizons.
    C. more problematic when the current coupons being reinvested are relatively small.

109. A duration gap is *most accurately* described as a difference between a bond's:
    A. Macaulay duration and effective duration.
    B. duration and the bondholder's investment horizon.
    C. actual change in value and the change estimated using duration and convexity.

Questions 110 through 115 relate to Derivatives. (9 minutes)

110. Jack Cheney, CFA, purchases a Swenson, Inc., October 80 put option for a premium of $5. Cheney holds the option until the expiration date when Swenson stock sells for $78 per share. At expiration, the loss on the contract is:
    A. $2.
    B. $3.
    C. $5.

111. Which of the following statements about call options is *least accurate*?
    A. The buyer of a call option has an obligation to perform.
    B. A call option is in the money when the strike price is below the stock price.
    C. The lower the strike price relative to the stock's underlying price, the more the call option is worth.

©2014 Kaplan, Inc.

112. A bank borrows for 360 days and simultaneously lends the proceeds for 90 days. This transaction creates a synthetic forward rate agreement (FRA) *closest to* a:
   A. long position in a 90-day FRA on 270-day LIBOR.
   B. long position in a 90-day FRA on 360-day LIBOR.
   C. short position in a 360-day FRA on 90-day LIBOR.

113. An investor buys a stock for $40 per share and simultaneously sells a call option on the stock with an exercise price of $42 for a premium of $3 per share. Ignoring dividends and transaction costs, what is the maximum profit the writer of this covered call can earn at expiration?
   A. $2.
   B. $3.
   C. $5.

114. Which of the following statements about futures and forwards is *most accurate*? Futures:
   A. are subject to default risk, but forwards are not.
   B. are individualized contracts, but forwards are standardized.
   C. require that traders post margin in order to trade, but forwards typically require no cash transaction until the delivery date.

115. Derivatives markets are *most likely* to:
   A. reduce transactions costs.
   B. increase speculation and risk.
   C. provide arbitrage opportunities to investors.

Questions 116 through 120 relate to Alternative Investments. (7.5 minutes)

116. To exit an investment in a portfolio company through a trade sale, a private equity firm sells:
   A. shares of a portfolio company to the public.
   B. the portfolio company to another private equity firm.
   C. the portfolio company to one of the portfolio company's competitors.

117. An investor can gain exposure to alternative investments by purchasing:
   A. convertible bonds of a high-yield issuer.
   B. a mortgage-backed security.
   C. an exchange-traded fund that tracks an emerging market index.

118. Which of the following is *least likely* a benefit of fund of funds (FOF) investing?
   A. FOFs may permit access to otherwise unavailable hedge funds.
   B. FOFs allow investors to diversify the risks of holding a single hedge fund.
   C. The fee is generally quite reasonable since the investor only pays the manager of the FOF.

119. A private equity firm that provides equity capital to a publicly traded company to finance the company's restructuring, but does not take the company private, is *best* described as engaging in:
    A. angel investing.
    B. mezzanine financing.
    C. private investment in public equity.

120. Which provision of a hedge fund's incentive fees is designed to prevent investors from paying multiple incentive fees for the same performance?
    A. Hurdle rate.
    B. High water mark.
    C. 2-and-20 structure.

©2014 Kaplan, Inc.

Exam 1
Morning Session Answer Key

To get valuable feedback on how your score compares to those of other Level I candidates, use your Username and Password to gain online access at Schweser.com and select "Performance Tracker" from your dashboard.

1.	C	31.	B	61.	A	91.	B
2.	C	32.	A	62.	C	92.	B
3.	C	33.	A	63.	B	93.	C
4.	A	34.	A	64.	C	94.	C
5.	A	35.	C	65.	A	95.	A
6.	A	36.	A	66.	B	96.	C
7.	C	37.	A	67.	C	97.	A
8.	C	38.	C	68.	B	98.	A
9.	A	39.	A	69.	B	99.	B
10.	C	40.	C	70.	A	100.	C
11.	A	41.	B	71.	A	101.	B
12.	A	42.	A	72.	C	102.	C
13.	C	43.	B	73.	B	103.	C
14.	C	44.	A	74.	A	104.	A
15.	B	45.	C	75.	B	105.	A
16.	B	46.	B	76.	C	106.	B
17.	B	47.	B	77.	A	107.	A
18.	A	48.	B	78.	B	108.	A
19.	B	49.	A	79.	A	109.	B
20.	A	50.	C	80.	A	110.	C
21.	C	51.	C	81.	B	111.	B
22.	C	52.	A	82.	B	112.	C
23.	B	53.	A	83.	A	113.	C
24.	B	54.	B	84.	C	114.	C
25.	A	55.	C	85.	C	115.	A
26.	A	56.	B	86.	A	116.	C
27.	B	57.	A	87.	C	117.	A
28.	C	58.	B	88.	B	118.	C
29.	C	59.	A	89.	A	119.	A
30.	B	60.	B	90.	C	120.	A

©2014 Kaplan, Inc.

Exam 1
Morning Session Answers

Answers referencing the Standards of Practice address Study Session 1, LOS 1.b, c and LOS 2.a, b, c, except where noted.

1. **C** Using the CFA designation in a fictitious name that conceals the owner's identity is a violation of Standard VII(B) Reference to CFA Institute, the CFA Designation, and the CFA Program. Because the social media message is intended to induce trading in a security, it is a violation of Standard II(B) Market Manipulation. Posting the message does not violate Standard III(B) Fair Dealing because it does not favor some clients' interests over others.

2. **C** A change in investment recommendation by a well-known and influential analyst is likely to affect the market price and is considered material information, so acting on this information before it has been released is prohibited by Standard II(A) Material Nonpublic Information. Because the member does not work for the analyst's firm, this is not addressed by Standard III(B) Fair Dealing. Having a reasonable basis does not apply to a member's own personal trades.

3. **C** Under Standard I(C) Misrepresentation, Winkler must identify Thompson as having developed the original model to avoid the prohibition against plagiarism. The only permitted exception is using factual information published by recognized financial and statistical reporting services such as S&P.

4. **A** Both ownership of Braden stock and the possible consulting work present potential conflicts of interest for Smith and must be disclosed within the report to comply with Standard VI(A) Disclosure of Conflicts.

5. **A** Standard I(A) Knowledge of the Law requires members and candidates to comply with the strictest requirement among the law where they reside, the law in the area where they do business, and the Code and Standards. In this case, the Code and Standards is the strictest. Standard III(B) Fair Dealing prohibits members and candidates from withholding shares in oversubscribed IPOs from clients for their own benefit.

6. **A** Standard IV(B) Additional Compensation Arrangements requires that members and candidates obtain written consent from their employers to enter into the agreement for additional contingent compensation from a client. Harris only received verbal consent. The concern is that such an arrangement might induce Harris to give partiality to this client's portfolio over those of her other clients.

7. **C** To be compliant with GIPS, firms must make compliant presentations available to prospects, on request, for any composite the firm has offered in the last five years, even for composites that have been terminated. (Study Session 1, LOS 4.d)

8. **C** Cantor violated Standard V(A) Diligence and Reasonable Basis because she did not have a reasonable and adequate basis for recommending clients buy HLC. Watson's enthusiasm and claim that HLC stock will perform well are not consistent with Cantor's conclusions. She must perform her own analysis before changing her investment recommendation. She has also violated Standard I(B) Independence and Objectivity because she has not exhibited the independence of analysis and thought that is required by the Standard.

9. **A** The actions are not in violation of the Standards. Under Standard IV(A) Loyalty, the use in new employment of knowledge and experience gained in previous employment is not prohibited. Hayes recreated the supporting records as required by Standard V(C) Record Retention.

10. **C** The first requirement of the Code of Ethics is that members and candidates "act with integrity, competence, diligence, respect, and in an ethical manner with the public, clients, prospective clients, employers, employees, colleagues in the investment profession, and other participants in the global capital markets." Knowing the applicable laws and regulations is required by Standard I(A) Knowledge of the Law. Standard VII(A) Conduct as Participants in CFA Institute Programs requires members and candidates not to compromise the integrity of CFA Institute.

11. **A** According to Standard IV(A) Loyalty, the interests of a member or candidate's employer are secondary to protecting the interests of clients and the integrity of capital markets. In this circumstance, whistleblowing is justified. As long as his motivation is clearly not for personal gain, he may, according to the Standards, violate employer confidentiality in this case. While he is required to dissociate from the suspect activity by Standard I(A) Knowledge of the Law, he is not prohibited by the Standards from reporting it unless a stricter local law applies.

12. **A** Black is in possession of material nonpublic information, and her most appropriate course of action is to inform her supervisor (or the firm's compliance officer) of what she has learned. She may not simply share the information with prospective buyers; if her firm determines that the information affects the value of the debentures, they must revise and recirculate the prospectus. Failing to do so may violate Standard I(C) Misrepresentation. Not informing her employer may be detrimental to her firm's interests and reputation if proceeding with the new issue without disclosure would violate regulations or laws.

13. **C** If a Professional Conduct Program inquiry finds that a member has violated the Code and Standards, CFA Institute may impose sanctions, which include public censure, suspension of membership in CFA Institute and use of the CFA designation, and revocation of a member's CFA charter. CFA Institute does not impose fines. (Study Session 1, LOS 1.a)

14. **C** Standard VI(C) Referral Fees requires members and candidates to disclose any compensation received for referrals and the nature of the compensation, to their employers and to any clients or prospects they refer to others with the expectation of compensation in any form.

©2014 Kaplan, Inc.

15. **B** The information received by Jenkins is covered by Standard II(A) Material Nonpublic Information, under which members who possess material nonpublic information related to the value of a security are prohibited from trading, or causing others to trade in, that security. For purposes of compliance with Standard II(A), Jenkins may attempt to achieve public dissemination of the information and may inform his compliance officer of the information. However, under no circumstances should Jenkins share material nonpublic information with other investment personnel. Sharing such information may cause others to trade on the information in violation of Standard II(A).

16. **B** Woods has misrepresented Lam's experience. They don't really have an "experienced international team." That would include analysts, researchers, back office capabilities and experience, and the firm's investment committee as well. It is not a violation of the Standard on performance presentation to include the results of the newly hired managers as long as it is clear they achieved their performance at their previous firm. Fair dealing has not been violated because no clients were disadvantaged in favor of others.

17. **B** According to Standard II(A) Material Nonpublic Information, the use of security analysis combined with nonmaterial nonpublic information to arrive at significant conclusions is allowable under the mosaic theory.

18. **A** All fee-paying discretionary accounts must be included in composites, but including non-fee-paying accounts is not required. The other statements are requirements for compliance. (Study Session 1, LOS 4.a)

19. **B** With monthly payments, we need a monthly rate:

6% / 12 = 0.5%. Next, solve for the monthly payment. The calculator keystrokes are:

PV = 200,000; FV = 0; N = 360; I/Y = 0.5; CPT → PMT = –$1,199.10. The balance at any time on an amortizing loan is the present value of the remaining payments. There are 312 payments remaining after the 48th payment is made. The loan balance at this point is: PMT = –1,199.10; FV = 0; N = 312; I/Y = 0.5; CPT → PV = $189,228.90.

Note that only N has to be changed to calculate this new present value; the other inputs are unchanged. (Study Session 2, LOS 5.f)

20. **A** What is a bond question doing here? CFA Institute examiners can and will insert material from other topics as they see fit. This is just a reminder to be on your guard!

First, find the yield on the note at time of purchase. The appropriate calculator steps are:

PV = –10,440; FV = 10,000; PMT = 600; N = 5; CPT → I/Y = 4.9842%. Next, value the note at a yield of 3.9842% with four years to maturity.

FV = 10,000; PMT = 600; N = 4; I/Y = 3.9842; CPT → PV = $10,731.99.

Finally, calculate the holding period return. The formula is:

$$R_t = \frac{P_t - P_{t-1} + D_t}{P_{t-1}}$$

$$R_t = \frac{\$10,731.99 - \$10,440 + \$600}{\$10,440} = 8.5\%$$

(Study Session 2, LOS 6.c and Study Session 16, LOS 53.a, f)

21. C $\dfrac{195}{160} - 1 = 0.21875$, or 21.88%

A longer approach is to calculate the holding period return for each stock for the year, then weight the returns using beginning values.

$$\text{Stock A} = \frac{20-10}{10} = 100\%$$

$$\text{Stock B} = \frac{60+1-50}{50} = 22\%$$

$$\text{Stock C} = \frac{110+4-100}{100} = 14\%$$

$$\left(\frac{10}{160}\right)(100\%) + \left(\frac{50}{160}\right)(22\%) + \left(\frac{100}{160}\right)(14\%) = 0.06250 + 0.06875 + 0.08750 = 0.21875, \text{ or } 21.88\%$$

(Study Session 2, LOS 7.e)

22. C From least to most information, the ordering of measurements scales is nominal, ordinal, interval, and ratio. (Study Session 2, LOS 7.a)

23. B $G = [(1.10)(0.85)(1.00)(1.05)]^{0.25} - 1$

$G = (0.98175)^{0.25} - 1 = 0.9954 - 1 = -0.00459 \approx -0.5\%$

Note: Taking a number to the 0.25 power is the same as taking the fourth root of the number. (Study Session 2, LOS 7.e)

24. B The mean absolute deviation is the mean of the absolute values of the differences between each number and the mean. Because the mean is (45 + 20 + 30 + 25) / 4 = 30, the mean absolute deviation is $\dfrac{15+10+0+5}{4} = 7.5$. (Study Session 2, LOS 7.g)

25. A As long as the investor earns at least a 5% return over the next year, the value of her portfolio after deducting the $100,000 down payment will not fall below $950,000. We first calculate the SFRatio for each of the two possible portfolios. We know that:

$$\text{SFRatio} = \frac{[E(R_p) - R_L]}{\sigma_p}$$

$$\text{SFRatio}_1 = \frac{17-5}{15} = 0.8$$

$$\text{SFRatio}_2 = \frac{12-5}{10} = 0.7$$

$$\text{SFRatio}_3 = \frac{8-5}{6} = 0.5$$

The SFR is the number of standard deviations that the minimum return is below the mean (expected) return. The optimal portfolio is the one with the greatest SFR as it has the lowest probability of a return below the minimum. Based on the SFRatio, the investor would prefer Portfolio 1. (Study Session 3, LOS 9.n)

                                            ©2014 Kaplan, Inc.

26. **A**   Triangles are thought to be continuation patterns, suggesting that the trend will continue in the same direction it was going when the triangle pattern formed. An RSI above 70 is thought to indicate an overbought condition, which can be a warning sign that the current uptrend is not sustainable. An uptrend line should act as a support level in an uptrend when the price approaches the trendline from above. If an uptrend line acts as a resistance level, the price must have broken down through the trendline, which is a sign that the uptrend may be ending. (Study Session 3, LOS 12.c, d, e)

27. **B**   An unbiased estimator has an expected value equal to the true value of the population parameter. A consistent estimator is more accurate the greater the sample size. An efficient estimator has the sampling distribution that is less than that of any other unbiased estimator. (Study Session 3, LOS 10.g)

28. **C**   According to Chebyshev's inequality, the proportion of the observations within 3 standard deviations of the mean is at least $1 - (1 / 3^2) = 0.89$ or 89%. This holds for any distribution, regardless of the shape. (Study Session 2, LOS 7.h)

29. **C**   Using the addition rule for probabilities, P(analyst or positive) = P(analyst) + P(positive) − P(analyst and positive). P(A or positive) = 130 / 200 + 110 / 200 − (70 / 200) = 0.65 + 0.55 − 0.35 = 0.85. Alternatively, CEOs that predict positive impact = 40, analysts = 130, Prob (CEO positive or analyst) = (40 + 130) / 200 = 85%. (Study Session 2, LOS 8.f)

30. **B**   There are many reasons that a statistically significant result may not be economically significant (meaningful). Besides transactions costs, we must consider the risk of the strategy as well. For example, although the mean abnormal return to the strategy over the 5-year sample period is greater than transactions costs, abnormal returns for various sub-periods may be highly variable. In this case the risk of the strategy return from month to month or quarter to quarter may be too great to make employing the strategy in client accounts economically attractive. (Study Session 3, LOS 11.e)

31. **B**   In simple random sampling, each item in the population has an equal chance of being selected. The analyst's method meets this criterion. (Study Session 3, LOS 10.c)

32. **A**   Nonparametric tests can be used in a variety of instances where the assumptions required for parametric tests cannot be sustained. A runs test can be used to test for the randomness of a sample. Both of the other tests are parametric because they test the value of a parameter of the underlying distribution. (Study Session 3, LOS 11.k)

33. **A**   The TRT/PSG cross rate is 5.5 × 8.0 = 44 TRT/PSG. Because the answer choices are quoted as PSG/TRT, we need to invert this result: 1 / 44 = 0.0227 PSG/TRT. (Study Session 6, LOS 21.d)

34. **A**   Because aggregate income is the same as aggregate output, measuring GDP by summing incomes or expenditures should produce the same value, except for a statistical discrepancy that results from using different data sources. The sum-of-value-added method of calculating GDP records the sum of the increases in value of goods and services at each stage of their production and distribution. The resulting total for GDP is the same as that reached by the value-of-final-output method because the sum of value added to a good at all stages of processing is equal to its selling price. Both methods calculate GDP based on expenditures. (Study Session 5, LOS 17.a, b)

35. **C** The J-curve effect refers to a plot of the trade deficit over time when the domestic currency depreciates (the foreign currency appreciates). The trade deficit gets worse initially but then improves over time, either because export and import demand are more elastic in the long run or because existing contracts for future delivery are fixed in foreign currency terms in the short run. (Study Session 6, LOS 21.j)

36. **A** Promoting economic growth and reducing world poverty are among the primary goals of the World Bank. The IMF primarily promotes the growth of international trade, supports exchange rate stability, and provides a forum for cooperation on monetary problems internationally. The WTO has a primary focus on reaching trade agreements and settling trade disputes. (Study Session 6, LOS 20.j)

37. **A** The quantity theory of money hypothesizes that a change in the money supply, at full employment, will cause a proportional change in the price level because velocity and real output will be unaffected. According to the equation of exchange, MV = PY, output of goods and services produced, *Y*, at full employment cannot change, so the price level, *P*, must increase. (Study Session 5, LOS 19.c)

38. **C** In a conventional fixed peg arrangement, a country pegs its currency within a margin of ±1% versus another currency or a basket that includes the currencies of its major trading or financial partners. Market-determined exchange rates are a characteristic of an independently floating exchange rate regime. (Study Session 6, LOS 21.i)

39. **A** Quantity supplied is zero at P = 17, and quantity supplied at P = 25 is 80. The area of the producer surplus triangle is $1/2 \times (25 - 17) \times 80 = 320$. (Study Session 4, LOS 13.j)

40. **C** Like all price searchers, monopolists will expand output until marginal revenue equals marginal cost. Monopolists do not charge the highest possible price which would be the price resulting in only one sale. A monopolist seeks to maximize profit, not price. (Study Session 4, LOS 16.d)

41. **B** Regardless of whether a tax is imposed on suppliers or consumers, the relative burden of the tax to each depends on the relative elasticities of supply and demand. Since demand is relatively less elastic than supply, the burden of the tax will be greater on consumers than on producers. These burdens are equivalent to decreases in producer and consumer surpluses. Total consumer and producer surpluses will be reduced by the amount of the resulting deadweight loss in addition to the total amount of tax collected. (Study Session 4, LOS 13.k, l)

42. **A** Inflation that is unexpected, or higher than expected, shifts wealth from lenders to borrowers. Unexpected deflation has the opposite effect. Because interest rates include a premium for expected inflation, an inflation rate that matches expectations does not shift wealth from lenders to borrowers. (Study Session 5, LOS 19.g)

43. **B** The supply curve for a firm under perfect competition is its marginal cost curve above average variable cost. As long as price exceeds AVC, the firm will produce up to the quantity where MC = Price, which is also MR in this case. (Study Session 4, LOS 16.c)

44. **A** Long-run aggregate supply is related to the level of technology and the available quantities of labor and capital. If the prices of productive inputs increase, short-run aggregate supply decreases (the SRAS curve shifts to the left), but long-run aggregate supply (potential real GDP) is unaffected. (Study Session 5, LOS 17.h, m)

©2014 Kaplan, Inc.

45. **C**   The matching principle holds that expenses should be accounted for in the same performance measurement period as the revenue they generate. (Study Session 8, LOS 25.d)

46. **B**   The description of the percentage-of-completion method is accurate. The completed contract method under U.S. GAAP recognizes revenue only when the entire project is complete. The installment method recognizes profit in proportion to cash collected. (Study Session 8, LOS 25.b)

47. **B**   Auditors issue a qualified opinion when there is a material instance of noncompliance with applicable accounting standards. An unqualified opinion means the auditors believe there is reasonable assurance that the financial statements are free of error and in compliance with applicable accounting standards. An adverse opinion is only issued when the auditors believe the financial statements as a whole are not fairly presented. (Study Session 7, LOS 22.d)

48. **B**   Declaring a stock dividend decreases retained earnings and increases contributed capital by the same amount, leaving total shareholders' equity unchanged. Issuing preferred stock increases both contributed capital and shareholders' equity. Increasing authorized shares does not increase contributed capital and shareholders' equity until the additional shares are issued. (Study Session 8, LOS 26.f and Study Session 11, LOS 38.a)

49. **A**

Net income	+100
Adjustment for noncash and nonoperating items:	
Depreciation	+25
Deferred taxes (increase)	+17
Profit from sale of equipment	−5
Adjustment for working capital items:	
Accounts receivable (decrease)	+30
Inventory (increase)	−17
Accounts payable (increase)	+10
Wages payable (decrease)	−5
Cash flow from operations	+$155

Dividends paid are CFF, not CFO. (Study Session 8, LOS 27.f)

50. **C**   Interest income is considered an operating cash flow under U.S. GAAP. (Study Session 8, LOS 27.a)

51. **C**   Dilution occurs since the exercise price for the warrants ($45) is less than the average market price for the shares ($50). The incremental number of shares outstanding is found from:

$$\left(\frac{\text{market price} - \text{exercise price}}{\text{market price}}\right) \times \text{\# warrants} = \left(\frac{50 - 45}{50}\right) \times 120{,}000 = 12{,}000$$

Number of shares to use in diluted EPS calculation = 500,000 + 12,000 = 512,000. (Study Session 8, LOS 25.g, h)

52. **A**   As an example, start with CA = 2, CL = 1, and Inv = 1.2. We begin with a current ratio of 2 and a quick ratio of 0.8. If the firm increases short-term bank debt (a current liability) by 1 to buy inventory (a current asset) of 1, both the numerator and denominator increase by 1, resulting in $\frac{3}{2} = 1.5$ (new current ratio) and $\frac{3 - 2.2}{2} = 0.4$ (new quick ratio). (Study Session 8, LOS 28.b)

53. **A** With an operating lease, the entire lease payment is recorded as rent expense and classified as an operating cash outflow. A finance lease results in a lower current ratio than an operating lease because the current portion of the principal repayment component will be added to current liabilities. The lessor does not recognize any profit at the inception of a direct financing lease. (Study Session 9, LOS 32.h)

54. **B** U.S. GAAP requires R&D costs to be expensed. IFRS requires research costs to be expensed, but development costs may be capitalized if certain criteria are met. (Study Session 9, LOS 30.a, b)

55. **C** LIFO will result in lower net income than FIFO in the current period, during a period of rising prices. The other choices will tend to increase current period earnings. (Study Session 9, LOS 29.c, 30.a, c)

56. **B** Securities that can be converted to common stock are said to be dilutive to earnings if conversion would result in lower earnings per share. A simple capital structure has only common stock or only common stock and nonconvertible stock. It contains no securities that could ever become or create common stock, even antidilutive ones. Whether warrants are antidilutive depends on the average stock price over the reporting period, not the value at the reporting date. (Study Session 8, LOS 25.h)

57. **A** Since this company has a simple capital structure, basic and diluted EPS are equal. The numerator equals net income − preferred dividends = 210,000 − (11,000 shares × 0.10 dividend × 100 par) = 210,000 − 110,000 = 100,000. The weighted average shares outstanding = 22,500 − (5,000 shares repurchased × 0.50 midyear) = 22,500 − 2,500 = 20,000. Then, basic EPS = diluted EPS = $\dfrac{100,000}{20,000}$ = $5 per share.

    (Study Session 8, LOS 25.g)

58. **B** FIFO companies have higher net income, lower COGS, higher inventory, and higher taxes. (Study Session 9, LOS 29.e)

59. **A** Under IFRS, inventory values are revalued upward only to the extent they were previously written down. In this case, that is from €25,000 back up to the original value of €28,000. The increase is reported as gain for the period. (Study Session 9, LOS 29.f)

60. **B** Remeasurements (actuarial gains and losses, difference between actual return and expected return on plan assets) are recognized as other comprehensive income under IFRS and are not amortized. (Study Session 9, LOS 32.j)

61. **A** Management may attempt to increase reported earnings in the current period by capitalizing an expense. Capitalizing a lease would decrease earnings in the current period compared to recording an operating lease. Classifying a nonrecurring gain as recurring income would not increase net income because it already includes nonrecurring gains. (Study Session 10, LOS 33.h)

62. **C** Deferred tax liability refers to balance sheet amounts that are created when tax expense is greater than taxes payable. (Study Session 9, LOS 31.a)

63. **B** EBT / EBIT is the interest burden, the second component in the extended DuPont equation. It shows that more leverage does not always lead to higher ROE. As leverage rises, so does the interest burden. The positive effects of leverage can be offset by the higher interest payments that accompany higher levels of debt. Net income / EBT is called the tax burden and is equal to (1 − tax rate). The higher the tax rate, the lower the ROE level. EBIT / revenue is called the EBIT margin or operating margin. (Study Session 8, LOS 28.d)

 ©2014 Kaplan, Inc.

64. **C**   Issuing debt results in a cash inflow from financing. Payment of debt at maturity has no effect on cash flow from operations but decreases cash flow from financing by the face value of the debt. (Study Session 9 LOS 32.a, b)

65. **A**   The liability method (SFAS 109 of U.S. GAAP) takes a balance sheet approach and adjusts deferred tax assets and liabilities to future tax rates. An increase in the tax rate increases the value of both deferred tax assets and deferred tax liabilities. (Study Session 9, LOS 31.e)

66. **B**   When a question does not specify which accounting standards apply, candidates are instructed to assume International Financial Reporting Standards (IFRS). According to IFRS, property held for the purpose of earning rental income is classified as investment property. However, when a property is transferred from owner-occupied to investment property, a firm using the fair value model must treat any increase in the property's value as a revaluation. That is, the firm may only recognize a gain on the income statement to the extent that it reverses a previously recognized loss. (Study Session 9, LOS 30.k)

67. **C**   Under U.S. GAAP, an asset is considered impaired when its book value is greater than the sum of the estimated undiscounted future cash flows from its use and disposal. (Study Session 9, LOS 30.h)

68. **B**   The four general categories are: (1) scale and diversification, (2) operational efficiency, (3) margin stability, and (4) leverage. Larger companies and those with more different product lines and greater geographic diversification are better credit risks. High operating efficiency is indicative of a better credit risk. Stable profit margins indicate a higher probability of repayment and thus, a better credit risk. Firms with greater earnings in relation to their debt level are better credit risks. While the availability of collateral certainly reduces lender risk, it is not one of the general categories used by credit rating agencies to determine *capacity* to repay. Specifically, they would consider (1) several specific accounting ratios and (2) business characteristics. The availability of collateral falls into neither category. (Study Session 10, LOS 34.c)

69. **B**   The cost of preferred stock is calculated as the preferred dividend divided by the market price, not the par value. (Study Session 11, LOS 36.g)

70. **A**   We know that at a 14% discount rate, the NPV of Project X is zero and the NPV of Project Y is greater than zero. There is no well-defined relationship between the required rate of return and ordinary payback. If Project Y is smaller in size, its NPV may be smaller than that of Project X. (Study Session 11, LOS 35.d, e)

71. **A**   Financing costs should not be included in incremental cash flows. They are reflected in the weighted average cost of capital (WACC). New business at other branches is a positive externality and the $150,000 to sell the property is an opportunity cost. (Study Session 11, LOS 35.b)

72. **C**   To use the pure-play method, an asset beta is calculated by removing the effects of leverage (delevering) from the comparable company's equity beta, then a project beta is estimated by adjusting the asset beta (relevering) based on the capital structure of the company that is evaluating the project. (Study Session 11, LOS 36.i)

73. **B**   An increase in days of receivables outstanding, other things equal, will lengthen both the operating and cash conversion cycles, indicating poorer working capital management. An increase in days of payables outstanding, other things equal, would decrease the cash conversion cycle. A decrease in cash and marketable securities could simply indicate better management of cash (e.g., buying back its common stock or investing excess cash in profitable business opportunities or securities). (Study Session 11, LOS 39.c)

74. **A** There are benefits to both an annually elected board and a board with staggered multiple-year terms so neither can be considered a "requirement." An annually elected board provides flexibility to nominate new board members in response to changes in the marketplace. Staggered boards may provide better continuity of board expertise and leadership but are more difficult to replace. (Study Session 11, LOS 40.b)

75. **B** Capital component breakpoint = $\dfrac{\text{value at which component's cost of capital changes}}{\text{component's weight in WACC}}$

Debt breakpoint = $\dfrac{\$200,000}{0.40}$ = $500,000

(Study Session 11, LOS 36.k)

76. **C** An increase in debt will increase interest expense, which will decrease net income but not operating income, which is calculated before subtracting interest expense. For a profitable firm, the decrease in net income will be offset by the decrease in equity from the repurchase of common stock, so that ROE increases. The effect of the increase in financial leverage will, however, increase the variability of ROE for a given change in operating earnings. (Study Session 11, LOS 37.c)

77. **A** A portfolio that plots on the capital market line with less risk than the market portfolio must include a positive allocation to the risk-free asset. Such a portfolio is called a lending portfolio because investing in the risk-free asset represents lending at the risk-free rate. (Study Session 12, LOS 43.b)

78. **B** Steeply sloped risk-return indifference curves indicate that a greater increase in expected return is required as compensation for assuming an additional unit of risk, compared to less-steep indifference curves. The more risk-averse Smith will choose an optimal portfolio with lower risk and a lower expected return than the less risk-averse Jones's optimal portfolio. (Study Session 12, LOS 42.h)

79. **A** E(R) = 7% + 0.9(11% − 7%) = 10.6%. Because the expected return of 10% is less than the required return of 10.6%, the security is overvalued. (Study Session 12, LOS 43.h)

80. **A** The correlation between the two stocks is:

$\rho_{A,B}$ = COV$_{A,B}$ / ($\sigma_A \times \sigma_B$) = 0.001 / (0.05 × 0.08) = 0.001 / (0.004) = 0.25

Note that the formula uses the standard deviations, *not the variances*, of the returns on the two securities. (Study Session 12, LOS 42.b)

81. **B** The three major steps in the portfolio management process are planning, execution, and feedback. Rebalancing the portfolio to its desired asset allocation is part of the feedback step. (Study Session 12, LOS 41.d)

82. **B** Portfolio 1 does not lie on the efficient frontier because it has a lower return than Portfolio 2 but has equal risk. Portfolio 4 does not lie on the efficient frontier because it has higher risk than Portfolio 3 but has the same return. (Study Session 12, LOS 42.g)

83. **A** Variance is a measure of total risk. (Study Session 12, LOS 43.c)

84. **C** Greenbaum's expected return for the coming year is (62 / 54) − 1 = 14.8%. Its risk premium relative to the risk-free rate is 14.8% − 8.0% = 6.8%. The market risk premium is 12% − 8% = 4%. Therefore, the beta of Greenbaum must be 6.8 / 4.0 = 1.7. (Study Session 12, LOS 43.e)

85. **C** Asset classes add value to a portfolio when they have unique risk/return profiles, and they have relatively low or negative correlations to one another. One of the benefits of asset allocation and diversification is to minimize unsystematic risk. Rebalancing policies are often established in the IPS, but establishing the strategic asset allocation will not necessarily prevent overweighting or underweighting due to market changes or tactical asset allocations. (Study Session 12, LOS 44.g)

86. **A** Financial markets are said to be operationally efficient if participants can achieve their desired purposes with low transactions costs. Markets are said to be informationally efficient if prices reflect new information rapidly, and allocationally efficient if resources are allocated to their most productive uses. (Study Session 13, LOS 45.k)

87. **C** The weak form of the EMH implies that an investor cannot earn positive abnormal returns on average using technical analysis (market information), after adjusting for transaction costs and taxes. Evidence has shown that insiders can achieve positive abnormal returns on average, but this relates to the strong form of the EMH. (Study Session 13, LOS 47.e)

88. **B** REIT indexes represent a convenient way to invest in real estate. Commodity indexes are based on futures prices of commodities, and are not replicated by investing in the commodities themselves. Hedge fund indexes are biased upward because hedge funds are not required to disclose their performance to index providers and poorly performing funds are less likely to do so (self-selection bias). (Study Session 13, LOS 46.j)

89. **A** A company's book value per share is typically not equal to its intrinsic value per share, since book value is based on the historical cost of assets. Intrinsic value is the present value of the security's future cash flows. The market value of a share is the cumulative investors' estimation of this intrinsic value, and market value is usually somewhat in line with the intrinsic value. (Study Session 14, LOS 48.g)

90. **C** *Step 1*: Determine the discount rate. 7.50% − 0.75% = 6.75%.

    Step 2: Value the preferred. $V_P = \dfrac{\text{dividend}}{k_p} = \dfrac{\$6.00}{0.0675} = \$88.89$.

    (Study Session 14, LOS 50.d)

91. **B** Price at which a margin call will occur:

    original price × [(1 − initial margin) / (1 − maintenance margin)]

    = [$32.00 × (1 − 0.5)] / (1 − 0.25) = $16.00 / 0.75 = $21.33

    (Study Session 13, LOS 45.f)

92. **B** ER = RFR + beta(R_M − RFR)

    k = E(R) = 0.05 + 1(0.15 − 0.05) = 0.15

    Retention (b) = (1 − dividend payout ratio) = 1 − 0.4 = 0.6

    g = (ROE)(b) = (0.15)(0.6) = 0.09

    $\text{Value} = \dfrac{D_1}{k-g} = \dfrac{\$2.50}{0.15-0.09} = \$41.67$

    (Study Session 14, LOS 50.e)

93. **C**   The consumer staples industry is best classified as non-cyclical and defensive. Energy and technology are best classified as cyclical industries. (Study Session 14, LOS 49.c, i)

94. **C**   If markets are efficient, investors should not earn consistently superior returns from technical trading rules such as a contrary opinion strategy. A stock price will decrease on a report of an increase in earnings if that increase is less than investors expected based on all the information previously available. An analyst's recommendations could be for stocks with more than market risk, or the analyst's industry may outperform for some period of time. Both could account for outperformance even though markets are efficient. (Study Session 13, LOS 47.e)

95. **A**   The security being described here is preferred stock (preference shares). In the event of liquidation of a firm, the claims of preferred equity shareholders are senior to the claims of common stockholders but subordinated to the claims of debt holders. Preferred shares typically have no voting rights. (Study Session 14, LOS 48.a)

96. **C**   Equal-weighted index portfolios require rebalancing after each return period because differences in returns among securities will drive the security weightings away from equal weighting. Changes in the security prices automatically adjust the weights in price- and value-weighted index portfolios to their correct values, so funds that track price- and value-weighted indexes do not require frequent rebalancing. (Study Session 13, LOS 46.f)

97. **A**   This is essentially a two-stage dividend discount model (DDM) problem. Discounting all future cash flows, we get:

$$P_0 = \frac{1.00}{(1.103)^5} + \frac{1.25}{(1.103)^6} + \frac{(1.25)^2}{(1.103)^7} + \left[\frac{(1.25)^3}{(0.103-0.05)(1.103)^7}\right] = \$20.647$$

Note that the constant growth formula can be applied to dividend 8 (1.25^3) because it *will* grow at a constant rate (5%) forever. (Study Session 14, LOS 50.e)

98. **A**   The SPV in a securitization is a separate legal entity and thereby bankruptcy-remote from the seller, which means the seller's creditors do not have a claim against the pool of assets underlying an ABS. As a result, the ABS may have a higher credit rating than the seller's corporate bonds. (Study Session 15, LOS 54.b)

99. **B**   Inclusion of a call feature will decrease the duration of a fixed income security. The other choices increase duration. (Study Session 16, LOS 55.e)

100. **C**   At the time of purchase, the coupon rate = the market rate, so the bond traded at par. One year later, with interest rates unchanged, the bond would still trade at par, or $1,000. Thus, there would be no gain or loss from the sale. (Study Session 15, LOS 53.b)

101. **B**   Intangible assets that can be sold, such as trademarks, provide collateral of good quality. A credit analyst should view as low-quality collateral any assets that are likely to be written down in value if a firm encounters financial distress, such as goodwill and deferred tax assets. (Study Session 16, LOS 56.e)

102. **C**   First find the yield to maturity (YTM) of the first bond and use it in the second bond calculation. The calculator sequence to determine the YTM is: PV = –701.22; FV = 1000; PMT = 80; N = 20; CPT → I/Y = 12.00%. We discount the cash flows of the second bond at 12.00%. The calculator steps are: PV = –701.22; FV = 1,000; N = 5; I/Y = 12; CPT → PMT = $37.12. (Study Session 15, LOS 53.a, b)

©2014 Kaplan, Inc.

103. **C**   Convexity adjustment to $\%\Delta P = \frac{1}{2}$ convexity measure $\times (\Delta YTM)^2 \times 100$

$= \frac{1}{2}(120)(-0.0025)^2(100) = 0.0375\%$. (Study Session 16, LOS 55.i)

104. **A**   During economic contractions, the probability of default increases for lower-quality issues and their yields increase. When investors anticipate an economic downturn, they tend to sell low-quality issues and buy high-quality issues, causing credit spreads to widen. (Study Session 16, LOS 56.h, j)

105. **A**   Supranational bonds are issued by multilateral agencies such as the World Bank or International Monetary Fund. Bonds that trade outside the jurisdiction of any one country are known as global bonds. Bonds that pay coupons in a different currency than their principal are known as dual-currency bonds. (Study Session 15, LOS 51.a, 52.e)

106. **B**   Investment grade bonds are BBB– and above. This bond is rated BB, which is below BBB–. (Study Session 15, LOS 52.a, and Study Session 16, LOS 56.c)

107. **A**   The value of a bond calculated using appropriate spot rates is its no-arbitrage value. If no arbitrage opportunities are present, this value is equal to the market price of a bond. (Study Session 15, LOS 53.c)

108. **A**   Effective duration and effective convexity capture the effects from changes in a bond's cash flows when the yield changes. For this reason, they are the appropriate measures of interest rate sensitivity for bonds with embedded options. (Study Session 16, LOS 55.b, c)

109. **B**   Bonds W and Y are most likely callable, and Bonds X and Z are most likely putable. If the option-adjusted spread is less than the zero-volatility spread, the embedded option has a negative value to the bondholder (e.g., a call option), and if the option-adjusted spread is greater than the zero-volatility spread, the embedded option has a positive value to the bondholder (e.g., a put option). Zero-volatility spreads adjust for the fact that nominal spreads (between the yields to maturity of two bonds) are theoretically correct only when the spot yield curve is flat. All of these bonds' zero-volatility spreads are nearly identical to their government spreads, which suggests the spot yield curve is approximately flat. (Study Session 15, LOS 51.f, 53.i)

110. **C**   The probability-weighted average calculated by the analyst is the option's value after one period. To estimate the option's value today, this result must be discounted by one period. (Study Session 17, LOS 58.n)

111. **B**   Baker's net cost of the position is 60 + 4 = \$64 per share. At exercise she receives \$60 per share. Her net loss on the position is –4(100) = –\$400. (Study Session 17, LOS 59.b)

112. **C**   Candidate 1 is incorrect. In the futures markets, margin is a performance guarantee. It is money deposited by both the long and the short. There is no loan involved (as opposed to in the equity markets) and thus no interest charges. Candidate 2 is correct. (Study Session 17, LOS 57.c)

113. **C**   The put holder will exercise the option at expiration whenever the stock's price is less than the exercise price. (Study Session 17, LOS 57.c, 58.i)

114. **C** Forward and futures prices may differ for otherwise identical contracts if interest rates are positively or negatively correlated with futures prices. The difference arises from the fact that futures are marked to market daily while forwards are not. A futures contract holder can earn interest on mark-to-market gains and faces an opportunity cost of interest of mark-to-market losses. (Study Session 17, LOS 58.f)

115. **A** Decreasing volatility of returns on the underlying stock will decrease option values for both puts and calls. An increase in the risk-free rate increases the values of call options on equities and decreases the values of put options on equities. (Study Session 17, LOS 58.k)

116. **C** Backfill bias refers to bias introduced by including the previous performance data for firms recently added to a benchmark index. (Study Session 18, LOS 60.c)

117. **A** Leveraged buyouts are the predominant activity pursued by private equity funds. Convertible arbitrage and activist shareholder strategies are more typically associated with hedge funds. (Study Session 18, LOS 60.b)

118. **C** Hedge funds do not typically trade on exchanges. (Study Session 18, LOS 60.d)

119. **A** While commodity futures retain the risk and correlation characteristics of the underlying commodities, the investor does not incur storage costs. Derivatives cannot have higher correlation with spot prices than the commodity itself, as its price is the spot price. Convenience yield is a benefit of owning the actual commodities. (Study Session 18, LOS 60.d)

120. **A** Investors require a liquidity premium for investments that are illiquid. Private equity funds are typically illiquid and may require lockup periods. Real estate investment trusts and exchange-traded funds are publicly traded and usually highly liquid. (Study Session 18, LOS 60.g)

©2014 Kaplan, Inc.

Exam 1
Afternoon Session Answer Key

To get valuable feedback on how your score compares to those of other Level I candidates, use your Username and Password to gain online access at Schweser.com and select "Performance Tracker" from your dashboard.

1. B	31. B	61. B	91. A
2. C	32. A	62. C	92. C
3. B	33. A	63. B	93. C
4. B	34. C	64. A	94. C
5. A	35. C	65. A	95. C
6. C	36. A	66. A	96. A
7. A	37. B	67. B	97. A
8. A	38. C	68. B	98. C
9. B	39. A	69. B	99. B
10. A	40. B	70. B	100. C
11. B	41. B	71. B	101. B
12. B	42. A	72. A	102. B
13. A	43. C	73. A	103. C
14. A	44. A	74. C	104. B
15. A	45. B	75. A	105. C
16. A	46. C	76. B	106. B
17. B	47. A	77. B	107. A
18. A	48. B	78. C	108. A
19. B	49. A	79. A	109. C
20. A	50. A	80. B	110. B
21. C	51. C	81. B	111. A
22. C	52. B	82. A	112. C
23. C	53. B	83. C	113. A
24. A	54. C	84. B	114. C
25. C	55. B	85. B	115. B
26. C	56. A	86. A	116. A
27. A	57. A	87. A	117. A
28. A	58. B	88. A	118. C
29. A	59. A	89. B	119. B
30. A	60. A	90. A	120. B

Exam 1
Afternoon Session Answers

Answers referencing the Standards of Practice address Study Session 1, LOS 1.b, c and LOS 2.a, b, c, except where noted.

1. **B** Schute has violated the Standard by not taking steps to ensure that the nonpublic information he has received as part of his investment banking work was not shared with others in the firm.

2. **C** Under Standard VII(B) Reference to CFA Institute, the CFA Designation, and the CFA Program, candidates in the CFA Program may appropriately reference their participation in the CFA Program. However, to be considered a candidate, individuals must be registered to take the next scheduled CFA examination. Therefore, Wellington, who intends to register for the next exam, but has not done so, has violated Standard VII(B). Wellington may indicate that he passed Level II of the CFA Program and the year in which he passed, but he is not a candidate unless he is registered for the next exam or awaiting exam results. Standard VII(A) Conduct as Participants in CFA Institute Programs addresses issues that concern the validity and security of the exams and the integrity and reputation of the CFA designation and CFA Institute.

3. **B** Global Investment Performance Standards represent ethical reporting standards, but compliance with GIPS is not a requirement of CFA Institute membership or to sit for the CFA examination. (Study Session 1, LOS 3.a)

4. **B** Michaels has violated Standard IV(C) Responsibilities of Supervisors, which requires him to make reasonable efforts to detect and prevent violations of compliance procedures. Simply making employees aware of the rules is not enough. Monitoring of employee trades, duplicate confirms, establishing blackout periods, or preclearance of employee trades are all methods that would have revealed the problem prior to the external audit. Michaels has not violated Standard I(D) Misconduct because his actions did not exhibit dishonesty or lack of integrity.

5. **A** Because the family account is a client account, it should be treated as any other client account would be. Waiting until after the firm buys shares would violate Standard VI(B) Priority of Transactions. There is no requirement that a firm's recommendations be make public.

6. **C** To comply with Standard IV(B) Additional Compensation Arrangements, because the additional compensation is contingent on future performance, Nelson must disclose this additional compensation to her employer and must receive written consent, which can be email or any other form of communication that can be documented.

7. **A** Anderson has violated Standard I(C) Misrepresentation by representing the work of another as his own in the report. The use of third-party research is not necessarily a violation of Standard I(B) Independence and Objectivity or Standard V(A) Diligence and Reasonable Basis. Using a research firm that is approved by his company is permitted as long as he has no knowledge that the work is of less than good quality.

©2014 Kaplan, Inc.

8. **A**   Because the itinerary required charter flights due to a lack of commercial transportation, River Casino can appropriately provide them. While Standard I(B) Independence and Objectivity recommends that members pay their own room costs, it is not required and it is not unusual for members to accept accommodations.

9. **B**   To comply with GIPS, portfolios must be assigned to composites before the returns are known; assigning them at the end of the year is not acceptable. The composite return must be asset weighted not a simple average (equal-weighted). Asset weighting will ensure that the performance reported will be representative of (if not exactly equal to) the performance of all the accounts assigned to a single composite over the reporting period. (Study Session 1, LOS 3.b, 4.a)

10. **A**   Smart violated both Standards. Smart violated Standard III(B) Fair Dealing because she not deal fairly and objectively with all clients and prospects when disseminating investment recommendations, giving priority to some of the firm's clients by trading for her clients first before issuing the report. She also sold her own shares before issuing the report, which violated Standard VI(B) Priority of Transactions. Smart did not give clients an opportunity to react to and benefit from her recommendation before she personally benefited from her research.

11. **B**   Whatever his motivation, Jacobs' attempt to manipulate the market price of Timeco shares with the intent to deceive market participants (in this case, his own client) constitutes a violation of Standard II(B) Market Manipulation.

12. **B**   Under Standard III(D) Performance Presentation, members and candidates must make reasonable efforts to ensure that investment performance information is fair, accurate, and complete. Rex has misled his potential clients by not disclosing that the first two years of his performance record were achieved at another firm. There is no prohibition against presenting simulated results as long as the fact that the results are simulated, rather than actual, is disclosed.

13. **A**   If Roberts suspects someone is engaging in activities that are illegal or violate the Code and Standards, Standard I(A) Knowledge of the Law requires him to dissociate from the activities if he cannot remedy the situation. In this situation, the teammate is acting within the applicable laws but is violating CFA Institute Standards of Professional Conduct. When the Code and Standards are stricter than applicable law, the Code and Standards apply to members and candidates. However, Roberts is not required by the Code and Standards to report violations of laws or the Code and Standards to CFA Institute or to governmental regulators, although it may be prudent or even required by law that he do so.

14. **A**   Government bonds are default risk free but are subject to price risk. Thus, Blush misrepresented the expected performance of the fund and therefore violated Standard I(C) Misrepresentation.

15. **A**   Standard VII(A) Conduct as Participants in CFA Institute Programs does not prohibit members and candidates from expressing negative opinions about CFA Institute or the CFA program. Disclosing exam content and misrepresenting information on the annual PCS are violations of Standard VII(A).

16. **A** Members and candidates who are in advisory relationships with clients should document unsuccessful attempts to update client information and circumstances. Because risk is to be evaluated in a portfolio context, there is no prohibition against the purchase of a security that is risky on a stand-alone basis, as long as the risk of the client's overall portfolio is consistent with their ability and willingness to assume investment risk. While lack of client information could make suitability a difficult question, Standard III(C) Suitability does not prohibit managing assets for clients who withhold information about their financial circumstances and needs.

17. **B** Standard VI(C) Referral Fees requires members and candidates to disclose any referral fees they will earn from successful referrals as well as the nature of the compensation. Here Rogers must disclose that he will receive a percentage of management fees on an ongoing basis.

18. **A** Bell is permitted to share confidential client information with another firm employee who is also working for the client's benefit, so sharing this information with his assistant is not a violation of Standard III(E) Preservation of Confidentiality

19. **B** We can treat these cash flows as a 35-year annuity due of $20,000 per year plus a 10-year annuity due of an additional $30,000 per year. With calculator in BGN mode:

   $20,000 per year for 35 years: N = 35, PMT = 20,000, I/Y = 4, FV = 0; CPT PV = −388,224

   $30,000 per year for 10 years: N = 10, PMT = 30,000, I/Y = 4, FV = 0; CPT PV = −253,060

   Total: $641,284 (Study Session 2, LOS 5.f)

20. **A** Geometric mean = $[(1.10)(1.14)(1.12)(1.10)(0.90)(1.12)]^{1/6} - 1 = 0.0766$, or 7.66% (Study Session 2, LOS 7.e)

21. **C** There are 415 members of the group in favor of the continuing education requirement. 180 of these are candidates, so the probability is 180 / 415 = 43.37%. Note that this question is quite similar to those where we apply Bayes' Theorem. The priors here are the probabilities that a member of the group is a charterholder or is a candidate. Both of these are 1,000 / 2,000 = 50%. Given the information that the member of the group favors continuing education, we can update the probability that that group member is a candidate to 43.37%. (Study Session 2, LOS 8.d)

22. **C** When constructing samples, researchers must be careful not to include just survivors (e.g., surviving companies, mutual funds, or investment newsletters). Since survivors tend to be those that have done well (by skill or chance), funds that have 10-year track records will exhibit performance histories with upward bias—mutual fund companies regularly discontinue funds with poor performance histories or roll their assets into better performing funds. Time period bias occurs when the period chosen is so short that it shows relationships that are unlikely to recur, or so long that it includes fundamental changes in the relationship being observed. A 10-year period typically includes a full economic cycle and is likely to be appropriate for this test. Look-ahead bias is present if the test relates a variable to data that were not available at the points in time when that variable's outcomes were observed. (Study Session 3, LOS 10.k)

23. **C** A normal distribution is a *continuous* symmetric probability distribution. (Study Session 3, LOS 9.a, e, j)

24. **A** A binomial random variable has an expected value or mean equal to *np*.
   Mean = 12(0.4) = 4.8. (Study Session 3, LOS 9.f)

 ©2014 Kaplan, Inc.

25. **C** The standard normal random variable, denoted Z, has mean equal to 0 and variance equal to 1. (Study Session 3, LOS 9.l, m)

26. **C** Portfolio X: SFRatio $= \dfrac{12-5}{14} = 0.50$

    Portfolio Y: SFRatio $= \dfrac{17-5}{20} = 0.60$

    Portfolio Z: SFRatio $= \dfrac{22-5}{25} = 0.68$

    According to the safety-first criterion, Portfolio Z, with the largest ratio (0.68), is the best alternative. (Study Session 3, LOS 9.n)

27. **A** The appropriate test is an F-test, where the larger sample variance (Index L) is placed in the numerator. (Study Session 3, LOS 11.j)

28. **A** Events J and K are dependent. By the multiplication rule, joint probability $P(JK) = P(J|K) \times P(K)$, or $P(JK) = P(K|J) \times P(J)$. Events are independent if $P(J|K) = P(J)$ and $P(K|J) = P(K)$. This implies that for independent events, $P(JK) = P(J) \times P(K)$. If this condition is not met, events J and K are dependent. If events J and K are mutually exclusive, their joint probability is zero. The information given is consistent with this but not sufficient to conclude that this is the case. (Study Session 2, LOS 8.g)

29. **A** The 20 quarters he has used are a sample of all the possible outcomes for the quarterly returns on the index. The difference between the true population parameter (mean index return) he is trying to estimate and the sample statistic he has calculated is called the sampling error. The arithmetic mean is the appropriate estimator of the next period's return. (Study Session 2, LOS 7.m, and Study Session 3, LOS 10.b)

30. **A** The significance level of a test is the probability that a true null hypothesis will be rejected by chance because the test statistic is from a sample and may take on a value that is outside the range of critical values because of sampling error. Choice B is incorrect because the probability of making a correct decision also must account for the probability of failing to reject a false null hypothesis. (Study Session 3, LOS 11.c)

31. **B** The lognormal distribution is most appropriate for modeling asset prices because the values cannot be less than zero and are not bounded on the upside. A binomial distribution allows only two possible outcomes over a period.
    (Study Session 3, LOS 9.o)

32. **A** Calculate the NPV as in any other project. Discount the cash flows back at a rate of 10%. $CF_0 = -200,000$; $CF_1 = 50,000$; $CF_2 = 60,000$; $CF_3 = 70,000$; $CF_4 = 80,000$; $CF_5 = -20,000$; I/Y = 10; CPT $\rightarrow$ NPV = -\$10,144. (Study Session 2, LOS 6.a)

33. **A** Increases in expected future incomes will decrease savings, which will decrease the supply of financial capital and increase the equilibrium interest rate. If the demand for financial capital rises, interest rates also rise; so both changes tend to increase the equilibrium interest rate. (Study Session 5, LOS 19.d)

34. **C** Potential expansion multiplier $= \dfrac{1}{\text{required reserve ratio}} = \dfrac{1}{0.2} = 5$

    $(100)(5) = 500$

    (Study Session 5, LOS 19.c)

35. **C** At a minimum wage above the equilibrium wage, there will be an excess supply of workers, since firms will not employ all the workers who want to work at the minimum wage. Firms will substitute other productive inputs for labor and use more than the economically efficient amount of capital. The result is increased unemployment because even though there are workers willing to work for less than the minimum wage, firms cannot legally hire them. (Study Session 4, LOS 13.k, l)

36. **A** The opportunity cost of one unit of leather for Ymer is 20 / 25 = 0.80 units of cheese, and the opportunity cost of one unit of cheese is 25 / 20 = 1.25 units of leather. The opportunity cost of one unit of cheese for Hokah is 30 / 35 = 0.86 units of leather, and the opportunity cost of one unit of leather is 35 / 30 = 1.167 units of cheese. Ymer has an absolute advantage in both cheese and leather, but has a comparative advantage only in leather. (Study Session 6, LOS 20.c)

37. **B** An industry with a downward-sloping long-run industry supply curve is a decreasing-cost industry. In such an industry, input costs decrease as output quantities increase. In the short run, this causes firms to earn economic profits. In the long run, these economic profits attract new entrants to the industry, which reduces the equilibrium selling price of the industry's output. (Study Session 4, LOS 15.i)

38. **C** Average cost pricing is meant to force a natural monopolist to reduce price to where the firm's average total cost intersects the market demand curve. This results in higher output and a lower price than would prevail for an unregulated natural monopoly. (Study Session 4, LOS 16.e)

39. **A** We can calculate the current USD/EUR cross rate as 104.2 / 76.6 = 1.3603 USD/EUR. The original USD/EUR cross rate was 100 / 80 = 1.2500 USD/EUR. Thus, the USD has depreciated relative to the EUR. While it is correct to say that the EUR has appreciated 4.2% relative to the JPY (104.2 / 100 − 1) = 4.2%, it is not correct to say that the JPY has depreciated by the same percentage. To calculate the percentage change in the JPY relative to the EUR, we need to invert the quotes. One year ago, the quote was 0.0100 EUR/JPY and now the quote is 0.0096 EUR/JPY. (0.0096 / 0.0100 − 1) = 0.0403 or 4.0% depreciation in the JPY relative to the EUR. (Study Session 6, LOS 21.c, d)

40. **B** Colluding restricts output and puts upward pressure on price, but cheating actually increases output and ultimately, if enough cheating occurs, puts downward pressure on the price. Colluders cheat to increase their share of the profits. (Study Session 4, LOS 16.d)

41. **B** Decreasing costs of factors of production cause a supply curve to increase (shift to the right). An increase in wages would shift the supply curve to the left. A decrease in the price of cars is represented as movement along the supply curve to a lower quantity supplied. (Study Session 4, LOS 13.c)

42. **A** The LM curve illustrates a positive relationship between real income and the real interest rate, holding the real money supply constant. The IS curve illustrates a negative relationship between real income and the real interest rate, holding the marginal propensity to save constant. (Study Session 5, LOS 17.f)

43. **C** An inferior good is one that experiences a decline in demand when income rises. (Study Session 4, LOS 14.f)

                    ©2014 Kaplan, Inc.

44. **A** According to the Keynesians, policymakers can use the budget to diminish aggregate demand through restrictive fiscal policy. Reducing government expenditures and/or increasing tax rates should lead to a decline in the expected size of the budget deficit or an increase in the budget surplus. (Study Session 5, LOS 19.s)

45. **B** Firms usually support the idea of having a single set of reporting standards because having one set of standards would reduce the cost and the time spent on reporting. Disagreement among different standard-setting bodies and regulatory authorities does hamper agreement on a single set of standards, as does political pressure from business groups and others who would be affected by changes in reporting standards. (Study Session 7, LOS 24.c)

46. **C** Foreign currency translation gains and losses are not reported on the income statement as a component of net income, but affect owners' equity because they are included as other comprehensive income. The other items are included on the income statement so they affect both net income and owners' equity. (Study Session 8, LOS 25.l)

47. **A**

Sale of common stock	45
Issuance of bonds	25
Financing cash flows	$70

(Study Session 8, LOS 27.f)

48. **B** Since the value of newly released DVDs will typically fall most rapidly in the first year after their release, some form of accelerated depreciation is appropriate. The declining balance method is the only accelerated depreciation method among the answer choices. Straight-line depreciation is appropriate when the decrease in value is uniform over an asset's life. Units-of-production depreciation assumes that there is a given amount of service that an asset will provide. (Study Session 8, LOS 25.d)

49. **A** When a firm has a controlling interest (>50%) in a subsidiary, but less than 100% ownership, it includes (consolidates) the assets and liabilities of that firm on its own balance sheet. Noncontrolling (or minority) interest in the equity section of the balance sheet represents the portion of the subsidiary that is not owned by the reporting firm. (Study Session 8, LOS 26.d)

50. **A** FCFF = Cash flow from operations + interest expense net of tax − net capital expenditures

FCFF = $800 + 80(1 − 0.35) − 40 + 30 = $842

Depreciation and amortization do not have to be added when calculating FCFF from CFO. They are added when calculating FCFF from net income. (Study Session 8, LOS 27.i)

51. **C** Securities held with the intent to profit over the short term are classified as trading securities, and changes in their market values are reflected in their balance sheet values and also reported on the income statement. Debt securities issued by the firm, and debt securities that the firm intends to hold until maturity, are both reported at amortized cost, not market value. Debt and equity securities that the firm does not expect to hold to maturity or to sell in the near term are marked to market on the balance sheet, but unrealized gains and losses do not affect the income statement. (Study Session 8, LOS 26.e)

52. **B** IFRS and U.S. GAAP both require discontinued operations to be reported on the income statement separately from continuing operations and net of tax. U.S. GAAP permits unusual and infrequent items to be treated as extraordinary items, but IFRS does not permit extraordinary items. Fixed assets can be revalued upward under IFRS but not under U.S. GAAP. (Study Session 8, LOS 25.e, 26.d)

53. **B** COGS FIFO = COGS LIFO − (ending LIFO reserve − beginning LIFO reserve)

    COGS FIFO = 27,000 − (1,400 − 1,200) = $26,800. (Study Session 10, LOS 34.e)

54. **C** The listing of all the journal entries in order of their dates is called the general journal. The general ledger sorts the entries in the general journal by account. "Trial ledger" is not part of an accounting system. (Study Session 7, LOS 23.f)

55. **B** When the capital structure contains options or warrants, the treasury stock method uses the average price. In this situation, the warrants are antidilutive because the exercise price of the warrant ($25) is higher than the market price of the stock ($20). Thus, warrants are excluded. Otherwise, common shares would be reduced.

    original shares of common stock $= 1,000,000 \left(\dfrac{12}{12} \right)$

    Then add the impact of the bond conversion:

    $(10,000)(20) \times (6/12) = 100,000$

    Thus, the adjusted denominator for fully diluted EPS is:

    1,000,000 + 100,000 = 1,100,000 (Study Session 8, LOS 25.g, h)

56. **A** During periods of rising prices, the last units purchased are more expensive than the existing units. Under LIFO, the cost of the last units purchased is assigned to cost of goods sold. This higher cost of goods sold results in lower income, as compared to the FIFO method. As the name suggests, the weighted average method is based on mathematical averages rather than timing of purchase/use. Thus, cost of goods sold using this method falls between that of LIFO and FIFO. (Study Session 9, LOS 29.e)

57. **A** If convertible bonds are dilutive, interest expense multiplied by (1 − tax rate) must be added back to the numerator to calculate diluted EPS. (Study Session 8, LOS 25.g, h)

58. **B** Net income is higher with capitalization because it does not decrease by the full amount spent, as it would with expensing. Capitalizing an expenditure changes its cash flow classification from an operating cash outflow to an investing cash outflow. As a result, CFO is higher and CFI is lower than they would be if the expenditure had been immediately expensed. Total cash flow, however, is unaffected (assuming the tax treatment of the expenditure is independent of the financial reporting treatment). Equity is higher in the period of the expenditure with capitalization. Assets are higher because they include the capitalized asset. Debt is unaffected by the decision to capitalize or expense. Thus, the debt-to-equity and debt-to-assets ratios are lower with capitalization. (Study Session 9, LOS 30.a)

59. **A** The three-part DuPont approach is as follows: net profit margin × asset turnover × leverage ratio, where the leverage ratio is assets-to-equity. (Study Session 8, LOS 28.d)

60. **A** Impairment writedowns are reported losses "above the line" and are included in income from continuing operations. (Study Session 8, LOS 25.e)

 ©2014 Kaplan, Inc.

61. **B**   Material changes in the firm's cost of debt capital should be included in the Management Discussion and Analysis section of the financial statements. If the firm does not use fair value reporting of debt obligations, net income and shareholders' equity are not affected by changes in the market value of the firm's debt, and disclosing its gain or loss in market value is not required. (Study Session 9, LOS 32.e)

62. **C**   Deferred tax assets and liabilities are adjusted for changes in expected tax rates under the liability method. (Study Session 9, LOS 31.e)

63. **B**   Whether a lease is an operating or a finance (capital) lease, both U.S. GAAP and IFRS require disclosure of the minimum lease payments for each of the next five years and the sum of minimum lease payments more than five years in the future. (Study Session 9, LOS 32.i)

64. **A**   Under IFRS, past service costs (changes in defined benefit plan obligations that result from a change in the plan's terms) are reported as part of service costs, a component of net income. Under U.S. GAAP, past service costs are recognized in other comprehensive income and amortized over time to the income statement. (Study Session 9, LOS 32.j)

65. **A**   Ineffective internal controls over accounting may provide opportunities for low-quality financial reporting. (Study Session 10, LOS 33.e)

66. **A**   Sensitivity analysis is based on hypothetical ("what if") questions about a single variable, such as "what if sales decline by 10%?" Simulation is a technique in which probability distributions for key variables are assumed and a computer is used to generate a distribution of outcomes based on repeated random selection of values for the key variables. Scenario analysis is based on one or more specific scenarios (a specific set of outcomes for key variables), which include changes in multiple variables. (Study Session 8, LOS 28.f)

67. **B**   Securitizing accounts receivable means the firm sells them to a special purpose vehicle that will issue asset-backed securities. This transaction will remove these accounts receivable from the firm's balance sheet. Using the proceeds to retire long-term debt will decrease liabilities by the same amount. Shareholders' equity is not affected. Therefore, the debt-to-equity ratio will decrease. The current ratio will decrease because accounts receivable (a current asset) decrease while current liabilities remain unchanged (or decrease only by any current portion of the debt paid down). The interest coverage ratio will increase because paying down long-term debt will decrease interest expense. (Study Session 8, LOS 26.h, 28.b, and Study Session 15, LOS 54.b)

68. **B**   Lessors that are dealers or manufacturers of the leased assets typically recognize sales revenue at the inception of a lease and thus account for their leases as sales-type capital (finance) leases. Dealers of high-value items that can be distinguished one from another, such as large earth movers, typically use specific identification to account for inventory. (Study Session 9, LOS 29.b, 32.h)

69. **B**   Business risk is the combination of sales risk, which is the variability of a firm's sales, and operating risk, which is the additional variability in operating earnings (EBIT) caused by fixed operating costs. (Study Session 11, LOS 37.a)

70. **B**   For a board to be independent, it should not have a majority of members who are firm executives. Board members should not be closely aligned with customers, suppliers, or pension advisors since their interests may conflict with those of shareholders. The board should meet regularly *outside* the presence of management. (Study Session 11, LOS 40.c)

71. **B** The investment opportunity schedule is a downward sloping curve of the internal rates of return (expected returns) of potential projects ranked from highest to lowest. This curve intersects the company's upward sloping marginal cost of capital curve at an amount of capital where the marginal project's IRR just equals the firm's cost of capital. The firm should accept projects with IRRs that exceed the marginal cost of capital (lie to the left of the intersection) and reject projects with IRRs less than the marginal cost of capital (lie to the right of the intersection). (Study Session 11, LOS 36.d)

72. **A** An increase in the weighted average collection period indicates that customers are taking longer to pay their outstanding accounts. This represents a drag on the company's liquidity. A vendor that changes its payment terms from "net 30" to "net 60" is allowing the company 60 days to pay instead of 30. This extension of trade credit is a source of liquidity for the company. An inventory turnover ratio that is increasing relative to the industry average is a sign of good inventory management, which can also be a source of liquidity for a company. (Study Session 11, LOS 39.a, f)

73. **A** The earnings yield on the firm's shares is $2 / $25 = 8%. Because both the firm's after-tax yield on excess cash and its after-tax cost of borrowing are less than the earnings yield, financing a share repurchase either with excess cash or with debt will increase earnings per share. (Study Session 11, LOS 38.d)

74. **C** Using the CAPM approach, the estimated cost of common equity = 3% + 0.89(12% − 3%) = 11%. Using the dividend discount model approach, the growth rate = (0.3)(0.2) = 6% and the estimated cost of common equity = $3 / $50 + 6% = 12%. To get a cost of common equity of 14%, Harlan most likely added a risk premium to Cyrene's bond yield. (Study Session 11, LOS 36.h)

75. **A** The cash conversion cycle is equal to the operating cycle minus the number of days of payables. If Quixote is extending the time it takes to pay its suppliers, its number of days of payables will increase, and its cash conversion cycle will decrease. Its operating cycle (days of inventory plus days of receivables) is unaffected by the increase in days of payables. Changes in inventory or receivables management would affect both the operating cycle and the cash conversion cycle. (Study Session 11, LOS 39.c)

76. **B** If the total undiscounted cash flows from two projects are equal, their NPV profiles intersect the vertical axis at the same value. The NPV profile will have a steeper slope for Project Smith, which has more of its cash inflows occurring later in its life, and therefore the IRR of Project Smith (its intersection with the horizontal axis) must be less than the IRR of Project Jones. The NPV for Project Jones will be greater at any rate of discount, and Project Jones will be preferred over the entire range. However, if the discount rate applied to the cash flows is greater than the IRR of Project Jones, both projects will have negative NPVs and the company should reject both of them. (Study Session 11, LOS 35.e)

77. **B** Other Board experience can be beneficial. Being a supplier to the firm may present the board member with a conflict of interest. A substantial stock position in the firm would align the board member's interests closely with those of other shareholders. (Study Session 11, LOS 40.d)

78. **C** Active management seeks to identify mispriced assets, which are likely to earn abnormal returns. A security that plots above the security market line (SML) is undervalued (i.e., expected to earn a return that is higher than it would if it were priced at its equilibrium price, given its systematic risk). (Study Session 12, LOS 43.h)

©2014 Kaplan, Inc.

79. **A**   Property and casualty insurers typically have a short-term time horizon, since claims are expected in the near term, and low risk tolerance. (Study Session 12, LOS 41.b)

80. **B** $(1+\text{HPR})^{1/n} - 1 = (1+1.70)^{1/20} - 1 = 0.050916$ (Study Session 12, LOS 42.a)

81. **B**   The investment guidelines section typically contains information about specific types of assets prohibited in the portfolio and the permissible use, if any, of leverage and derivatives. (Study Session 12, LOS 44.b)

82. **A**   Of the five categories of investment constraints, the four matters listed are related to Pope's time horizon (years to retirement), liquidity needs (available cash), legal and regulatory factors (required copies of account statements to Pope's compliance officer), and unique needs and preferences (no investments in Lower Pannonia). None of these constraints address Pope's tax situation or the taxable status of the investment account. (Study Session 12, LOS 44.e)

83. **C**   This statement is not correct; the standard deviation of returns for the resulting portfolio is a weighted average of the returns standard deviation of the risk-free asset (zero) and the returns standard deviation of the risky-asset portfolio. (Study Session 12, LOS 43.a)

84. **B**   From the fact that $\text{beta}_i = \text{Cov}_{i,mkt} / \text{Var}_{mkt}$, we have $\text{Cov}_{i,mkt} = \text{beta}_i \times \text{var}_{mkt}$.

$\text{Cov}_{i,mkt} = 1.2 \times 0.14^2 = 0.02352$. (Study Session 12, LOS 43.e)

85. **B**   Risk-return indifference curves slope upward because risk-averse investors will only take on more risk if they are compensated with greater expected returns. The more risk-averse the investor, the steeper the indifference curves. Indifference curves are nonlinear because utility theory assumes investors require larger increments of expected return for each additional unit of risk. (Study Session 12, LOS 42.h)

86. **A**   This grouping is most likely the result of a cluster analysis and may have arisen by chance. The two firms clearly offer different products and services. An industrial machinery manufacturer is likely to be a cyclical firm, while a grocery retailer is likely to be a non-cyclical firm. (Study Session 14, LOS 49.b, c)

87. **A**   Value-weighted indexes do not need to be adjusted for stock splits because the market capitalization of the company remains the same. (Study Session 13, LOS 46.e)

88. **A**   The numerator of the formula for the P/E is the payout ratio, which is unchanged (both expected earnings and dividends increase by the same percentage). The denominator $(k - g)$ doubles from 3% to 6%, which will decrease the P/E by half. (Study Session 14, LOS 50.h)

89. **B** $k = \text{RFR} + \beta(R_M - \text{RFR}) = 0.08 + 1.2(0.13 - 0.08) = 0.08 + 0.06 = 0.14$

$$P_0 = \frac{P_1 + D_1}{1+k} = \frac{25 + 1.10}{1.14} = \$22.89$$
(Study Session 14, LOS 50.e)

90. **A**   In an equity swap, one party pays a fixed amount periodically in return for a payment that is calculated using a specific amount and the return on a stock or portfolio of stocks. (Study Session 13, LOS 45.c)

91. **A**   Asset-based models are often used to value natural resources companies and companies that are being liquidated. Because Visser is unprofitable, an earnings multiplier model or a dividend discount model such as the Gordon growth model may not produce a meaningful value for the firm. (Study Session 14, LOS 50.b)

92. C Value @ t = 2 = $\dfrac{D_3}{k-g} = \dfrac{D_0(1+g)^3}{k-g} = \dfrac{\$6.25(1.07)^3}{0.12-0.07} = \$153.13$
    (Study Session 14, LOS 50.e)

93. C Management buyout refers to a situation where an investor group that includes the firm's key management purchases all the outstanding shares (not just a controlling interest) of a public company in order to take it private. Once this is done, the shares are no longer registered for public trading and, as a result, are no longer traded on exchanges or in other public markets. (Study Session 14, LOS 48.c)

94. C The maturity phase of an industry life cycle is not typically characterized by excess capacity or price competition. The conditions described may be consistent with a concentrated industry (typically characterized by low levels of price competition, since firms in the industry seek to avoid it) that is moving into the decline phase of an industry life cycle (excess capacity leads to aggressive price cutting, especially when barriers to exit are high). These conditions could also be consistent with an industry that is moving into the shakeout phase (characterized by developing excess capacity and intense price competition) following the growth phase (during which price competition is low). (Study Session 14, LOS 49.h)

95. C $P_2 = \dfrac{D_3}{k-g} = \dfrac{2.25(1.2)^2}{0.15-0.05} = 32.40$

    $P_0 = \dfrac{\$2.25}{1.15} + \dfrac{2.70}{(1.15)^2} + \dfrac{32.40}{(1.15)^2} = \$28.50$
    (Study Session 14, LOS 50.e)

96. A Restrictions on short sales remove some of the selling pressure on overvalued securities that would otherwise drive their market values down toward their intrinsic values in an efficient market. Market inefficiency caused by high transactions costs or restrictions on arbitrage trading may allow market values that are different from intrinsic values to persist both for overvalued and undervalued securities. (Study Session 13, LOS 47.b, c)

97. A The investor is short the stock and will experience losses if the stock price increases. A stop buy order at $44 will execute if the stock price rises to $44 or higher. A limit buy order at $44 would execute immediately because the stock price is less than $44. (Study Session 13, LOS 45.e, h)

98. C This question can be answered without calculations. Since the spot rates are less than the coupon rate, the price must be greater than par value, so C is the only possible correct choice.

    This is a four-period bond with $50 cash flows each period. Divide each spot rate by two to get the semiannual rate.

    PV_1: N = 1; I/Y = 3.00; FV = $50; CPT → PV   = $48.54
    PV_2: N = 2; I/Y = 3.25; FV = $50; CPT → PV   = $46.90
    PV_3: N = 3; I/Y = 3.50; FV = $50; CPT → PV   = $45.10
    PV_4: N = 4; I/Y = 3.75; FV = $1,050; CPT → PV = $906.23

    or $\dfrac{50}{1.03} + \dfrac{50}{1.0325^2} + \dfrac{50}{1.035^3} + \dfrac{1,050}{1.0375^4} = \$1,046.77$

    Sum to get $1,046.77. (Study Session 15, LOS 53.c)

©2014 Kaplan, Inc.

99. **B** The change in price due to a change in yield is only approximate because the calculation of effective duration does not reflect all of the curvature of the price-yield curve (convexity). It is a linear approximation of a non-linear relation. (Study Session 16, LOS 55.b)

100. **C** Issuing securitized bonds from a special purpose entity allows a corporation to dedicate the assets' cash flows to specific debt issues. This enables the issue to receive a higher credit rating than that of the corporation. (Study Session 15, LOS 51.d, 54.b)

101. **B** Rollover risk is the risk that an issuer who relies on the commercial paper market as a funding source may not be able to issue new commercial paper when an outstanding issue matures. Default risk and reinvestment risk are faced by bondholders. (Study Session 15, LOS 52.f)

102. **B** Because the price-yield relationship for an option-free bond is convex, interest rate risk as measured by duration changes when a bond's YTM changes. An increase in YTM reaches a flatter part of the price-yield curve, from which changes in yield will have relatively smaller effects on the bond's value. (Study Session 16, LOS 55.e)

103. **C** $\sqrt{\dfrac{(1.07)^4}{(1.05)^2}} - 1 = 0.0904$, or $\dfrac{(4 \times 7) - (2 \times 5)}{2} = 9$ as an approximation

 (Study Session 15, LOS 53.h)

104. **B** EBIT / interest is a coverage ratio and debt / capital is a leverage ratio. Higher interest coverage and lower leverage are favorable for creditworthiness. Of the three companies given, Knight has the highest interest coverage and Lawrence has the lowest leverage. EBIT / revenue (operating profit margin) is a profitability ratio and revenue / assets (asset turnover) is an operating ratio. (Study Session 8, LOS 28.e, Study Session 9, LOS 32.k, and Study Session 16, LOS 56.f, g)

105. **C** The term structure of yield volatility refers to the volatility of interest rates at different maturities. If the term structure of yield volatility is downward sloping, short-term interest rates are more volatile than long-term interest rates. (Study Session 16, LOS 55.j)

106. **B** This bond has no cash flows for the first five years. It then has a $100 cash flow for years 6 through 10. Additionally, the accrued interest ($500) that wasn't paid in the first five years would have to be paid at the end, along with the principal. A financial calculator using the CF/NPV worksheet can handle this type of problem. The required inputs are $CF_0 = 0$, $CF_1 = 0$, $F_1 = 5$, $CF_2 = 100$, $F_2 = 4$, $CF_3 = 1{,}600$, $F_3 = 1$, NPV, I = 10%, CPT = 813.69. Note that CF_3 is made up of the principal ($1,000) plus the remaining $100 coupon plus the accrued interest ($500) that was not paid during the first five years of the bond's life. (Study Session 15, LOS 53.a)

107. **A** Current yield = annual coupon / bond price. A pure discount bond is a zero-coupon bond, which has a current yield of zero. (Study Session 15, LOS 53.f)

108. **A** Floating-rate securities are subject to interest rate risk because their coupon rates are not reset continuously. The longer the time until the security's next reset date, the greater its potential price fluctuation away from par value (to a discount or premium). Other reasons that the price can differ from par include caps and floors on the floating rate, changes in the issuer's credit risk that are not reflected in the coupon's quoted margin over LIBOR, and changes in the market's required margin for the firm's level of credit risk. A decrease in the required margin would be likely to cause the security to trade at a premium rather than a discount. Liquidity risk is much less likely to change than default risk and market interest rates. (Study Session 15, LOS 51.e, 53.f)

109. **C** Prepayment rates will most likely increase if mortgage rates decrease. Increasing prepayments will decrease the weighted average life of the pass-through security. (Study Session 15, LOS 54.d)

110. **B** Ignoring the convenience yield (a nonmonetary benefit of holding the asset) will result in a forward price that is above the no-arbitrage forward price. To profit from this mispricing, an arbitrageur would borrow at the risk-free rate (i.e., take a short position in the risk-free asset), purchase the underlying asset, and take a short position in the forward contract. (Study Session 17, LOS 58.a, c)

111. **A** Normally, options with greater time to expiration are worth more than otherwise identical options that are nearer to expiration. However, in some circumstances, this relationship may not hold for European puts. For example, if the price of the underlying asset goes to zero, the European put with less time to expiration may be worth more because the put holder will receive the exercise price earlier. (Study Session 17, LOS 58.k)

112. **C** Replication of a swap with off-market FRAs is used to determine the value of an interest rate swap and to establish the swap price such that its value is zero at initiation. (Study Session 17, LOS 58.h)

113. **A** When the stock's price (S) – the strike price (X) is positive, a call option is in the money. 35 – X = 3, so X = 32. (Study Session 17, LOS 59.a)

114. **C** Both put and call writers (sellers) have an obligation to honor the terms of the option if it is exercised. Option holders (buyers) have the right, not the obligation, to exercise under the terms of the agreement. The holder pays a premium for this right, while the writer receives a premium for this obligation. A forward contract imposes an obligation on both the buyer and seller to exchange the underlying asset. (Study Session 17, LOS 57.b)

115. **B** An asset underlying put and call options can be replicated with a long European call option, a short European put option, and a long position in a risk-free bond that pays the exercise price on the expiration date. (Study Session 17, LOS 58.l)

116. **A** Compared to traditional investments, alternative investments exhibit less liquidity, less regulation, and less transparency. As a group, alternative investments generally have relatively low return correlations with traditional investments. (Study Session 18, LOS 60.a)

117. **A** The description relates best to the early stage wherein the capital that is supplied helps speed up product development and also helps pay for the beginning of a marketing campaign. (Study Session 18, LOS 60.d)

 ©2014 Kaplan, Inc.

118. **C** Quantitative directional strategies employ technical analysis and may have net long or short exposure. A market neutral strategy maintains approximately equal values in long and short positions and is typically based on fundamental analysis. Special situations strategy is an event-driven strategy that involves investing in firms that are selling divisions or assets, distributing capital, or issuing or repurchasing securities. (Study Session 18, LOS 60.d)

119. **B** In a hedge fund's fee structure, a hard hurdle rate means that incentive fees are earned only on returns in excess of the benchmark return. A soft hurdle rate means that incentive fees are calculated on the entire return, but are only paid if the return exceeds the hurdle rate. A high water mark specifies that incentive fees are only paid on returns that increase an investor's account value above its highest previous value. (Study Session 18, LOS 60.f)

120. **B** Investing in farmland may provide income over the life of the investment from crops produced and sold. Investing in commodities typically does not provide income. Commodities and real estate investments such as farmland may both provide a hedge against inflation. Direct investments in real estate are less liquid than investments in commodities, which are typically made through highly liquid exchange-traded derivatives. (Study Session 18, LOS 60.d)

EXAM 2
MORNING SESSION ANSWER KEY

To get valuable feedback on how your score compares to those of other Level I candidates, use your Username and Password to gain online access at Schweser.com and select "Performance Tracker" from your dashboard.

1.	B	31.	B	61.	B	91.	B
2.	A	32.	A	62.	A	92.	C
3.	C	33.	B	63.	A	93.	B
4.	B	34.	C	64.	B	94.	C
5.	A	35.	B	65.	C	95.	A
6.	A	36.	A	66.	C	96.	B
7.	C	37.	A	67.	C	97.	A
8.	A	38.	C	68.	A	98.	B
9.	B	39.	C	69.	C	99.	A
10.	C	40.	A	70.	B	100.	C
11.	B	41.	C	71.	A	101.	C
12.	C	42.	C	72.	A	102.	A
13.	B	43.	B	73.	B	103.	C
14.	B	44.	B	74.	A	104.	B
15.	C	45.	C	75.	C	105.	C
16.	A	46.	C	76.	C	106.	A
17.	B	47.	A	77.	B	107.	A
18.	B	48.	C	78.	C	108.	A
19.	B	49.	A	79.	A	109.	C
20.	C	50.	B	80.	B	110.	A
21.	A	51.	A	81.	A	111.	B
22.	A	52.	A	82.	C	112.	A
23.	B	53.	B	83.	B	113.	B
24.	C	54.	A	84.	A	114.	A
25.	C	55.	C	85.	A	115.	C
26.	B	56.	A	86.	C	116.	A
27.	B	57.	C	87.	B	117.	C
28.	C	58.	A	88.	A	118.	A
29.	B	59.	B	89.	A	119.	B
30.	C	60.	A	90.	B	120.	B

©2014 Kaplan, Inc.

Exam 2
Morning Session Answers

Answers referencing the Standards of Practice address Study Session 1, LOS 1.b, c and LOS 2.a, b, c, except where noted.

1. **B** Members can accept or reject a disciplinary sanction proposed by the Professional Conduct Program staff. If the member rejects the sanction, the matter is referred to a hearing before a disciplinary review panel of CFA Institute members. The other statements are accurate. (Study Session 1, LOS 1.a)

2. **A** In this case, Miguel has not violated the standards. For a gift from a client in appreciation of past service or performance, informing his supervisor verbally is sufficient. Standard I(B) Independence and Objectivity requires disclosure prior to accepting the gift "when possible," but in cases such as this when there is short notice, notification afterward is permitted.

3. **C** Roberts violated Standard III(E) Preservation of Confidentiality by revealing his business relationship with Roberts without permission. Because the information that Roberts' plans to sell his home is not received as part of his professional relationship with Roberts, it is not covered by the Standard.

4. **B** Watson's excessive drinking is unfortunate but we have no evidence that it has affected his work, professional integrity, judgment, or reputation. His arrest for public intoxication occurred while he was away from work. If he commits an act involving fraud or dishonesty, he would violate the Standard on misconduct.

5. **A** GIPS require a firm to show a GIPS-compliant history for a minimum of five years, or since inception of the firm or the composite if in existence for less than five years. If Reliable has been in business for less than five years, it may still claim compliance with GIPS on a since-inception basis, provided the firm follows all other aspects of compliance. The other choices are requirements for a firm to claim compliance with GIPS. (Study Session 1, LOS 4.a)

6. **A** The recommended procedures for compliance with Standard I(B) Independence and Objectivity include the recommendation that analysts on company visits pay their own travel expenses and use commercial transportation if it is available.

7. **C** Brett violated both the Code of Ethics and Standard VII(A) Conduct as Participants in CFA Institute Programs. By writing down information from the Candidate Body of Knowledge and taking it into the exam room, she compromised the integrity of the exam, whether she used the notes or not. Her actions are also in violation of the Code of Ethics by not acting "with integrity, competence, diligence, respect, and in an ethical manner."

8. **A** The requirement that members and candidates place their clients' interests before their employer's or their own is in Standard III(A) Loyalty, Prudence, and Care. The other choices are included in the CFA Institute Code of Ethics.

9. B   Kramer violated Standard V(B) Communication with Clients and Prospective Clients. The problem is with the word "will." Kramer should have used "is estimated to be" to separate fact from opinion. Statistical estimates of future events are subject to change and should not be presented as certainties. She need not give complete details of the statistical model but should indicate its general characteristics and the important factors involved in her projections.

10. C   Standard III(B) Fair Dealing requires that all clients be treated fairly. Members and candidates should not discriminate against any client. A family member who is a fee-paying client should not be treated differently from other clients when taking investment action. Following up changes in recommendations with phone calls to larger clients is not a violation of the Standard if the changes have been disseminated fairly.

11. B   Thompson has not violated Standard II(B) Market Manipulation by posting his firm's projections for Ibex. A firm's recommendation of a security may increase its price without any intent to mislead the market. The firm has disseminated the details of the offering to its clients fairly, so Thompson may call individual clients without violating the Standard III(B) Fair Dealing.

12. C   According to Standard VI(A) Disclosure of Conflicts, Elliott should disclose his beneficial ownership of Tech to his employer and to clients and prospects because such ownership could interfere with his ability to make unbiased and objective recommendations. Selling his shares or declining to write the report are not required and are more extreme than simply disclosing the potential conflict.

13. B   Mendoza has not violated the Standards of Practice or GIPS. Because the presentation was introductory and brief, Mendoza was not required to give any supporting documentation, but he made it available to clients and prospective clients upon request. His claim of GIPS compliance on the information sheet is appropriate. (Study Session 1, LOS 3.c)

14. B   Telling a selected group of analysts new information does not constitute public disclosure, and therefore acting or causing others to act on this information is a violation of Standard II(A) Material Nonpublic Information. Recommending the sale of a stock rated as a "hold" is not a violation of Standard III(B) Fair Dealing.

15. C   Standard III(C) Suitability requires that members and candidates update client information (the IPS) at least annually. The IPS can be updated more frequently if there are significant changes in the investment strategy or client characteristics.

16. A   To comply with Standard III(E) Preservation of Confidentiality, Johnson must not discuss with her charitable foundation anything regarding her client and her client's intentions. It does not matter that her client intends to give money to charities in the near future.

17. B   Standard III(A) Loyalty, Prudence, and Care does not require the voting of all proxies. A cost-benefit analysis may support the conclusion that the voting of all proxies is not beneficial to the client in light of the time and effort required. Voting on nonroutine issues that have a material impact is required.

18. B   According to Standard I(A) Knowledge of the Law, Gold must comply with the most strict of the laws of Country T, laws of Country U, and the CFA Standards of Practice. In this case, the most strict rules are those in the Standards of Practice. Standard VI(C) Referral Fees requires the disclosure of all referral fees and Standard II(A) Material Nonpublic Information prohibits acting or causing others to act on the basis of material non-public information.

   ©2014 Kaplan, Inc.

19. **B** It's best to break this problem into parts to accommodate the change in the interest rate.

    Money in the fund at the end of ten years based on deposits made with initial interest of 5%:

    (1) The total value in the fund at the end of the fifth year is $3,152.50:
        PMT = −1,000; N = 3; I/Y = 5; CPT → FV = $3,152.50. (calculator in END mode)

    (2) The $3,152.50 is now the present value and will then grow at 4% until the end of the tenth year. We get: PV = −3,152.50; N = 5; I/Y = 4; PMT = −1,000; CPT → FV = $9,251.82

    (Study Session 2, LOS 5.e)

20. **C** With more than one compounding period per year, $FV_N = PV\left(1 + \dfrac{r_s}{m}\right)^{mn}$

    $PV = \$5,000; r_s = 6\%; m = 12; \dfrac{r_s}{m} = \dfrac{6\%}{12} = 0.5\%; n = 3; m \times n = 12 \times 3 = 36$.

    To compute FV_3, enter PV = −5,000; I = 0.5; PMT = 0; and N = 36 to get $5,983.40.
    (Study Session 2, LOS 5.d)

21. **A** A *t*-distribution with sufficiently high degrees of freedom is approximately normal and a normal distribution has thinner tails compared to a *t*-distribution. The less the degrees of freedom, the fatter the tails. (Study Session 3, LOS 10.i)

22. **A** $R_1 = -10/100 = -10\%; R_2 = +9/90 = +10\%$

    geometric mean $= \sqrt{(0.9)(1.1)} - 1 = -0.005$ or -0.5%

    An alternative way to get the geometric mean is:

    $\left(\dfrac{\text{ending value}}{\text{beginning value}}\right)^{\frac{1}{n}} - 1 = \text{geometric mean return}$

    $\sqrt{\dfrac{99}{100}} - 1 = -0.005$ or -0.5%

    (Study Session 2, LOS 7.e)

23. **B** $R_L = \dfrac{2.0 + 151 - 150}{150} = 0.02$

    Choose Portfolio X because it has the larger safety-first ratio, $(0.10 - 0.02)/0.14 = 0.57$.

    Note: $\text{SFRatio(B)} = \dfrac{0.12 - 0.02}{0.20} = 0.50$

    (Study Session 3, LOS 9.n)

24. **C**   To find the money-weighted rate of return, equate the present value of inflows to the present value of outflows and find the discount rate that makes them equal.

t = 0:	Buy 500 shares @ $22	=	−$11,000

t = 1:	$0.42 × 500 shares	=	+$210
	Buy 500 shares @ $24.75	=	−$12,375
	Net cash flow	=	−$12,165

t = 2:	$0.42 × 1,000 shares	=	+$420
	Buy 600 shares @ $31.25	=	−$18,750
	Net cash flow	=	−$18,330

t = 3:	Sell 1,000 shares @ $35.50	=	+$35,500
	Sell 600 shares @ $36.00	=	+$21,600
	Net cash flow	=	+$57,000

    Find the IRR with CFs as follows:
    $CF_0 = -11,000$; $CF_1 = -12,165$; $CF_2 = -18,330$; $CF_3 = 57,100$.
    The final result is IRR = 18.49%. (Study Session 2, LOS 6.d)

25. **C**   The up-move factor equals one plus the percentage increase when the variable goes up, and the down-move factor is equal to one divided by the up-move factor. (Study Session 3, LOS 9.g)

26. **B**   No calculations are really necessary here since the MMY involves no compounding and a 360-day year, the BEY requires compounding the quarterly HPR to a semiannual rate and doubling that rate, and the EAY requires compounding for the entire year based on a 365-day year. A numerical example of these calculations based on a 90-day holding period yield of 1.3% is: the money market yield is 1.3% × 360 / 90 = 5.20%, the bond equivalent yield is $2 \times [1.013^{182.5 / 90} - 1] = 0.0531 = 5.31\%$, which is two times the effective semiannual rate of return, and the effective annual yield is $1.013^{365 / 90} - 1 = 0.0538 = 5.38\%$. Calculating the semiannual effective yield using 180 days instead of 182.5 does not change the order. (Study Session 2, LOS 6.e)

27. **B**   P(good economy and bear market) = 0.60 × 0.20 = 0.12. The other statements are true. The P(normal market) = (0.60 × 0.30) + (0.40 × 0.30) = 0.30. Given that the economy is poor, the probability of a normal or bull market = 0.30 + 0.20 = 0.50. (Study Session 2, LOS 8.f)

28. **C**   Expected value = (0.4)(10%) + (0.4)(12.5%) + (0.2)(30%) = 15%

    Variance = $(0.4)(10 - 15)^2 + (0.4)(12.5 - 15)^2 + (0.2)(30 - 15)^2 = 57.5$

    Standard deviation = $\sqrt{57.5} = 7.58\%$

    (Study Session 2, LOS 8.m)

29. **B**   We can view this problem as the number of ways to choose three analysts from five analysts when the order they are chosen matters. The formula for the number of permutations is:

    $$\frac{n!}{(n-r)!} = \frac{5!}{2!} = 5 \times 4 \times 3 = 60$$

    On the TI financial calculator: 5 2nd nPr 3 = 60.

    (Study Session 2, LOS 8.o)

©2014 Kaplan, Inc.

30. **C** Choice A is downgrade risk; choice B is default risk. (Study Session 3, LOS 9.n, and Study Session 16, LOS 56.a)

31. **B** Rejecting the null hypothesis when it is true is a Type I error. The probability of a Type I error is the significance level of the test and one minus the significance level is the confidence level. The power of a test is one minus the probability of a Type II error, which cannot be calculated from the information given. (Study Session 3, LOS 11.c)

32. **A** Type I error is rejecting the null hypothesis when it is true. The power of a test is the probability of rejecting the null hypothesis when it is false. $H_A: X \neq 0$ indicates a two-tailed test, while $H_A: X < 0$ or $H_A: X > 0$ indicates a one-tailed test. (Study Session 3, LOS 11.b, d)

33. **B** Real business cycle theory, which derives from applying utility theory and budget constraints to macroeconomic models, is associated with the New Classical school. (Study Session 5, LOS 18.c)

34. **C** If the quantity supplied at a given price is greater than the quantity demanded, then that price is greater than the equilibrium price. A price ceiling on electricity set above the equilibrium price will have no effect because the quantity supplied equals the quantity demanded at a price less than this legal maximum. A minimum wage causes a loss of efficiency (quantity of labor supplied is greater than the quantity demanded) when it is set above the equilibrium wage for unskilled workers. Increased search time is an example of an inefficiency that results from a rent ceiling below the equilibrium rent level. (Study Session 4, LOS 13.k, l)

35. **B** Arbitrage-free forward rate = 1.3382 USD/EUR × (1.025 / 1.035) = 1.3253 USD/EUR. (Study Session 6, LOS 21.h)

36. **A** The demand curve (price as a function of Q_D) is found by inverting the demand function:

$$P_{gas} = 20 + 2/15\ P_{bus} - 1/15 Q_D$$

The slope of this function (for any positive value of P_{bus}) is –1/15, or –0.0667. (Study Session 4, LOS 13.g)

37. **A** Demand curves are not observable so a monopolist must search for the profit maximizing price. Because demand information is not perfect, a monopolist is a price searcher. The other statements are false. Although a monopolist can earn positive economic profits in the long run, they are not guaranteed; if average total costs exceed price, the monopolist will experience economic losses. A monopolist maximizes *profit*, not revenue, where marginal revenue equals marginal cost. (Study Session 4, LOS 16.b, d, e)

38. **C** With exchange rate targeting, a central bank's ability to increase the value of the domestic currency is limited by the amount of foreign reserves the country has available to buy its own currency in the foreign exchange market. While inflation targeting and interest rate targeting have limitations (e.g., liquidity trap conditions may exist, interest rates are bounded by zero), the central bank's resources are not typically a limitation. (Study Session 5, LOS 19.l, n)

39. **C** From an initial equilibrium, an increase in real money balances will leave households and businesses with more money than they wish to hold, so they will purchase interest-bearing securities, driving their prices up and yields down until a new equilibrium short-term rate is established. (Study Session 5, LOS 19.d)

40. **A** An increase in expected future incomes will cause consumers to increase current expenditures (reduce current savings) in anticipation of the higher future incomes. An increase in the money supply will tend to decrease interest rates which will lead to increased consumer spending on durable goods and increased investment by businesses. Both effects increase aggregate demand. (Study Session 5, LOS 17.h)

41. **C** Either higher-than-expected or lower-than-expected inflation can cause producers to misinterpret unexpected changes in the price level as signals of increases or decreases in demand, and produce more or less than the equilibrium quantity of output. (Study Session 5, LOS 19.g)

42. **C** In the Heckscher-Ohlin model, the source of comparative advantage is the relative amounts of labor and capital that are available in each country. Countries with more capital available relative to labor available will have a comparative advantage in producing capital-intensive goods, while countries with more labor available relative to capital will have a comparative advantage in labor-intensive goods. (Study Session 6, LOS 20.d)

43. **B** Firms' demand curves are perfectly elastic (horizontal) in a market characterized as perfect competition, so that marginal revenue is equal to price and a firm maximizes profit by producing the output quantity at which marginal cost equals price. In monopoly markets or under monopolistic competition, firm demand curves are downward sloping so that marginal revenue is less than price. (Study Session 4, LOS 16.f)

44. **B** If demand is inelastic, the percentage change in quantity demanded is smaller than the percentage change in price; quantity demanded is relatively unresponsive to price changes. A price increase increases total expenditures on a good. (Study Session 4, LOS 13.m)

45. **C** These are examples of items that are typically treated as extraordinary under U.S. GAAP. There is no provision for accounting for an item as extraordinary under IFRS. Accounting errors are corrected with prior-period adjustments, which are made by restating results for any prior periods that are presented in the current financial statements. Discontinued operations are not classified as unusual or infrequent items and are reported (net of taxes) after net income from continuing operations but before net income. (Study Session 8, LOS 25.e)

46. **C** Borrowing funds to purchase capital equipment will result in an increase in assets (equipment) and in liabilities (debt). The accrual of the salaries that are owed, but not paid, as of month-end will increase expenses and increase liabilities (accrued salary expense). Therefore, these two transactions taken together will result in the greatest increase in liabilities. (Study Session 7, LOS 23.c)

47. **A** Cash received from issuing securities is a financing cash flow. Income taxes paid are operating cash flows under U.S. GAAP. Interest and dividends received and interest paid are considered operating cash flows under U.S. GAAP, but dividends paid are considered financing cash flows. (Study Session 8, LOS 27.a, c)

48. **C** The easiest way to calculate CFO here is total cash flow − cash flow from investing − cash flow from financing = $13,000 + 5,000 + 4,250 = $22,250. Alternatively, CFO = $50,000 − 3,250 − 17,000 − 7,000 − 500 = $22,250. (Study Session 8, LOS 27.f)

 ©2014 Kaplan, Inc.

49. **A**   Cash conversion cycle (CCC) = days of sales outstanding + days of inventory on hand − number of days of payables. Days of sales outstanding = 365 / receivables turnover = 365 / 11 = 33.18; 365 / 12 = 30.42. This means the CCC decreases by 2.76 days. (Study Session 8, LOS 28.b)

50. **B**   Besides the annual SEC filings, an analyst should examine a company's quarterly or semiannual filings. These interim filings typically update the major financial statements and footnotes, but are not necessarily audited. Annual reports to shareholders and press releases are written by management and are often viewed as public relations or sales materials. (Study Session 7, LOS 22.e)

51. **A**   Basic EPS *does not* consider potential dilution from convertible bonds.
Original shares = 2,000,000(12) = 24,000,000
+ Stock dividend = 200,000(12) = 2,400,000
+ New shares = 100,000(3) = 300,000

$$\frac{sum}{12} = \frac{26,700,000}{12} = 2,225,000$$

Alternatively, 2 million (1.1) + (¼) (100,000) = 2.225 million. (Study Session 8, LOS 25.g)

52. **A**   Meeting or exceeding its own earnings guidance is a possible motivation for management to issue low-quality financial reports. Inadequate board oversight and wide ranges of acceptable accounting treatments are more appropriately viewed as opportunities for issuing low-quality financial reports. (Study Session 10, LOS 33.d, e)

53. **B**   In the absence of taxes, there is no difference in cash flow between LIFO and FIFO. In addition, using LIFO would result in lower working capital (inventory is lower). Using LIFO would result in lower net income because of a *lower* gross margin (cost of goods sold is higher). (Study Session 9, LOS 29.h)

54. **A**   Screening for high dividend yield stocks will likely include a disproportionately high number of financial services firms as such firms typically have higher dividend payouts. A screen to identify firms with low P/E ratios will likely exclude growth firms from the sample as high expected earnings growth leads to high P/Es. (Study Session 10, LOS 34.d)

55. **C**   A ratio that is highly variable, but consistently greater than one, is not necessarily indicative of low-quality earnings. Operating cash flow that is less than net income (ratio less than one) or declining over time may indicate low quality earnings from aggressive accounting or accounting irregularities. (Study Session 10, LOS 33.i)

56. **A**   Under IFRS, if the outcome of a long-term contract cannot be estimated reliably, the firm should expense costs when incurred, recognize revenue to the extent of the costs, and recognize profit only when the contract is complete. The firm does not need to recognize a loss when expenses are greater than cash collected, but would need to recognize a loss if it determined that a loss on the contract was likely. (Study Session 8, LOS 25.b, c)

57. **C**   Useful lives and salvage values of long-lived assets are management estimates that may vary among companies. Companies typically do not disclose data about estimated salvage values, except when estimates are changed. (Study Session 9, LOS 30.c)

58. **A**   Interest and dividends received are reported as income, regardless of the balance sheet classification of marketable securities. (Study Session 8, LOS 26.e)

59. **B** Straight line depreciation is (100,000 + 10,000 + 5,000 − 25,000) / 6 = 15,000 each year. Double-declining balance depreciation in the second year is: 115,000 (2/3)(1/3) = 25,556. The difference is $10,556. Remember that salvage value is not part of the declining balance calculation. (Study Session 8, LOS 25.d, and Study Session 9, LOS 30.d)

60. **A** A decrease in the accounts receivable amount on the balance sheet indicates that cash collections exceed revenues (sales). This increases operating cash flow because receivables are being collected. An increase in the accounts payable amount on the balance sheet indicates that purchases from suppliers exceed cash payments. This increases operating cash flow because the cash was not used to pay the suppliers. (Study Session 8, LOS 27.f)

61. **B** The most useful estimates of inventory and cost of sales are those that best approximate current cost. Whether prices are increasing or decreasing, FIFO provides a better estimate of inventory values, and LIFO provides a better estimate of cost of sales. If prices are stable, there is no difference between LIFO and FIFO estimates of inventory or cost of sales. (Study Session 9, LOS 29.e)

62. **A** Working capital equals current assets minus current liabilities and is lower under a finance lease because the current portion of the finance lease increases current liabilities. Total asset turnover is lower because total assets are higher under a finance lease. Companies with finance leases report higher debt-to-equity ratios because liabilities increase and equity is unchanged at lease inception and lower in the early years of the lease. Return on equity is lower with a finance lease because the numerator, net income, is decreased proportionally more than the denominator, equity, from the greater expense of a finance lease in its early years. Over the life of the lease, the expenses are equal. (Study Session 9, LOS 32.h, k)

63. **A** Warranty expense should be recorded when the inventory item covered by the warranty is sold. A deferred tax asset is created when warranty expenses are accrued on the financial statements but are not deductible on the tax returns until the warranty claims are paid. The full amount of the obligation, $100,000, is recorded as an expense, with a deferred tax asset of $30,000. Note that a deferred tax asset results when taxable income is more than pretax income and the difference is likely to reverse (warranty will be paid) in future years. (Study Session 9, LOS 31.d)

64. **B** Diluted EPS = [NI − preferred dividends + convertible interest (1 − t)] / [weighted average shares + convertible debt shares].

    100(1,000)(6%)(1 − 0.4) = $3,600; convertible debt shares = 50(100) = 5,000

    $$\frac{\$15,000 - \$10,000 + \$3,600}{2,000 + 5,000} = \$1.23$$

    (Study Session 8, LOS 25.g)

65. **C** Noncurrent assets are those that will not be used up during the next year or during the firm's operating cycle. Firm investment is typically in assets that are longer term in nature. (Study Session 8, LOS 26.d)

©2014 Kaplan, Inc.

66. **C** The initial liability is the amount received from the creditor, not the par value of the bond.

    N = 8; I/Y = 11/2 = 5.5; PMT = 500,000; FV = 10,000,000; CPT → PV = $9,683,272.

    The interest expense is the effective interest rate (the market rate at the time of issue) times the balance sheet liability. $9,683,272 × 0.055 = $532,580.

    The value of the liability will change over time and is a function of the initial liability, the interest expense and the actual cash payments. In this case, it increases by the difference between the interest expense and the actual cash payment: $532,580 − $500,000 = $32,580 + $9,683,272 = $9,715,852. *Tip:* Knowing that the liability will increase is enough to select choice C without performing this last calculation. Entering N = 7 and solving for PV also produces $9,715,852. (Study Session 9, LOS 32.b)

67. **C** On a horizontal common-size balance sheet, the divisor is the first-year values so they are all standardized to 1.0 by construction. Trends in the values of these items as well as the relative growth in these items are readily apparent. A vertical common-size balance sheet expresses all balance sheet accounts as a percentage of total assets and does not standardize the initial year. (Study Session 8, LOS 28.a)

68. **A** The increase in the valuation allowance tells us that the company has decreased its estimate of its future profitability and thus its ability to realize the benefits of its deferred tax assets. A longer period for recognition of unearned revenue would not affect the temporary differences reflected in deferred tax assets. Increasing the estimate of assets' useful lives would tend to slow financial statement depreciation relative to depreciation for tax, which would increase deferred tax liability going forward, other things constant. Decreases in the carrying values of both a DTL and a DTA may reflect a decrease in the tax rate. (Study Session 9, LOS 31.g)

69. **C** Changing the inventory accounting method has no immediate cash flow effects and therefore should not change a firm's short-term forecast (typically 4 to 6 weeks) of its net cash position. However, because the average cost inventory method will result in lower gross profit compared to FIFO, it will also result in decreased taxes. The firm's long-term forecast (typically 3 to 5 years) of its net cash position should reflect a decrease in cash outflows for taxes, and consequently greater net cash in future periods. (Study Session 9, LOS 29.e and Study Session 11, LOS 39.d)

70. **B** It is not uncommon for individuals to be members of the boards of directors of more than one firm. This is acceptable as long as they maintain independence and act in the interests of the firms' shareholders. A strong corporate code of ethics should discourage the company from awarding consulting contracts or finder's fees to board members or relatives of board members. (Study Session 11, LOS 40.f)

71. **A** The appropriate method for estimating the cost of equity for a firm in a developing market is to add a country risk premium (CRP) to the market risk premium, so the revised CAPM equation becomes: $k_{ce} = R_F + \beta[E(R_{MKT}) - R_F + CRP]$. The CRP is the sovereign yield spread (between yields on the country's government bonds and a developed country's government bonds) adjusted for the volatility of the developing country's equity market. An alternative approach is to add the CRP (not the sovereign yield spread) to the cost of equity as calculated from the CAPM. (Study Session 11, LOS 36.j)

72. **A**   Factoring refers to the sale of receivables without recourse; that is, the risk that the firm's customers will not pay, or will not pay in a timely manner, is borne by the factor, who purchases the receivables. Thus, the amount the factor will pay per dollar of receivables is lower (higher discount or interest rate) if the credit quality of the firm's credit customers is lower. (Study Session 11, LOS 39.g)

73. **B**   The degree of financial leverage (DFL) is the percent change in earnings per share for a given percent change in operating income. The degree of operating leverage (DOL) is the percent change in operating income for a given percent change in sales. The degree of total leverage (DTL) is the percent change in earnings per share for a given percent change in sales, and is the product of DOL and DFL. Based on the information given, Smith has a higher DFL than Jones, but we cannot conclude that Smith has a higher DTL than Jones. (Study Session 11, LOS 37.b)

74. **A**   The correct treatment of flotation costs according to the CFA Curriculum is to include their cost in the initial cash outflow of the project. Since flotation costs are included in the initial outlay, they decrease the NPV by an amount that is unaffected by the discount rate, and the discount rate and cost of capital are not adjusted for flotation costs. (Study Session 11, LOS 36.l)

75. **C**   An increase in the tax rate will reduce Thompson's after-tax cost of debt (other things equal) and therefore reduce its WACC. With a relatively lower cost of debt the firm will likely change its capital structure to include more debt and less equity (i.e., to increase its financial leverage). (Study Session 11, LOS 36.b)

76. **C**   The payment of a stock (as opposed to a cash) dividend does not affect the firm's total equity or net income, but will decrease its earnings per share because it increases the number of shares outstanding. (Study Session 11, LOS 38.a)

77. **B**   Restrictions on particular investment choices must be listed in the constraints section of the IPS. This investor must abide by his employer's policies, which is an example of a legal and regulatory factor. The appendix to an IPS usually lists items such as the rebalancing policy and strategic asset allocation that might change more frequently than a constraint. (Study Session 12, LOS 44.e)

78. **C**   Property and casualty insurers may need to distribute funds at any time if a disaster occurs. Endowment funds have a very long horizon, as they are often expected to operate in perpetuity with only annual distributions representing a relatively small percentage of the fund value. Defined benefit plans have an investment horizon based on the years to retirement of currently covered workers and the years they (and their beneficiaries) are expected to live after retirement. (Study Session 12, LOS 41.b)

79. **A**   The market model is expressed as: $R_i = \alpha_i + \beta_i R_m + \varepsilon_i$. In this model, beta ($\beta_i$) measures the sensitivity of the rate of return on an asset (R_i) to the market rate of return (R_m). (Study Session 12, LOS 43.d)

80. **B**   The correlation between the returns of the two assets is:

$$\frac{Cov_{AB}}{\sigma_A \sigma_B} = \frac{0.03735}{\sqrt{0.031} \times \sqrt{0.045}} = 1.$$

Therefore, the standard deviation of the portfolio returns is a weighted average of the standard deviations of returns for the two assets: $0.3\sqrt{0.031} + 0.7\sqrt{0.045} = 20.13\%$.

Since the correlation of returns is +1, there are no diversification benefits. (Study Session 12, LOS 42.e)

©2014 Kaplan, Inc.

81. **A**   Open-end funds redeem existing shares or issue new shares in accordance with investor demand. Closed-end fund shares are fixed in number and trade on exchanges as though they were common stock. (Study Session 12, LOS 41.e)

82. **C**   Using the CAPM, the required rate of return for each stock is:

$E(R_X)$ = 4% + 1.0(10% − 4%) = 10.0%.

10.0% − 10.0% = 0.0% properly valued.

$E(R_Y)$ = 4% + 1.6(10% − 4%) = 13.6%.

16.0% − 13.6% = 2.4% undervalued.

$E(R_Z)$ = 4% + 2.0(10% − 4%) = 16.0%.

16.0% − 16.0% = 0.0% properly valued.

(Study Session 12, LOS 43.h)

83. **B**   According to the CAPM, rational, risk-averse investors will optimally choose to hold a portfolio along the capital market line. This can range from a 100% allocation to the risk-free asset to a leveraged position in the market portfolio constructed by borrowing at the risk-free rate to invest more than 100% of the portfolio equity value in the market portfolio. The global minimum variance portfolio lies below the CML and is not an efficient portfolio under the assumptions of the CAPM. (Study Session 12, LOS 42.g)

84. **A**   Based on the CAPM, the portfolio should earn: E(R) = 0.05 + 1.5(0.10) = 20%. On a risk-adjusted basis, this portfolio lies on the security market line (SML) and thus is earning a risk-adjusted rate of return equivalent to that of the market portfolio. (Study Session 12, LOS 43.g)

85. **A**   For investment horizons of over one year, the geometric mean return over the five years is the best estimator. Geometric mean return = $[(1.11)(1.05)(0.87)(1.08)(1.09)]^{1/5} - 1$ = 3.604%. For a 2-year holding period the expected return is then $(1.03604)^2 - 1$ = 7.34%. (Study Session 2, LOS 7.m and Study Session 12, LOS 42.a)

86. **C**   g = (1 − payout)(ROE) = (1 − 0.40)(16%) = 9.6%

$$k = \frac{\$1.50(1.096)}{\$40} + 0.096 = 13.7\%$$

(Study Session 14, LOS 50.e)

87. **B**   The following formula indicates the stock price that will trigger a margin call:

$$\text{long} = \frac{(\text{original price})(1 - \text{initial margin \%})}{1 - \text{maintenance margin}} = \frac{(\$50)(1 - 0.50)}{1 - 0.25} = \$33.33$$

(Study Session 13, LOS 45.f)

 Professor's Note: An intuitive way to solve minimum margin problems for equity accounts is based on the fact that while the margin amount changes with stock price changes after purchase, the loan amount does not. Stock price is $50, loan is $25, when the margin is 25% the loan must be 75% (of share price). $25 / 0.75 = $33.33.

88. **A** Operational efficiency refers to low transactions costs in a securities market. Informational efficiency means prices change rapidly to reflect new information without predictable bias and rates of return are, on average, proportional to risk. (Study Session 13, LOS 45.k)

89. **A** Price-weighted index $= \dfrac{4+10}{2} = 7$. A price-weighted index is not affected by a split. The divisor is adjusted to account for the price change.

$$\text{Value-weighted index} = 100 \times \dfrac{\$4(50)+\$5(20)}{\$2(50)+\$10(10)} = 150$$

(Study Session 13, LOS 46.e)

90. **B** Required return = 5% + 1.1(8%) = 13.8%

Sustainable growth = 18%(1 − 0.4) = 10.8%

$$\dfrac{P_0}{E_1} = \dfrac{0.40}{0.138-0.108} = 13.33.$$

(Study Session 14, LOS 50.c, h)

91. **B** Free cash flow-based valuation techniques are appropriate for valuing shares of a firm that does not pay dividends. The Gordon growth model and two-stage dividend discount model are appropriate for valuing shares of dividend-paying firms. (Study Session 14, LOS 50.f)

92. **C** The shakeout industry life-cycle stage is characterized by slowing (but still positive) growth, intense competition, and declining profitability, as demand begins to approach market saturation. In contrast, the decline industry stage is characterized by negative growth. The lack of brand loyalty among customers suggests the industry has not yet reached the mature stage. (Study Session 14, LOS 49.h)

93. **B** Dividend payout = 1 − earnings retention rate = 1 − 0.4 = 0.6

$R_S = R_f + \beta(R_M - R_f)$ = 0.06 + 1.2(0.11 − 0.06) = 0.12

g = (retention rate)(ROE) = 0.4(0.12) = 0.048

$$P/E = \dfrac{\text{dividend payout ratio}}{k-g} = \dfrac{0.6}{0.12-0.048} = 8.33$$

Price = E(P/E) = $4(8.33) = $33.32

(Study Session 14, LOS 50.c, h)

94. **C** Both technology and housing firms tend to be quite cyclical, that is, their profits are very sensitive to changes in overall growth. The profits of telecommunications firms, on the other hand, are less economically sensitive. (Study Session 14, LOS 49.c)

95. **A** Behavioral finance studies how market anomalies can arise from psychological traits that affect investor behavior and cause investors to make systematic errors such as exiting profitable positions too soon and holding unprofitable positions too long. (Study Session 13, LOS 47.g)

©2014 Kaplan, Inc.

96. **B**   Since the index is price weighted, the value of the stocks will match the index performance. Total returns includes dividend yield, however, and since dividends are not included in the performance of the index itself, the portfolio will outperform the index by the amount of the dividend yield. (Study Session 13, LOS 46.b)

97. **A**   One of the disadvantages of present value models such as the Gordon growth model is that the required rate of return on equity must be estimated. Neither an enterprise value multiplier model nor an asset valuation model requires an explicit estimate of the required rate of return. (Study Session 14, LOS 50.k)

98. **B**   Because the coupon rate is greater than its yield to maturity, the bond price is at a premium to par value. If the yield remains unchanged, the price will decrease toward par value along its constant-yield price trajectory. (Study Session 15, LOS 53.b)

99. **A**   Default risk is the possibility that the issuer will fail to meet its obligations under the indenture, for which investors demand a premium above the return on a default-risk-free security. Bond ratings indicate default risk. Downgrade risk is the risk that a bond will be reclassified as a riskier security by a credit rating agency. Credit spread risk is the risk that the default risk premium on a bond can increase. (Study Session 16, LOS 56.a, d)

100. **C**   A callable bond is made up of a straight bond and a written call option. An increase in volatility increases the value of the call option and decreases the value of the callable bond. On the other hand, a putable bond is made up of an option-free (or straight) bond and a long put option. An increase in volatility increases the value of the put option and therefore increases the value of the putable bond. (Study Session 15, LOS 51.f, and Study Session 17, LOS 58.k)

101. **C**   The name "medium-term note" does not imply anything about the original maturity of the security. (Study Session 15, LOS 52.f)

102. **A**   Portfolio duration is an approximation of the price sensitivity of a portfolio to parallel shifts of the yield curve (yields for all maturities increase or decrease by equal amounts). Key rate duration may be used to estimate interest rate risk for non-parallel shifts in the yield curve. (Study Session 16, LOS 55.d, f)

103. **C**   "Top-heavy" refers to a capital structure that includes a high percentage of secured bank debt. A firm with a top-heavy capital structure may be limited in its access to additional bank borrowing, which increases the likelihood of default if the firm encounters financial distress. (Study Session 16, LOS 56.j)

104. **B**   First calculate V– and V+, the bond's value at 7.25% and 8.75% yields to maturity. The bond values are $1,052.70 and $950.69, respectively:

N = 20; I/Y = 7.25 / 2 = 3.625; PMT = 40; FV = 1,000; CPT PV = –1052.70

N = 20; I/Y = 8.75 / 2 = 4.375; PMT = 40; FV = 1,000; CPT PV = –950.69

$$D = \frac{V_- - V_+}{2V_0(\Delta y)} = \frac{1,052.70 - 950.69}{2(1,000)(0.0075)} = 6.8.$$

(Study Session 16, LOS 55.b)

105. **C** $4y1y = \dfrac{(1.055)^5}{(1.04)^4} - 1 = 0.1172$

        Note: 5(5.5) – 4(4) = 11.5%. (Study Session 15, LOS 53.h)

106. **A**   Interpolated spreads (I-spreads) are spreads to swap rates. (Study Session 15, LOS 53.i)

107. **A**   We know that: $r_{BD} = \dfrac{D}{F}\left(\dfrac{360}{t}\right)$

        D = $1,000,000 – $987,845 = $12,155
        F = $1,000,000
        t = 78 days

        Substituting we get: $r_{BD} = \dfrac{\$12,155}{\$1,000,000}\left(\dfrac{360}{78}\right) = 0.0561$

        (Study Session 2, LOS 6.e)

108. **A**   Covered bonds are an obligation of the corporation that issues them but their interest and principal payments are provided by a pool of assets that are legally recognized as bankruptcy-remote. They are different from securitized bonds, which are issued by a special purpose vehicle. (Study Session 15, LOS 51.d, 54.b)

109. **C**   An agency RMBS is said to extend when prepayments of the underlying mortgages are slower than expected. A decrease in interest rates would tend to accelerate prepayments, resulting in contraction. Agency RMBS are not typically structured with tranches. Exhaustion of a support tranche is a source of extension risk for a planned amortization class of a CMO. (Study Session 15, LOS 54.d, e, f)

110. **A**   Because the right to exercise a call option early is not valuable when the underlying asset does not pay any cash flows, the value of an American call option is equal to the value of an otherwise identical European call option. (Study Session 17, LOS 58.o)

111. **B**   The net cost of the position is 40 – 3 = $37. If the stock price at expiration is ≥44, the gain on the position is $7. If the stock price were to fall to zero, the investor would lose $37. (Study Session 17, LOS 59.b)

112. **A**   Before expiration, an option can have a price greater than its exercise or intrinsic value. This amount by which an option's price is greater than its exercise value is referred to as its time value. (Study Session 17, LOS 58.j)

113. **B**   The counterparties do not exchange the notional principal on an interest rate swap. (Study Session 17, LOS 57.c)

114. **A**   Convenience yield refers to the nonmonetary benefits of holding an asset, for example being in a position to sell an overvalued asset that is difficult to sell short. Convenience yield does not include monetary benefits such as interest and dividend income. The costs of holding the asset, net of the monetary and nonmonetary benefits of holding it, is referred to as the net cost of carry. (Study Session 17, LOS 58.d)

115. **C**   If the margin account balance falls below the maintenance margin level, the account must be brought back up to the initial margin amount. (Study Session 17, LOS 57.c)

©2014 Kaplan, Inc.

116. **A** The asset-based approach uses either the liquidation values or fair market values of assets. The discounted cash flow approach involves calculating the present value of expected future cash flows. The comparables-based approach uses market or private transaction values of similar companies to estimate multiples of EBITDA, net income, or revenue. (Study Session 18, LOS 60.e)

117. **C** Because a hedge fund database only includes the more stable funds that have survived, the risk measure of hedge funds as an asset class is biased downward. (Study Session 18, LOS 60.e)

118. **A** Real estate and commodities offer potential hedges against inflation because rents, property values, and commodity prices tend to increase with inflation in the long term. (Study Session 18, LOS 60.d)

119. **B** In a secondary sale, a private equity firm sells one of its portfolio companies to a group of investors or another private equity firm. (Study Session 18, LOS 60.d)

120. **B** The notice period is the time within which a hedge fund must fulfill a request for redemption of shares. The period during which investors may not redeem shares is called a lockup period. (Study Session 18, LOS 60.d)

Exam 2
Afternoon Session Answer Key

To get valuable feedback on how your score compares to those of other Level I candidates, use your Username and Password to gain online access at Schweser.com and select "Performance Tracker" from your dashboard.

1. B	31. C	61. B	91. B
2. C	32. A	62. A	92. C
3. A	33. A	63. C	93. C
4. A	34. C	64. B	94. C
5. A	35. A	65. A	95. B
6. C	36. B	66. A	96. B
7. C	37. A	67. A	97. B
8. A	38. B	68. B	98. B
9. B	39. B	69. B	99. B
10. A	40. C	70. C	100. C
11. B	41. B	71. A	101. C
12. A	42. C	72. C	102. A
13. A	43. C	73. C	103. C
14. C	44. B	74. C	104. B
15. A	45. A	75. B	105. C
16. B	46. C	76. C	106. B
17. B	47. C	77. C	107. B
18. A	48. B	78. A	108. A
19. C	49. C	79. A	109. A
20. B	50. B	80. B	110. A
21. C	51. B	81. A	111. A
22. B	52. C	82. B	112. B
23. B	53. A	83. A	113. B
24. A	54. A	84. A	114. C
25. C	55. A	85. C	115. B
26. C	56. B	86. A	116. B
27. C	57. C	87. B	117. B
28. C	58. C	88. B	118. A
29. B	59. B	89. A	119. A
30. B	60. C	90. A	120. B

©2014 Kaplan, Inc.

Exam 2
Afternoon Session Answers

Answers referencing the Standards of Practice address Study Session 1, LOS 1.b, c and LOS 2.a, b, c, except where noted.

1. **B** According to Standard VII(B) Reference to the CFA Institute, the CFA Designation, and CFA Program, citing an expected date for completing a level of the CFA Program is a misuse of the CFA designation.

2. **C** All investment personnel in this example are subject to the CFA Institute Code and Standards as part of the firm's established policies. The candidate's reference to her Level III status and the inclusion of such information in her biographical information is not in violation of the CFA Institute Code and Standards. Candidates may clearly reference their participation in the CFA program, provided such reference does not imply the achievement of any type of partial designation. The analyst is considered a candidate since she is registered to take the next scheduled examination. The Code and Standards prohibit using material nonpublic information. Since the Code and Standards are *stricter* than the local law, they must be followed by the analyst. The junior analyst failed to exercise diligence and thoroughness in making investment recommendations and failed to have a reasonable and adequate basis for such recommendations.

3. **A** Standard VI(B) Priority of Transactions recommends, but does not require, that a member or candidate obtain pre-clearance from his or her supervisor before participating in an equity IPO. Guidance for Standard III(B) Fair Dealing states that members and candidates distributing IPO shares must distribute shares in an oversubscribed IPO to clients and may not withhold shares for themselves.

4. **A** To comply with Standard IV(B) Additional Compensation Arrangements, Bryant must obtain written consent from her employer before undertaking the independent consulting project. Bryant must also provide a description of the types of services being provided, the length of time the arrangement will last, and the compensation she expects to receive for her services.

5. **A** Standard V(C) Record Retention requires members to maintain records of the data and analysis they use to develop their research recommendations. Recommendations may be brief, in capsule form, or simply a list of buy/sell recommendations. A list of recommendations may be sent without regard to suitability, including both safe income stocks and aggressive growth stocks, for example.

6. **C** Standard IV(C) Responsibilities of Supervisors indicates that a member should decline supervisory responsibility in writing until the firm adopts reasonable compliance procedures. Otherwise, Brooks cannot adequately exercise her responsibility.

7. **C** Standard III(D) Performance Presentation recommends that terminated accounts be *included* in historical performance calculations.

8. **A**   Standard V(B) Communication with Clients and Prospective Clients requires that Toma separate opinion from fact. Toma's statement that excess demand will persist into the foreseeable future is an opinion, not a fact. Toma has established a reasonable basis for his recommendation through his analysis. Suitability does not become an issue until a client chooses to act on Toma's recommendation.

9. **B**   Under Standard III(A) Loyalty, Prudence, and Care, the fiduciary duty in this case is to plan participants and beneficiaries, not shareholders or plan trustees.

10. **A**   According to Standard III(B) Fair Dealing, if a client places an order that goes against the firm's recommendation for that security, members and candidates should inform the client of the discrepancy between the order and the firm's recommendation before accepting the order.

11. **B**   Private equity is one of the nine major sections of the GIPS standards; the others are not. (Study Session 1, LOS 4.d)

12. **A**   The trader has carried out an arbitrage transaction. Because she did not exhibit any intent to distort prices or trading volume, the member did not violate Standard II(B) Market Manipulation. Standard III(B) Fair Dealing is concerned with fair treatment of clients and is not relevant to this transaction.

13. **A**   Hoffman has violated both Standard I(B) Independence and Objectivity, which specifically addresses the requirement of disclosure of the nature of any compensation from the subject company, and Standard VI(A) Disclosure of Conflicts, which, more generally, requires disclosure of any potential conflict of interest in research reports and investment recommendations.

14. **C**   To comply with Standard VI(A) Disclosure of Conflicts, both the market-making activities by the firm and the directorship held by a principal in the firm must be disclosed.

15. **A**   According to Standard II(A) Material Nonpublic Information, Farr is free to act under the mosaic theory because nonmaterial nonpublic information does not fall within the prohibition on trading based on material nonpublic information. He should keep detailed documentation of his analysis to document that he did not advise or act based on material nonpublic information.

16. **B**   GIPS require firms that claim compliance to maintain written documentation of their policies and procedures for complying with GIPS. Verification of GIPS compliance is optional. In order to initially claim compliance with GIPS, a firm must have a minimum of five years (or since firm inception) of GIPS-compliant data. After the first compliant presentation, another year of compliant performance must be added each year until the compliant performance history reaches at least ten years. (Study Session 1, LOS 3.c, 4.b)

17. **B**   Standard VI(C) Referral Fees states that members and candidates must disclose to employers and to affected prospects and clients, before entering into any formal agreement for services, any benefits received for the recommendation of services provided by the member.

18. **A**   Michaels has violated Standard II(A) Material Nonpublic Information. Members who possess material nonpublic information are prohibited from acting or causing others to act on that information. She may not share the information with anyone except designated supervisory or compliance employees within her firm. Disclosing to her supervisor, who is not identified as a designated supervisor of compliance issues, is not permitted.

   ©2014 Kaplan, Inc.

19. **C**   If *p* is the probability that an event occurs, then the odds for the event occurring are expressed as p / (1 − p), or the probability that the event occurs divided by the probability that the event does not occur. The odds against the event are expressed as the reciprocal of the odds for the event. (Study Session 2, LOS 8.c)

20. **B**   The investor has to ensure that the amount deposited now will grow into the amount needed to fund the perpetuity. With semiannual compounding, the effective annual rate (EAR) earned on funds in the account is:

$$EAR = \left(1 + \frac{annual\ rate}{2}\right)^2 - 1 = \left(1 + \frac{0.04}{2}\right)^2 - 1 = 0.0404 = 4.04\%$$

The present value of the perpetuity = \$25,000/0.0404 = \$618,811.88.

Note that since the first scholarship award is paid out in four years, the present value of the perpetuity represents the amount that must be in the account at time t = 3. We can find the required deposit from:

$$FV = -618{,}811.88;\ N = 3;\ I = 4.04;\ CPT \rightarrow PV = \$549{,}487.24\ or\ \frac{618{,}811.88}{1.0404^3}$$

(Study Session 2, LOS 5.c, d, e)

21. **C**   If a return distribution has positive excess kurtosis, statistical models that do not account for the fatter tails will underestimate the likelihood of very bad or very good outcomes. A distribution with positive skewness will have a mean greater than the median and larger average positive deviations than average negative deviations. (Study Session 2, LOS 7.j, k, l)

22. **B**   When testing hypotheses about the population mean, the sample standard deviation must be used in the denominator of the test statistic when the population standard deviation is unknown, the population is normal, and/or the sample is large. The statistic is a *t*-stat with n − 1 degrees of freedom. The numerator is the sampling error for the population mean if the true mean is μ_0 and the denominator is the standard error of the sample mean around the true mean. (Study Session 3, LOS 11.g)

23. **B**   Dividing the covariance between returns of two assets by the individual *standard deviations* of returns of the two assets yields the correlation coefficient. (Study Session 2, LOS 8.k)

24. **A**   The data are cross-sectional, which means that it is a sample of observations taken at a single point in time. Time-series data are observations taken at specific and equally spaced points in time (for example, the monthly returns on a specific stock for the period January 1 through December 31 of a given year). The sampling error is the difference between a sample statistic (here, the mean) and the corresponding population parameter, or 10.5 − 9.7 = 0.8. The sample statistic (here, the mean) is itself a random variable and has its own probability distribution. (Study Session 3, LOS 10.d)

25. **C**   Relative strength charts display the price of an asset relative to the price of another asset or benchmark over time. This type of chart is useful for demonstrating whether one asset class or market has outperformed or underperformed another. Candlestick charts and point-and-figure charts are generally used to display price patterns for a single asset or market over time. (Study Session 3, LOS 12.b, h)

26. **C** The standard deviation of two stocks that are perfectly positively correlated is the weighted average of the standard deviations: 0.5(18.9) + 0.5(14.73) = 16.82%. This relationship is true only when the correlation is one. Otherwise, you must use the formula:

$$\sigma_p = \sqrt{w_1^2\sigma_1^2 + w_2^2\sigma_2^2 + 2w_1w_2\sigma_1\sigma_2\rho_{1,2}}$$

(Study Session 2, LOS 8.l)

27. **C** The Sharpe measure for a portfolio is calculated as the (mean portfolio return – mean return on the risk-free asset)/portfolio standard deviation. The Sharpe measures for the three mutual funds are:

mutual fund P = (13 – 5) / 18 = 0.44
mutual fund Q = (15 – 5) / 20 = 0.50
mutual fund R = (18 – 5) / 24 = 0.54

Assuming that investors prefer return and dislike risk, they should prefer portfolios with large Sharpe ratios to those with smaller ratios. Thus, the investor should prefer mutual fund R. (Study Session 2, LOS 7.i)

28. **C** When order of selection matters, as it does here, use the permutation formula:

$$_nP_r = \frac{n!}{(n-r)!}$$

$_nP_r$ = 6! / (6 – 3)! = (6 × 5 × 4 × 3 × 2 × 1) / (3 × 2 × 1) = (6 × 5 × 4) = 120

(Study Session 2, LOS 8.o)

29. **B** The standard error of the sample mean can be estimated by dividing the population standard deviation by $\sqrt{n}$. (Study Session 3, LOS 10.e, f)

30. **B** Given that the population variance is unknown and the sample size is large, the 95% confidence interval for the population mean is:

$$\bar{x} \pm z_{\alpha/2}\frac{s}{\sqrt{n}}$$

The confidence interval is:

$$1.7 \pm 1.96\left(\frac{0.4}{\sqrt{100}}\right) = 1.7 \pm 1.96(0.04) = 1.7 \pm 0.0784 = 1.622 \text{ to } 1.778.$$

(Study Session 3, LOS 10.j)

31. **C** This is a test of the value of a single variance and is based on a test statistic with a performed via the chi-square distribution. (Study Session 3, LOS 11.j)

32. **A** The forecast resistance levels are one-half, five-eighths, and two-thirds of the price decrease from $180 to $100. All of these are Fibonacci ratios. Projecting from the breakout of an inverse head and shoulders pattern would more likely suggest a single price target or range than three different specific targets. Moving average convergence/divergence lines are unlikely to be used for price targeting because they are not on the same scale as prices. (Study Session 3, LOS 12.d, e, g)

©2014 Kaplan, Inc.

33. **A** Price discrimination involves a single product, not two alternatives. As long as the company faces a downward-sloping demand curve, can identify at least two groups of customers with different price elasticities of demand, and can prevent reselling between groups, the company can profit from price discrimination. (Study Session 4, LOS 16.b, d)

34. **C** Automatic stabilizers are built-in features that tend to automatically promote a budget deficit during a recession and a budget surplus during an inflationary boom, without a change in policy. (Study Session 5, LOS 19.o)

35. **A** Short-run equilibrium may occur above full employment, for example as a result of an increase in aggregate demand caused by a decrease in taxes. Both employment and the price level increase in the short run. Above-full employment causes upward pressure on wages that will reduce short-run aggregate supply until, in the long run, output returns to its full-employment level with a still-higher equilibrium price level. (Study Session 5, LOS 17.k)

36. **B** A firm will increase production if its marginal revenue is greater than its marginal cost, until it reaches the profit-maximizing output level at which marginal revenue equals marginal cost. Under perfect competition, marginal revenue equals price. (Study Session 4, LOS 15.f, 16.d)

37. **A** For the base period, three years ago, the real exchange rate is the same as the nominal exchange rate, 1.32 USD/EUR. The real exchange rate over the period has changed from 1.32 to 1.40 × (112 / 118) = 1.3288. This increase in the real USD/EUR exchange rate indicates that the base currency (EUR) has appreciated in real terms, so that eurozone goods are now more expensive in real terms to U.S. consumers. (Study Session 6, LOS 21.a)

38. **B** There is a market equilibrium at a price of 250, where $Q_S = 750$ and $Q_D = 750$. Although the supply curve is downward sloping, the equilibrium is stable because the supply curve intersects the demand curve from above—the slope of the supply curve (–1/3) is steeper than the slope of the demand curve (–1/5). (Study Session 4, LOS 13.f)

39. **B** Differentiated products are a feature of monopolistic competition markets. Interdependence is a characteristic of oligopoly markets. Horizontal demand curves facing producers are a feature of perfect competition. (Study Session 4, LOS 16.a)

40. **C** The Fisher effect states that a nominal interest rate is the sum of a real interest rate and the expected inflation rate. (Study Session 5, LOS 19.e)

41. **B** Falling money wages would cause businesses to increase (profit-maximizing) output levels at each price level for final goods and services. Changes in the price level of goods and services are represented by a movement along a short-run aggregate supply curve, not a shift in the curve. A rise in resource prices will decrease aggregate supply. An increase in government spending will shift the aggregate demand curve but not the aggregate supply curve. (Study Session 5, LOS 17.h)

42. **C** At the end or peak of an expansion, economic activity begins to slow, sales are less than planned, and excess inventory accumulates, increasing inventory-to-sales ratios. To reduce inventory-to-sales ratios to desired levels, firms decrease production, which is one of the causes of a contraction. (Study Session 5, LOS 18.b)

43. **C** In a descending price or Dutch auction, the government will sell bonds to the bidders who bid the lowest yields (highest prices) until all the bonds are sold. Bidder 1 receives 200 bonds at a yield of 5.25%, Bidder 2 receives 100 bonds at a yield of 5.30%, and Bidder 3 receives the remaining 200 bonds at a yield of 5.40%. (Study Session 4, LOS 13.i)

44. **B** In the short run, the average product of labor curve is first increasing and then decreasing as diminishing marginal returns to that factor take effect. In the short run, the marginal product of labor is first increasing and then decreasing when diminishing marginal returns take effect. The marginal product of labor curve will be above the average product of labor curve initially, and, at some point, will intersect the average product curve at its maximum. When the total product of labor begins to increase at a decreasing rate, the average product of labor will be decreasing. (Study Session 4, LOS 15.j)

45. **A** The $478,000 is unearned revenue, a liability. The $2.3 million owed to the government but not yet paid is income tax payable, also a liability. Deferred tax accounts arise from temporary differences between tax reporting and financial reporting. (Study Session 7, LOS 23.a, d)

46. **C** The installment method should be used when future cash collection cannot be reasonably estimated. For long-term projects, a firm should use percentage of completion when payment is reasonably assured and the firm can reliably estimate the project's outcome, and completed contract when the firm cannot estimate the outcome reliably. (Study Session 8, LOS 25.b)

47. **C** Use the direct method.

Collections from customers	$5,000
Cash expenses	−$2,000
Cash flow from operations	$3,000

Cash expenses are given. If you had been given COGS, you would need to adjust that for inventory changes to get cash expenses for inputs. Depreciation is a non-cash change.

Changes in depreciation are used with the indirect method. Net change in cash will reflect CFI and CFF, not just CFO. (Study Session 8, LOS 27.f)

48. **B** Using the indirect method requires adjusting for change in working capital accounts such as accounts receivable, inventory, and accounts payable. (Study Session 8, LOS 27.f)

49. **C** In a period of rising prices, LIFO results in higher COGS, lower inventory balances, and lower gross profit, as compared to FIFO. In a falling price environment, these effects are the opposite. Working capital (current assets minus current liabilities) is higher under FIFO in a rising price environment because inventories are higher. (Study Session 9, LOS 29.c, e)

50. **B** In the case where insurance premiums paid are not tax deductible, taxes would be higher so the effective tax rate (tax expense / pretax income) would be higher. Expenses on the income statement that are not deductible for tax and will not reverse are permanent differences and will not affect deferred tax items. (Study Session 9, LOS 31.i)

51. **B** Operating profit margin can be read directly from a common-size income statement. Asset turnover and return on equity mix balance sheet and income statement items. (Study Session 8, LOS 25.i, j, 28.b)

©2014 Kaplan, Inc.

52. **C**   Use the Treasury stock method:

    Step 1:   Determine the number of common shares created if the warrants are exercised = 100,000.

    Step 2:   Calculate the cash inflow if the warrants are exercised: (100,000)($50 per share) = $5,000,000.

    Step 3:   Calculate the number of shares that can be purchased with these funds using the average market price ($60 per share): 5,000,000 / 60 = 83,333 shares.

    Step 4:   Calculate the net increase in common shares outstanding from the exercise of the warrants: 100,000 − 83,333 = 16,667.

    Step 5:   Add the net increase in common shares from the exercise of the warrants to the number of common shares outstanding for the entire year: 1,000,000 + 16,667 = 1,016,667.

    (Study Session 8, LOS 25.g)

53. **A**   Unless impairment has been recognized, land is reported at historical cost and is not subject to depreciation. Increases in value are not reflected in balance sheet values under U.S. GAAP. (Study Session 8, LOS 26.e)

54. **A**   The income statement reports the amounts for each of the major line items within the general categories of revenues and expenses. The various accruals, adjustments, and management assumptions are implicit in the reported amounts but are not specifically explained in the income statement. Much of the detail contained in various accruals, adjustments, and management assumptions that go into the financial statements can be found in the footnotes to the statements and Management's Discussion and Analysis. Supplementary schedules contain additional information, including a more detailed breakdown of certain large account balances. (Study Session 7, LOS 22.c)

55. **A**   The income statement shows an extraordinary item, which is permitted under U.S. GAAP but not under IFRS. From this we can conclude that the firm reports under U.S. GAAP. U.S. GAAP requires dividends received to be classified as CFO, while IFRS allows them to be classified as either CFO or CFI. A firm reporting under U.S. GAAP may not revalue assets upward but may use LIFO. (Study Session 8, LOS 25.e, 26.e, 27.c)

56. **B**   The installment sales method of revenue recognition does not result in permanent differences between pretax and taxable income. Premium payments on life insurance of key employees is an expense on the financial statements, but is not deducted on tax returns. Tax exempt interest is recognized as revenue on the financial statements. These items result in permanent differences between pretax income and taxable income. (Study Session 9, LOS 31.f)

57. **C**   The IASB Conceptual Framework for Financial Reporting describes the two fundamental qualitative characteristics of financial statements as relevance and faithful representation. The Conceptual Framework lists timeliness, comparability, verifiability, and understandability as characteristics that enhance relevance and faithful representation. (Study Session 7, LOS 24.d)

58. **C**   For a firm using FIFO, gross profit is the same whether the firm uses a periodic or perpetual inventory system. For a firm using LIFO or average cost, gross profit can be different depending on the choice of inventory system. (Study Session 9, LOS 29.d)

59. **B** Operating leases are not recognized as liabilities and therefore the debt-to-equity ratio will be lower than a similar finance lease. Capitalizing a lease will increase the asset base and decrease asset turnover. Lease capitalization decreases the operating cash outflow and therefore increases operating cash flows (all else equal). (Study Session 9, LOS 32.g)

60. **C** When a firm capitalizes costs, it classifies the cash outflow as CFI rather than CFO. The result is higher CFO compared to expensing the same costs. (Study Session 9, LOS 30.a and Study Session 10, LOS 33.h)

61. **B** A mindset that allows rationalization is the third important condition underlying low-quality financial reporting. Poor financial controls are an example of opportunity and pressure to meet earnings expectations is a possible motivation. (Study Session 10, LOS 33.e)

62. **A** Banks often present liquidity-based balance sheets, which list all assets and liabilities in order of liquidity, because for banks this format is typically more relevant and reliable than a classified balance sheet. Firms in most other industries typically present classified balance sheets. (Study Session 8, LOS 26.c)

63. **C** When stated on a per-share basis, different companies' financial data cannot be compared meaningfully because they depend on the number of shares outstanding, which is unrelated to the companies' operating performance or profitability. Earnings per share and cash flow per share are inputs into valuation ratios such as price/earnings and price/cash flow, which may be used to compare different stocks. (Study Session 8, LOS 28.e)

64. **B** Under IFRS, when an asset is permanently impaired, it must be written down to its recoverable amount (greater of value in use or fair value less selling costs) in the period in which the impairment is recognized. (Study Session 9, LOS 30.h)

65. **A** This is a discount bond since the market interest rate at issuance exceeds the coupon rate. The initial liability is equal to the proceeds received when the bond was issued. We can find this amount from the following calculation: FV = 50,000,000; N = 10; I = 3.5; PMT = 1,500,000; CPT → PV = $47,920,848.67. Change N to 8 and calculate PV to get liability value at the beginning of the second year of the bond's life, 48,281,511. Interest expense for the next semiannual period is 48,281,511(0.035) = $1,689,853. The subsequent change in the market rate has no effect on the amortization of the discount. (Study Session 9, LOS 32.a, b)

66. **A** For firms that revalue assets upward, IFRS requires disclosure of the date the asset was revalued, how management determined its fair value, the asset's carrying value using the historical cost model, and (for intangible assets) whether the asset's useful life is finite or indefinite. Although assets and shareholders' equity will increase as a result of the revaluation, net income will not increase. The increase in the value of the asset is reported as a revaluation surplus in shareholders' equity. Amortization expense will not increase because indefinite-lived intangible assets are not amortized. (Study Session 9, LOS 30.e, g, j)

67. **A** Goodwill has an indefinite life and is not amortized. A trademark or other intangible asset that has an expiration date but is renewable at minimal cost is treated as having an indefinite life and is not amortized. The patent has a finite life and its cost will be amortized at the rate of $1 million each year over ten years under the straight-line method. (Study Session 9, LOS 30.f)

©2014 Kaplan, Inc.

68. **B**   Reducing the numerator and denominator by the same amount will increase a ratio that is greater than one and decrease a ratio that is less than one. (Study Session 8, LOS 28.b)

69. **B**   Selecting an external auditor (subject to shareholder approval) is a responsibility of the Board's audit committee. (Study Session 11, LOS 40.e)

70. **C** $k_{ce} = D_1/P_0 + g = (3)(1.05)/(31.50) + 0.05 = 0.15$ or 15%

$k_d(1 - t) = 10\%(1 - 0.4) = 6\%$

If the company has a debt-to-equity ratio of 0.5, it will have \$0.50 in debt for each \$1.00 in equity. V = debt + equity = 0.5 + 1 = 1.5. Therefore, the weight is 33.3% (0.5 / 1.5) for the debt component and 66.7% (1.0 / 1.5) for the equity component.

$$WACC = \frac{D}{V}(k_{debt})(1-t) + \left(\frac{E}{V}\right)k_s = 0.333(6.0\%) + 0.677(15\%) = 2\% + 10\% = 12\%.$$

(Study Session 11, LOS 36.h)

71. **A**   The 19th space is neither an incremental cost, nor an opportunity cost or a type of cannibalization. It is a sunk cost since the firm has already committed to parking for 20 taxis. The cost of the 19th parking space is not directly relevant to the capital budgeting decision. (Study Session 11, LOS 35.b)

72. **C**   Risky projects will seem relatively more attractive than they actually are, causing them to be undertaken a disproportionately high percentage of the times they are considered. (Study Session 11, LOS 36.a)

73. **C**   When companies that require shareholder attendance to vote hold their meetings on the same day but in different locations, it prevents shareholders from attending all the meetings and therefore exercising their full voting rights. (Study Session 11, LOS 40.g)

74. **C**   The firm should reject both projects.

	0	*1*	*2*	*3*	*4*	*5*	*6*
Project J:	−\$12,000	\$4,000	\$5,000	\$6,000			
Project K:	−\$20,000	\$3,000	\$3,000	\$3,000	\$5,000	\$8,000	\$8,000

Project J: I/Y = 12; CF_0 = (12,000); CF_1 = 4,000; CF_2 = 5,000; CF_3 = 6,000; CPT → NPV = −172.

Project K: same process. NPV = −1,025. (Study Session 11, LOS 35.d)

75. **B**   Given that they have the same amount of sales and Acme's receivables turnover (sales/average accounts receivable) is higher, Acme must have lower average accounts receivable than Butler. Given that they have equal quick ratios, subtracting accounts receivable from the numerators of the quick ratios of both firms will produce a cash ratio for Butler that is lower than the cash ratio for Acme. (Study Session 11, LOS 39.b)

76. **C**   The book value of Daker shares is (£140 million − £85 million) / 11 million = £5 per share. Repurchasing its shares at a price equal to book value will not change the book value of Daker shares. (Study Session 11, LOS 38.e)

77. **C**   The firm would not want to exhaust its capital budget on "bad" projects, (i.e., projects with IRR < cost of capital [NPV < 0]). They should continue to invest as long as the project's return is greater than the marginal cost of capital of the firm. When the project's IRR = cost of capital, the NPV = 0. This project will only make the firm larger; it will add nothing to the stock price. The investment opportunity schedule plots expected project returns from highest to lowest IRR. (Study Session 11, LOS 36.d)

78. **A**   Banks typically need to maintain excess reserves in order to meet regulatory requirements. As a result, a bank must invest in assets that are more conservative than those invested by other types of financial institutions. An endowment will usually have significant long-term spending requirements in addition to its current expenses. Thus, a college endowment should accept higher risk in order to attain the returns indicated by its mandate. A mutual fund company may invest in many types of securities depending on the type of funds being managed. Investments may range from conservative money market funds to more aggressive derivatives. Therefore, a mutual fund company's level of risk tolerance may be greater than or less than those of a bank or endowment. (Study Session 12, LOS 42.b)

79. **A**   Promised retirement payments from a defined benefit pension plan are an obligation of the sponsoring firm. A defined contribution plan does not promise a specific periodic payment after retirement and the firm's obligations are limited to its promised contributions to current employees' accounts. (Study Session 12, LOS 41.c)

80. **B**   Although the risk measure on the capital market line diagram is total risk, all portfolios that lie on the CML are well diversified and have only systematic risk. This is because portfolios on the CML are all constructed from the risk-free asset and the (well-diversified) market portfolio. Any portfolio, including single securities, will plot along the SML in equilibrium. Their unsystematic risk can be significant, but it is not measured on the SML diagram because unsystematic risk is not related to expected return. Both the CML and the SML reflect relations that hold when prices are in equilibrium. (Study Session 12, LOS 43.f)

81. **A**   Portfolio X has a lower expected return and a higher standard deviation than Portfolio Y. X must be inefficient. (Study Session 12, LOS 42.g)

82. **B**   In addition to the three factors of the Fama and French model, market-to-book, firm size, and excess returns on the market, Carhart added a momentum factor based on prior relative price performance. (Study Session 12, LOS 43.d)

83. **A**   An IPS requires an investor to consider and articulate his objectives and constraints. It also provides an objective standard by which the portfolio's performance will be judged by specifying a benchmark portfolio. Guidance for Standard III(C) Suitability requires members to prepare IPS when beginning advisory relationships with clients. Asset allocation is determined after strategy is developed and capital market conditions are assessed. (Study Session 12, LOS 41.d, 44.a)

84. **A**   Stock A: k_A = 8% + 1.5(7%) = 18.5%. Because the estimated return of 18.1% is less than the required return of 18.5%, Stock A is *overvalued*.

Stock B: k_B = 8% + 1.1(7%) = 15.7%. Because the estimated return of 15.7% equals the required return of 15.7%, Stock B is *properly valued*.

Stock C: k_C = 8% + 0.6(7%) = 12.2%. Because the estimated return of 12.5% is greater than the required return of 12.2%, Stock C is *undervalued*. (Study Session 12, LOS 43.h)

©2014 Kaplan, Inc.

85. **C** Stocks of cyclical firms, such as homebuilders, tend to have high systematic risk (i.e., high beta). Stocks of noncyclical firms, such as utility or health care companies, tend to respond less to changes in systematic risk factors (i.e., they have low betas). (Study Session 12, LOS 43.c, e, and Study Session 14, LOS 49.c)

86. **A** The price return on the index does not include cash dividends. Since the reinvested dividends will add to the number of shares of those stocks that pay dividends, Gomez's portfolio return (total return) will be higher than the price return on the index. The relative performance of high-priced and low-priced stocks does not affect this result. (Study Session 13, LOS 46.b)

87. **B** Good-till-cancelled is a validity instruction, which indicates when an order may be filled. Execution instructions include limit orders and market orders, as well as instructions regarding trade size and visibility. A clearing instruction indicates how to arrange final settlement of the trade. (Study Session 13, LOS 45.g)

88. **B** The owner of a sponsored DR share has the same voting rights and receives the same dividends as the owner of a common share of the firm. With an unsponsored DR, the depository bank retains the voting rights. A global depository receipt may be sponsored or unsponsored. (Study Session 14, LOS 48.d)

89. **A** Peer groups should include comparable companies with similar business activities. An analyst can appropriately include a company in multiple peer groups if the company's business activities are comparable to firms in more than one peer group. (Study Session 14, LOS 49.d)

90. **A** dividend payout = 1 − earnings retention rate = 1 − 0.6 = 0.4

$$R_S = R_f + \beta(R_{mkt} - RFR) = 0.05 + 1.0(0.10 - 0.05) = 0.10$$

g = (retention rate)(ROE) = (0.6)(0.10) = 0.06

$$P/E = \frac{\text{dividend payout}}{k-g} = \frac{0.4}{0.10-0.06} = 10$$

price = (E)(P/E) = (2)(10) = $20

Alternatively, dividend will be 40% of $2 earnings or $0.80, and $\frac{0.80}{0.10-0.06} = \$20$

(Study Session 14, LOS 50.e)

91. **B** The individual security weights in an equal-weighted index must be rebalanced periodically to restore equal weights as security prices change over time. The weights in a price-weighted index are determined by securities prices. Market capitalization-weighted indexes are self-adjusting to a large extent. (Study Session 13, LOS 46.c, f, k)

92. **C** Security market indexes may be used as benchmarks for the performance of active managers, but the index chosen should represent the universe of securities from which the manager is choosing. Here, an index of high yield bonds would be a more appropriate benchmark. (Study Session 13, LOS 46.g)

93. **C**   While an increase in a firm's ROE due to a sharp increase in earnings will, if unexpected, lead to an increase in the intrinsic value of its shares, an increase in a firm's ROE due to the repurchase of stock with debt will not necessarily increase the intrinsic value of the firm's shares, as any increase in ROE may be offset by an increase in the risk inherent in the firm's shares. (Study Session 14, LOS 48.h)

94. **C**   The short seller loses if the stock price increases. The other choices are accurate statements. (Study Session 13, LOS 45.e)

95. **B**   Bond indexes are more difficult to build and maintain than stock indexes for several reasons. Bonds in an index have to be replaced as they mature, so turnover is likely to be greater in a bond index than in a stock index. Many bonds lack the continuous trade data that exists for exchange-traded equities. (Study Session 13, LOS 46.i)

96. **B**   You can select the correct answer without calculating the share values. Royal is using a shorter period of supernormal growth and a higher required rate of return on the stock. Both of these factors will contribute to a lower value using the multistage DDM.

$$\text{Knight: } \frac{\$1(1.10)}{1.09} + \frac{\$1(1.10)^2}{1.09^2} + \frac{\$1(1.10)^3 / (0.09 - 0.04)}{1.09^2} = \$24.43$$

$$\text{Royal: } \frac{\$1(1.10)}{1.10} + \frac{\$1(1.10)^2 / (0.10 - 0.04)}{1.10} = \$19.33$$

Royal's valuation is $5.10 less that Knight's valuation. (Study Session 14, LOS 50.e)

97. **B**   An industry in the growth stage is usually characterized by increasing profitability, decreasing prices, and a low degree of competition among competitors. (Study Session 14, LOS 49.h)

98. **B**   The market value of the Treasury note is the present value of the remaining coupons plus the present value of the principal, discounted at the semiannual rates available from dividing each annual spot rate in the table by two.

$$\text{value of T-note} = \frac{\$25}{(1.015)} + \frac{\$25}{(1.0175)^2} + \frac{\$25}{(1.02)^3} + \frac{\$1,025}{(1.0225)^4} = \$1,010.05$$

At $1,008, the T-note is priced below the present value of its cash flows ($1,010) and is therefore underpriced. (Study Session 15, LOS 53.c)

99. **B**   An issuer of a callable bond must compensate the bondholder when the issue is sold by offering a higher coupon rate or accepting a lower price than if the call feature was not included. Convexity will typically be much less than for an option-free bond, and reinvestment risk is greater for callable bonds. (Study Session 15, LOS 51.f, and Study Session 16, LOS 55.h)

100. **C**   The bond equivalent yield rate on the par bond (Z) is 6% or a 3% semiannual rate. The equivalent quarterly rate, $1.03^{1/2} - 1 = 0.014889$. Security X makes 20 quarterly payments of $15 and 20 quarterly payments of $20. We need to use the cash flow function as follows: $CF_0 = 0$; $CF_1 = 15$; $F_1 = 20$; $CF_2 = 20$; $F_2 = 19$; $CF_3 = 1,020$; $F_3 = 1$; $I = 1.4889$; $CPT \rightarrow NPV = \$1,067.27$. Note that CF_3 contains the final quarterly payment of $20 along with the $1,000 face value payment. (Study Session 15, LOS 53.f)

©2014 Kaplan, Inc.

101. **C** Yield spreads reflect the credit quality of bond issuers and the liquidity of the market for their bonds. Narrowing (decreasing) yield spreads reflect improving credit quality or more liquidity. Widening (increasing) yield spreads reflect deteriorating credit quality or less liquidity. Increased estimates of the recovery rate in the event of default represent an improvement in investors' assessment of the issuer's credit quality and are likely to narrow yield spreads on the issuer's bonds. (Study Session 16, LOS 56.a)

102. **A** The full price is clean price plus accrued interest. (Study Session 15, LOS 53.d)

103. **C** Reinvestment risk is a disadvantage of a sinking fund provision. Some bondholders will be repaid the bond principal earlier than the maturity date. If interest rates have declined since they bought the bonds, these bondholders will only be able to reinvest the returned principal at a lower rate of return. A sinking fund provision increases the credit quality of an issue and typically does not affect a bond's taxable status. (Study Session 15, LOS 51.e)

104. **B** Restricted subsidiaries are those whose cash flows and assets are designated to service the debt of their holding company. Classifying a subsidiary as restricted alleviates structural subordination by making holding company debt rank pari passu with the subsidiary's debt. (Study Session 16, LOS 56.j)

105. **C** If the prepayment speed is higher than the PAC collar, the support tranche receives more prepayments. The life of the support tranche will shorten. The PAC tranche *could* receive higher prepayments if the support tranche principal is fully repaid (i.e., a broken PAC). In this case, the support tranche is still outstanding, which means that hasn't happened yet. (Study Session 15, LOS 54.e)

106. **B** $\%\Delta price \approx -7.48(-0.0075) = 0.0561$
$\$1,018(1 + 0.0561) = \$1,075.11$ (Study Session 16, LOS 55.i)

107. **B** In a shelf registration, an entire issue is registered with securities regulators but the bonds are sold to the public over a period of time as the issuer needs to raise funds. In a serial bond issue, bonds with multiple maturity dates are issued at the same time. A waterfall structure is issued in tranches with differing priority of claims. (Study Session 15, LOS 52.c,f)

108. **A** If we want the 3-year forward rate in three years, the appropriate formula is:

$$3y3y = \left[\frac{(1+S_6)^6}{(1+S_3)^3}\right]^{1/3} - 1$$

S_6 = 6-year spot rate and S_3 = 3-year spot rate. (Study Session 15, LOS 53.h)

109. **A** This question does not require calculations. Because the return on reinvested coupon interest is less than the note's yield to maturity, the investor's realized yield on the note must be less than the YTM. Only Choice A can be correct. (Study Session 16, LOS 55.a)

110. **A** At expiration, the value to the holder (long position) of a put option on a stock is the greater of zero or the exercise price minus the stock price. If the stock price is greater than the exercise price, the value of a put option to the holder is zero and the holder will allow the option to expire unexercised. (Study Session 17, LOS 58.i)

111. **A** Powers is betting that the stock's price will not rise above $50. If she's right, she will pocket the $3.50 and lose nothing. If the stock rises above the strike price, she is losing all of the upside potential. Once the stock price rises above $53.50, the benefit of the strategy (i.e., the income generated by the option premium) is offset by the gain she has foregone on the stock. (Study Session 17, LOS 59.b)

112. **B** Restrictions on short sales may be an impediment to arbitrage when a security is overpriced relative to another security or derivative that has identical cash flows. Because arbitrage transactions are theoretically riskless, risk aversion should not be viewed as an impediment. The law of one price is the theory arbitrage trading will force two assets with the same cash flows toward the same price. (Study Session 17, LOS 57.e, 58.a)

113. **B** The put-call-forward parity relationship is the same as the standard put-call parity relationship, with the present value of the forward price substituted for the underlying asset. (Study Session 17, LOS 58.l, m)

114. **C** Over-the-counter derivatives are customized private contracts between counterparties. (Study Session 17, LOS 57.a)

115. **B** The price (or premium) of an option is its intrinsic value plus its time value. An out-of-the-money option has an intrinsic value of zero, so its entire premium consists of time value. Time value is zero at an option's expiration date. Time value is the amount by which an option's premium exceeds its intrinsic value. (Study Session 17, LOS 58.j, k)

116. **B** Returns on commodities over time have been lower than returns on global stocks or bonds, and price volatility has been higher. (Study Session 18, LOS 60.d)

117. **B** Macro strategy funds invest based on expected shifts of global economies, primarily in currency and interest rate derivatives. Quantitative directional funds take long and short positions in equities based on technical analysis. Event-driven funds seek to profit from investment strategies based on specific corporate events and one-time transactions. (Study Session 18, LOS 60.d)

118. **A** One of the ways to invest in real estate is by purchasing residential or commercial mortgage-backed securities. (Study Session 18, LOS 60.b)

119. **A** If a fund calculates a trading NAV, it will adjust market prices downward for securities in which it holds positions that are large relative to trading volume or total value outstanding and thus are less liquid. (Study Session 18, LOS 60.e)

120. **B** In the context of an LBO, mezzanine financing refers to debt that carries warrants or equity conversion features. This debt is typically subordinated to other bonds that are issued to finance the LBO. Committed capital is the investment of limited partners in a private equity fund and does not include debt that the fund issues to finance a particular LBO. (Study Session 18, LOS 60.d)

©2014 Kaplan, Inc.

Exam 3
Morning Session Answer Key

To get valuable feedback on how your score compares to those of other Level I candidates, use your Username and Password to gain online access at Schweser.com and select "Performance Tracker" from your dashboard.

1. B	31. B	61. C	91. A
2. C	32. B	62. C	92. C
3. A	33. C	63. A	93. B
4. A	34. C	64. B	94. B
5. A	35. A	65. C	95. C
6. B	36. B	66. A	96. B
7. B	37. A	67. C	97. C
8. A	38. B	68. B	98. B
9. A	39. B	69. A	99. B
10. C	40. C	70. B	100. B
11. A	41. B	71. B	101. B
12. A	42. C	72. B	102. B
13. A	43. B	73. A	103. C
14. C	44. B	74. A	104. C
15. A	45. C	75. C	105. B
16. B	46. C	76. C	106. B
17. C	47. B	77. C	107. A
18. A	48. C	78. C	108. B
19. B	49. C	79. C	109. C
20. C	50. B	80. C	110. C
21. B	51. A	81. A	111. A
22. A	52. A	82. B	112. B
23. A	53. B	83. B	113. B
24. B	54. A	84. B	114. C
25. A	55. B	85. B	115. A
26. A	56. C	86. B	116. B
27. B	57. C	87. A	117. B
28. C	58. A	88. C	118. A
29. C	59. A	89. A	119. A
30. A	60. B	90. A	120. C

Exam 3
Morning Session Answers

Answers referencing the Standards of Practice address Study Session 1, LOS 1.b, c and LOS 2.a, b, c, except where noted.

1. **B** Standard VI(C) Referral Fees requires members and candidates to disclose to clients and prospects any consideration or benefit received by the member for the recommendation of any service. "Soft dollars" refers to benefits received from client brokerage.

2. **C** Standard IV(C) Responsibilities of Supervisors explicitly states that speaking to the employee to determine the extent of the violations and receiving assurances that it will not be repeated is not enough. Finley must take positive steps to ensure that the violation will not be repeated, including promptly launching an investigation and limiting the employee's activities and/or increasing supervision of the employee until the results of the investigation are known.

3. **A** Stein violated Standard I(C) Misrepresentation by presenting material developed by another to her supervisor without disclosing that the work was not her own.

4. **A** Standard V(A) Diligence and Reasonable Basis states that if a consensus opinion has a reasonable basis, a member or candidate who disagrees with it does not have to dissociate from it but should document the difference of opinion.

5. **A** Under Standard IV(C) Responsibilities of Supervisors, if Klein clearly cannot discharge supervisory responsibilities because of an inadequate compliance system, he should decline in writing to accept the supervisory responsibility until the firm adopts reasonable procedures to allow him to adequately exercise such responsibility.

6. **B** Crocker is essentially using a soft-dollar arrangement to pay for research used in managing her clients' accounts. According to Standard III(A) Loyalty, Prudence, and Care, Crocker may pay higher fees without violating her fiduciary duty as long as the research benefits the firm's clients and the commission paid is reasonable in relation to the research and execution of services received.

7. **B** Standard IV(A) Loyalty does not prohibit former employees from contacting clients of their previous firm so long as the contact information does not come from the records of the previous employer or violate a noncompete agreement.

8. **A** Houser has not violated the Code and Standards. Guidance for Standard II(A) Material Nonpublic Information states that an analyst does not need to make his recommendations public just because investors would want to know about them, and is free to issue recommendations only to his clients. The guideline about what makes information material (i.e., investors would want to have the information before making an investment decision) applies to nonpublic information from the issuer of a security. An analyst covering the security, however, is not an insider with the issuing firm.

©2014 Kaplan, Inc.

9. A   To comply with Standard VI(A) Disclosure of Conflicts, members and candidates must make full disclosure of all matters that could impair their independence. Sell-side members and candidates should disclose to their clients any ownership in a security that they are recommending.

10. C   According to Standard IV(B) Additional Compensation Arrangements, members and candidates must obtain written permission from their employer before accepting an offer of compensation (for the performance of work done for their employer) in addition to what they receive from their employer and that is contingent on future performance.

11. A   Compliance requires that the firm follow local law and disclose the conflict between local law and GIPS. (Study Session 1, LOS 4.c)

12. A   Standard III(D) Performance Presentation requires that statements about performance be not only accurate but also fair and complete. While Vance's statement may be accurate in a technical sense, it is neither fair nor complete, and it seems intended to mislead prospects about Vance's past performance in managing equities accounts or selecting equity securities [and, thus, also likely violates Standard I(C) Misrepresentation]. While compliance with GIPS and its methods of composite construction and calculation are recommended, they are not required by the Standards.

13. A   It is not a violation of the Standards to present a recommended list of securities, some of which may not be suitable for some clients. It is permitted to present investment recommendations in capsule form as long as clients are informed that more information about the securities is available on request.

14. C   Farley is in violation of Standard VI(B) Priority of Transactions. Client transactions must take precedence over members' or candidates' trades. He should have submitted his personal trade order only after trading for his client. Standard III(B) Fair Dealing requires that Farley deal fairly with all clients when recommending securities or taking investment action. Since the endowment fund is Farley's only account, he has not disadvantaged any other client.

15. A   The Standards do not require that members put their employment ahead of their personal lives; these are issues between White and his employer. White's management of a fixed-income account does not compete with his employer's investment banking or equity-only account management business and is not expected to create a conflict with his employer. Therefore, it does not violate Standard IV(A) Loyalty or Standard IV(B) Additional Compensation Arrangements.

16. B   Dodd has most likely violated Standard III(B) Fair Dealing by giving Phillips an overgenerous allocation of the oversubscribed ("hot") new issue. The problem is not that he is offering compensation to a client to resolve a dispute but that by overallocating the IPO shares to Phillips, he is not treating his other clients fairly. Standard III(B) Fair Dealing requires that members and candidates not use shares of hot issues as an incentive to achieve a reward or benefit. The benefit in this case is that the dispute will be resolved. Dodd's actions do not exhibit any dishonesty that would violate Standard I(D) Misconduct, and Dodd is not receiving any additional compensation.

17. C   The nine major sections of the CFA Institute Global Investment Performance Standards are Fundamentals of Compliance, Input Data, Calculation Methodology, Composite Construction, Disclosures, Presentation and Reporting, Real Estate, Private Equity, and Wrap Fee/Separately Managed Account (SMA) Portfolios. (Study Session 1, LOS 4.d)

18. **A** Carson has not violated either Standard based on the information given. The suitability of an investment is to be determined based on the risk and return characteristics of the portfolio and not on the risk and return characteristics of each individual security. The fact that a security does not pay a dividend and has a beta higher than the market is not enough to determine its suitability in a portfolio context. The fact that regulators have called previously reported earnings into question does not necessarily mean that Carson's analysis was not diligent or that he did not have a reasonable basis for his selection of this security.

19. **B** With no interest paid on the original $5,000 loan, at 6% in five years the loan balance will be:

New loan balance = $5,000(1.06)^5 = $6,691.13 or PV = 5,000; I/Y = 6; N = 5; PMT = 0; CPT → FV = −$6,691.13.

$6,691.13 is the loan that has to be retired over the next five years. The financial calculator solution is:

PV = 6,691.13; I/Y = 6; N = 5; FV = 0; CPT → PMT. You obtain PMT = −1,588.45. (Study Session 2, LOS 5.e)

20. **C** N = 4; PMT = 0; PV = −4,000; FV = 6,520; CPT → I/Y = 12.99%,

or $\left(\dfrac{6{,}520}{4{,}000}\right)^{1/4} - 1 = 12.99\%$.

The question asks for the *effective* annual rate and gives the beginning and ending values. That the ending value was arrived at by monthly compounding is not relevant. (Study Session 2, LOS 5.c)

21. **B** Choice A describes a histogram, and Choice C describes a frequency polygon. (Study Session 2, LOS 7.d)

22. **A** holding period return (HPR) = $\dfrac{\text{ending value} + \text{dividends}}{\text{beginning value}} - 1$

$$HPR = \frac{10 + 50 + 105 + 2 + 4}{20 + 40 + 100} - 1 = 0.06875 = 6.875\%$$

(Study Session 2, LOS 6.c, 7.e)

23. **A** Calculate the mean: $\dfrac{25 + 15 + 35 + 45 + 55}{5} = 35$. To get the mean absolute deviation, sum the deviations around the mean (ignoring the sign), and divide by the number of observations $= \dfrac{10 + 20 + 0 + 10 + 20}{5} = 12$. (Study Session 2, LOS 7.g)

24. **B** $\text{mean} = \dfrac{5 + 10 + 15}{3} = 10$

population standard deviation $= \sqrt{\dfrac{(5-10)^2 + (10-10)^2 + (15-10)^2}{3}} = 4.0825$

$CV = \dfrac{\text{standard deviation}}{\text{mean}} = \dfrac{4.0825}{10} = 0.408$

(Study Session 2, LOS 7.i)

                                   ©2014 Kaplan, Inc.

25. **A** For the positively skewed distribution, the mode is less than the median, which is less than the mean. (Study Session 2, LOS 7.k)

26. **A** The probability of surviving to the end of the fifth year is the product of the probabilities of surviving in each year, or one minus the probability of failure. Therefore, the 5-year survival probability is $(1 - 0.25)(1 - 0.20)(1 - 0.20)(1 - 0.15)(1 - 0.10)$ = 0.3672.

   The present value of the expected payoff is $\dfrac{\$20,000(0.3672)}{1.25^5} = \$2,407.$

   (Study Session 2, LOS 8.i)

27. **B** The first year account return was $\dfrac{55}{42} - 1 = 31\%$. The second year return was $\dfrac{54}{55} - 1 = -1.8\%$. The geometric mean is $(1.31 \times 0.982)^{1/2} - 1 = 13.4\%$, which is the time-weighted return. Since only one asset was involved, $\left(\dfrac{54}{42}\right)^{1/2} - 1 = 13.4\%$ also gives the time-weighted return. To calculate the money-weighted return, use the cash flow function with Cf0 = −42,000, Cf1 = −55,000, and Cf2 = 54,000 × 2 = 108,000, and compute IRR, which is 7.73%. The money-weighted return is lower because the amount in the account was greater in the second period, when the return was poor. (Study Session 2, LOS 6.d)

28. **C** The binomial distribution is a discrete distribution, while the normal distribution is an example of a continuous distribution. Univariate distributions can be discrete or continuous. (Study Session 3, LOS 9.a)

29. **C** About 68% of all observations fall within ±1 standard deviation of the mean. Thus, about 68% of the values fall between 5 and 25. (Study Session 3, LOS 9.m)

30. **A** The central limit theorem holds for any distribution as long as the sample size is large (i.e., n > 30). (Study Session 3, LOS 10.e)

31. **B** The population variance is known (in this case 100), so the standard error of the sample mean is $\sigma/\sqrt{n} = \sqrt{100}/\sqrt{225} = 10/15 = 0.67$. (Study Session 3, LOS 10.f)

32. **B** The t-test must be used when the sample size is small, the population is normal, and the population variance is unknown. If the population is non-normal and the variance is unknown, there is no valid test statistic when the sample is small. (Study Session 3, LOS 11.d, f, g)

33. **C** Increased government borrowing would decrease, not increase, the profitability of corporate investment projects since it will tend to increase interest rates and required rates of return in general. (Study Session 5, LOS 19.q)

34. **C** If the domestic government collects the full value of the import license, a quota can have the same economic result as a tariff. Quota rents are the gains to those foreign exporters who receive import licenses under a quota if the domestic government does not charge for the import licenses. With respect to the importing country, import quotas, tariffs, and voluntary export restraints all decrease consumer surplus and increase producer surplus. (Study Session 6, LOS 20.e)

35. **A** The price coefficient of a complement in a demand function is negative. This means a decrease in the price of a complement to a good will increase the quantity demanded of that good. (Study Session 4, LOS 13.b)

36. **B** The manager's investment decisions are most consistent with expectations of a recessionary gap. In a recession, commodity prices and interest rates are likely to decrease. Decreasing interest rates should increase the prices of high-quality bonds. An inflationary gap would likely cause interest rates to increase, which would decrease bond prices. An inflationary gap or stagflation conditions would likely result in increasing commodity prices. (Study Session 5, LOS 17.i)

37. **A** The long-run production decision differs from the short-run production decision in that fixed costs can be changed in the long run but not the short run. Thus, short-run cost curves apply for a given size of a plant, and long-run cost curves can show costs for different size plants. (Study Session 4, LOS 15.h)

38. **B** To calculate the cross price elasticity of the quantity demanded of gasoline with respect to the price of bus travel, we must first calculate the quantity of gas demanded:

    $300 - 14(1.5) + 2(12) = 303$

    The cross elasticity is:

    $$\frac{\Delta Q_D}{\Delta P_{bus}} \times \frac{P_{bus}}{Q_D} = 2 \times \left(\frac{12}{303}\right) = 0.0792 \text{ or } 0.08$$

    (Study Session 4, LOS 13.m)

39. **B** In some cases, a monopolist may be unable to sell for a profit. Price may be insufficient to cover the per-unit cost of the monopolist, even when operating at the MR = MC rate of output. The monopolist faces a downward-sloping demand curve. (Study Session 4, LOS 16.a, b, d)

40. **C** These conditions characterize *monopolistic competition*. By contrast, monopolies and oligopolies have high barriers to entry and involve either a single seller (monopoly) or a small number of interdependent sellers (oligopoly). Similar to monopolistic competition, pure competition involves a large number of independent sellers. With pure competition, products are homogeneous (not differentiated), no barriers to entry exist (not low barriers to entry), and the demand schedule is horizontal (not downward sloping) and perfectly elastic (not highly elastic). (Study Session 4, LOS 16.h)

41. **B** The change from a forward premium to a forward discount means the forward rate expressed as PQR/XYZ was higher than the spot rate one year ago but is lower than the spot rate today. The relationship between spot rates, forward rates, and interest rates is:

    $$\frac{\text{forward}}{\text{spot}} = \frac{\left(1 + i_{price}\right)}{\left(1 + i_{base}\right)}$$

    Therefore, one year ago the PQR three-month interest rate was greater than the XYZ three-month interest rate, but today the XYZ three-month interest rate is greater than the PQR three-month interest rate. The forward discount today suggests the XYZ is expected to depreciate relative to the PQR, but the change from a forward premium to a forward discount does not imply that the XYZ has depreciated or appreciated. (Study Session 6, LOS 21.e, g)

 ©2014 Kaplan, Inc.

42. **C**   Accounting profit is often an unsatisfactory performance measure from an economic point of view because accounting costs generally do not include the opportunity costs of equity capital. Accounting costs do reflect the cost of depreciation. (Study Session 4, LOS 15.a)

43. **B**   Under the elasticities approach, a currency depreciation will lead to a greater reduction in a trade deficit when export demand and/or import demand are more elastic. The demand for luxury goods is relatively elastic, while the demand for goods without good substitutes or for goods that represent only a small portion of consumer expenditures is relatively inelastic. (Study Session 6, LOS 21.j)

44. **B**   At a minimum wage above the equilibrium wage, there will be an excess supply of workers. Firms substitute other productive resources for labor and use more than the economically efficient amount of capital. The result is increased unemployment and a decrease in economic efficiency. Firms may decrease the quality or quantity of the non-monetary benefits they previously offered to workers. (Study Session 4, LOS 13.k, l)

45. **C**   Paying off accounts payable from cash lowers current assets and current liabilities by the same amount. Because the current ratio started off above 1, the current ratio will increase. Because the quick ratio started off less than 1, it will decrease further. The other choices are incorrect. Buying fixed assets on credit decreases both ratios because the denominator increases, with no change to the numerator. Using cash to purchase inventory would result in no change in the current ratio but would decrease the quick ratio by decreasing the numerator. (Study Session 8, LOS 28.b)

46. **C**   cash conversion cycle (CCC) = days of sales outstanding + days of inventory on hand – number of days of payables

$$\text{number of days of payables} = \frac{365}{\text{payables turnover}} = \frac{365}{11} = 33.18 \text{ days}; \; \frac{365}{10} = 36.5 \text{ days}$$

Since the payables payment period increases by 3.32 days and receivables days increases by 5, CCC increases by 1.68 days. (Study Session 8, LOS 28.b)

47. **B**   Inventory turnover is cost of goods sold divided by average inventory. A manager who wishes to manipulate earnings or the balance sheet to show improvement in this ratio can either understate inventories, which would understate working capital and total assets, or overstate cost of goods sold, which would understate earnings. (Study Session 9, LOS 29.h; Study Session 10, LOS 33.h)

48. **C**   The three objectives of financial market regulation according to IOSCO are to (1) protect investors; (2) ensure the fairness, efficiency, and transparency of markets; and (3) reduce systemic risk. Because of the increasing globalization of securities markets, IOSCO seeks to attain uniform financial regulations across countries. (Study Session 7, LOS 24.b)

49. **C**   Sales revenue for which the product or service has yet to be delivered gives rise to a liability account, unearned revenue. This liability will be reduced as the product or service is actually delivered. (Study Session 8, LOS 26.e)

50. **B**

Sales	+$4,000	
Cash received from customers		+$4,000 (since no change in AR)
Cost of goods sold	−2,000	
Increase in inventory	−100	
Increase in accounts payable	+300	
Other cash input expenses	−500	
Cash paid for inputs		−2,300
Cash paid for taxes		−200
Cash flow from operations		+1,500

   (Study Session 8, LOS 27.f)

51. **A**   The analyst should add the U.S. GAAP firm's LIFO reserve to its balance sheet inventory and subtract the change in the LIFO reserve from its cost of goods sold. This adjustment will increase the firm's total assets and change its pretax income, income taxes, net income, and retained earnings (increasing them if the LIFO reserve increased, or decreasing them if the LIFO reserve decreased). These adjustments will change the firm's debt-to-equity ratio by changing total equity, and change the cash conversion cycle by changing inventories. The adjustments do not change current liabilities or current assets other than inventories, so the quick ratio is not affected. (Study Session 8, LOS 28.b, c and Study Session 10, LOS 34.e)

52. **A**   The required disclosures for long-lived assets under IFRS are more extensive than they are under U.S. GAAP. IFRS requires a reconciliation of beginning and ending carrying values for classes of long-lived tangible assets, while U.S. GAAP does not. (Study Session 9, LOS 30.j)

53. **B** $$ROE = \frac{\text{net income}}{\text{equity}} = \frac{0.16(1,500)}{(1-0.40)(2,000)} = 0.20, \text{ or } 20\%$$

   If the debt ratio (TD/TA) is equal to 40% and the firm has no preferred stock, the percentage of equity is 1 − 0.40, or 60%. (Study Session 8, LOS 28.b)

54. **A**   Shares issued post-split need not be adjusted for the split as they are already "new" shares. Options with an exercise price greater than the average share price do not affect diluted EPS. (Study Session 8, LOS 25.g)

55. **B**   Diluted EPS uses average price. Since the average price is greater than the exercise price, the warrants are dilutive.

   $$\frac{60-50}{60} \times 1,000,000 = 166,667$$

   (Study Session 8, LOS 25.g, h)

©2014 Kaplan, Inc.

56. **C** The cash conversion cycle is $(365/6) + (365/9) - (365/12) = 60.8 + 40.6 - 30.4 = 71$ days. ROA is lower than ROE when net income is positive and debt is present. Just the fact that a company has a high gross profit margin does not necessarily mean it will have a high net profit margin. For example, the company could have very high operating expenses and end up with a low net profit margin. (Study Session 8, LOS 28.b)

57. **C** Prior service costs arise when changes in the terms of a defined benefit pension plan increase the future benefits due to employees based on their prior employment with the company. (Study Session 9, LOS 32.j)

58. **A** FIFO COGS:
100 @ $210	= $21,000	
70 @ $225	= $15,750	
	$36,750	

    LIFO ending inventory:
Purchases	190
Sales	170
Balance	20 @ $210 = $4,200 (Study Session 9, LOS 29.c)

59. **A** Straight-line depreciation: $14 million / 7 = $2.0 million

    Accelerated depreciation: $14 million × 0.333 = $4.662 million

Difference in depreciation: $4.662 million − $2.0 million =	$2.662 million
× Tax rate	0.35
Increase in deferred tax liability	$931,700

    (Study Session 9, LOS 31.d)

60. **B** Depreciation methods are an example of a difference that may require an analyst to adjust financial statements to make them comparable. Acquisition goodwill is treated the same way under IFRS and U.S. GAAP: it is not amortized but is tested for impairment at least annually. Securities held for trading are reported at fair value with unrealized gains and losses reported on the income statement. (Study Session 10, LOS 34.e)

61. **C** Unrealized gains and losses on securities held for trading are included in net income. Unrealized gains and losses on securities available for sale are not reported in net income but are included in comprehensive income. Net income will show a $2 million loss from the securities held for trading. Shareholders' equity will reflect this loss as well as the $3 million unrealized gain from securities available for sale, for a net increase of $1 million. (Study Session 8, LOS 25.l)

62. **C** This transaction results in a reduction of debt and an increase in equity. However, since no cash is involved, it is not reported as a financing activity in the cash flow statement, but will be disclosed in the notes to the cash flow statement. (Study Session 8, LOS 27.b)

63. **A** Operating lease payments distinguish the fixed charge coverage ratio from the interest coverage ratio. The fixed charge coverage ratio is decreasing at the same time the interest coverage ratio is increasing, which means the company's operating lease payments are increasing. (Note that the years are presented right-to-left.) The increasing interest coverage ratio suggests earnings before interest and taxes are increasing more (or decreasing less) than the interest payments on the company's debt. The debt-to-capital ratio is essentially unchanged in the period shown, which implies that the company has not changed its capital structure significantly. (Study Session 8, LOS 28.b, c and Study Session 9, LOS 32.k)

64. **B** Cash flows are no different under the percentage-of-completion method compared with the completed-contract method. Income statement and balance sheet accounts will differ between the two firms. (Study Session 8, LOS 25.b)

65. **C** A specific explanatory paragraph that makes reference to (questions) the going concern assumption may be a signal of serious problems and call for close examination by the analyst. Therefore, in the absence of such a paragraph, there is no need for a close examination of the going concern assumption by the analyst. The objective of an audit is to enable the auditor to provide an opinion on the fairness and reliability of the financial statements. This is not the same as numerical accuracy. The auditor generally only provides reasonable assurance that there are no material errors in the financial statements, not an opinion about their numerical accuracy. An independent certified public accounting firm must be appointed by the audit committee of the company's board of directors, not by its management. Appointment of the auditors by management would reduce the level of perceived independence. (Study Session 7, LOS 22.d and Study Session 11, LOS 40.e)

66. **A** For growing firms, capitalizing results in higher net income compared to expensing. A capitalizing company classifies the costs of the capitalized assets as CFI outflows, while a company that expenses these costs classifies them as CFO outflows. Thus, Alfred's CFO will be higher and CFI lower than Canute's. Working capital is unaffected by the decision to capitalize or expense because the decision does not affect current assets or current liabilities. (Study Session 9, LOS 30.a)

67. **C** Accrued wages should be recorded as a liability (wages payable). Failing to record a liability for accrued wages will understate wage expense, which leads to an overstatement of net income. Since net income is overstated, retained earnings and owners' equity are both overstated. Assets are unaffected. (Study Session 7, LOS 23.e)

68. **B** When the PV of the lease payments is greater than the carrying value of an asset, the lessor records an immediate gross profit on sale equal to the excess of the PV over the carrying value, and the lease is termed a sales-type lease, not a direct financing lease. (Study Session 9, LOS 32.g)

69. **A** Since at breakeven sales, fixed costs + variable costs = revenue, variable costs for Rodgers at sales of $5 million must be $5 million – $2 million = $3 million, or 60% of sales. With sales of $7 million, variable costs are 0.6 × 7 million = 4.2 million. Operating income is then 7 million – 4.2 million – 2 million = $800,000.

    By assuming some arbitrary price for the product such as $1,000, this problem can be solved in units as well. Variable costs would be $600 per unit and operating income would be 7,000 (1,000 – 600) – 2 million = $800,000. (Study Session 11, LOS 37.e)

70. **B** The weights used to calculate WACC should be based on the firm's target capital structure. If the company does not provide information about its target capital structure, an analyst can use the company's current capital structure or the average capital structure weights for the industry. Similar size is not enough for the average weights for other companies to be relevant if those companies are not in the same industry. (Study Session 11, LOS 36.c)

71. **B** Information is typically not available to compare the aging of receivables between companies, among groups of companies, or within an industry. Receivables turnover can be calculated from the balance sheet. An aging schedule shows either the absolute or percentage amount of accounts receivable that are current and that are past due by various lengths of time. (Study Session 11, LOS 39.f)

©2014 Kaplan, Inc.

72. **B** No calculation is necessary. Assuming the tax treatment of the two alternatives is the same, a share repurchase results in the same shareholder wealth as a cash dividend payment of an equal amount. (Study Session 11, LOS 38.f)

73. **A** Since the net present value of the five projects is the expected increase in firm value from undertaking the projects, maximizing the NPV of the projects chosen will result in the selection of the optimal group of five projects. Since the profitability index is the ratio of the present value of the expected after-tax cash flows to the initial outlay, choosing the five projects with the greatest profitability indexes will identify the five projects with the greatest total present values and the projects with the greatest total net present values. (Study Session 11, LOS 35.c)

74. **A** Sunk costs are not to be included in investment analysis. Opportunity costs and the project's impact on taxes are relevant variables in determining project cash flow for a capital investment. (Study Session 11, LOS 35.b)

75. **C** An increase in the number of days of payables suggests a company is taking longer to pay its vendors. This reduces the cash conversion cycle and represents effective working capital management, a source of liquidity for a company. A decrease in days of payables would be a drag on liquidity because the company is paying its vendors more quickly, which uses cash. (Study Session 11, LOS 39.a, c)

76. **C** Regularly reviewing performance, independence, skills, and experience of existing board members is a responsibility of the Nominations Committee, not the Audit Committee. The other choices are positive characteristics of the Audit Committee. (Study Session 11, LOS 40.e)

77. **C** Beta, a measure of systematic risk, can be estimated as the slope coefficient from a regression based on the market model, $R_i = \alpha + \beta_i (R_{mkt} - R_f)$. This regression line is the security's characteristic line. (Study Session 12, LOS 43.e)

78. **C** A unique feature of ETFs is that they will create shares when institutional investors deposit securities that are included in the ETF basket and will redeem ETF shares for institutional investors. This is done to ensure an efficient and orderly market in the shares and to prevent the fund shares from trading at (much of) a premium or discount, thereby avoiding one of the pitfalls of closed-end funds. (Study Session 12 LOS 41.e)

79. **C** The important points in the determination of asset classes are that assets included in a class have similar performance characteristics and a relatively high correlation of returns between assets, and that returns of asset classes have relatively low correlations to realize the benefits of diversification across asset classes. Some asset classes, such as real estate and hedge funds, may be illiquid. The asset classes in the strategic allocation should be mutually exclusive and cover the universe of investable assets available to the fund manager(s) based on the client's objectives and constraints, not the broadest possible universe of asset classes. (Study Session 12, LOS 44.f)

80. **C** The Standards of Practice have very little to do with investment constraints. (Study Session 12, LOS 44.e)

81. **A** A risk-averse investor prefers less risk to more risk. The lower the correlation, the greater the risk reduction. Thus, a risk-averse investor would most prefer the portfolio with the lowest correlation coefficient and least prefer the one with the highest. Of the choices given, W and Y's correlation coefficient of +0.6 is the highest. (Study Session 12, LOS 42.d, f)

82. **B** The CAPM concludes that expected returns are a positive (linear) function of systematic risk. (Study Session 12, LOS 43.c)

83. **B** The SML and CML both intersect the vertical axis at the risk-free rate. The SML describes the risk/return tradeoff for individual securities or portfolios, whereas the CML describes the risk/return tradeoff of various combinations of the market portfolio and a riskless asset. (Study Session 12, LOS 43.b, f)

84. **B** Even risk-averse investors will prefer leveraged risky portfolios if the increase in expected return is enough to offset the increase in portfolio risk. Scott's portfolio selection implies that she is more risk averse than Fiona, has steeper indifference curves, and is willing to take on less additional risk for an incremental increase in expected returns than Fiona. (Study Session 12, LOS 42.h)

85. **B** The Sharpe ratio measures excess return per unit of total risk. The Treynor measure and Jenson's alpha are calculated with beta, not standard deviation, and are appropriate for analyzing portfolios based on systematic risk. (Study Session 12, LOS 43.h)

86. **B** A price-weighted index will put the most weight on Stock X, which had the worst performance. A price-weighted index will have a beginning value of (160 + 80 + 60) / 3 = 100 and an ending value of (136 + 100 + 66) / 3 = 100.67, for an increase of 0.67%. The percent change for a value-weighted index is (13,600 + 10,000 + 66,000) / (16,000 + 8,000 + 60,000) − 1 = 6.7%. The percent change for an equal-weighted index using the geometric mean is $[(1 - 0.15)(1 + 0.25)(1 + 0.1)]^{1/3} - 1 = 5.3\%$. (Study Session 13, LOS 46.d)

87. **A** High industry concentration refers to an industry that has a small number of firms, which often leads to less price competition, higher pricing power, and higher return on invested capital. High barriers to entry refer to industries where it is costly for new competitors to enter the industry, which allows companies already in the industry to maintain high profitability and prices. Low industry capacity refers to a situation where demand is greater than supply at current prices, which allows companies to maintain high prices and profits. (Study Session 14, LOS 49.g)

88. **C** Consumer discretionary goods purchases are very sensitive to economic cycles, while consumer staples are a non-cyclical industry. (Study Session 14, LOS 49.c, j)

89. **A** An investor cannot achieve positive abnormal returns on average by using technical analysis if prices fully reflect all available security market (price and volume) information. The weak form of the EMH assumes prices reflect this information, and the semistrong and strong forms assume prices reflect additional (non-market) information as well. (Study Session 13, LOS 47.e)

90. **A** First solve for D_5: $D_5 = (D_1)(1 + g)^n = \$1(1.05)^4 = \$1.216$

$$P_4 = \frac{D_5}{(k - g)} = \frac{\$1.216}{(0.15 - 0.05)} = \$12.16$$

or

$$P_0 = \frac{1}{0.15 - 0.05} = 10$$

$$P_4 = 10(1.05)^4 = \$12.16$$

(Study Session 14, LOS 50.e)

                    ©2014 Kaplan, Inc.

91. **A** By taking a short position in a put option, the investor has long exposure to the risk in the underlying asset. Because the value of a put option decreases when the price of the underlying asset increases, the value of a short position in a put increases when the price of the underlying increases. Both a short position in a call option and a long position in a put option increase in value when the price of the underlying asset decreases; that is, these option positions have short exposure to the risk of the underlying asset. (Study Session 13, LOS 45.e)

92. **C** $$P/E = \frac{\text{dividend payout ratio}}{k-g}$$

$$g = ROE \times \text{retention rate}$$

Increases in k reduce P/E. Increases in g or the dividend payout ratio increase P/E. (Study Session 14, LOS 50.e, h)

93. **B** Sales of newly issued securities take place in the primary market. Registration of shares sold in private placements of securities is not required. The secondary market refers to the markets in which previously issued securities are traded. (Study Session 13, LOS 45.i)

94. **B** Callable shares typically pay a higher dividend than noncallable shares because investors demand compensation for the fact that the call option limits investors' potential return. Callable shares are riskier than noncallable shares because the issuer has the option to buy back the shares at a fixed price. (Study Session 14, LOS 48.e)

95. **C** Asset-based valuation involves determining market values for the subject company's assets and liabilities to calculate the equity value. Compared to the other answer choices, a privately held metal fabrication company will likely have a larger proportion of physical assets relative to intangible assets, and market values for its physical assets should be relatively easier to obtain. An online news site is likely to have a relatively small physical asset base and relatively high intangibles, making this company difficult to value using asset-based valuation. A large multinational corporation is likely to be difficult to value using an asset-based valuation model, even if the company has a large physical asset base relative to its intangibles, because it may have extensive international assets. (Study Session 14, LOS 50.j)

96. **B** This is a supernormal growth stock valuation problem.

Step 1: Find the dividends in the supernormal growth period.

$D_1 = 1.00(1.20) = \$1.20$; $D_2 = 1.2(1.2) = \$1.44$; $D_3 = 1.44(1.15) = \$1.656$

Step 2: Use the constant growth model to find the price at the end of period 2.

$$P_2 = \frac{D_3}{k-g} = \frac{1.656}{0.10-0.06} = \$41.40$$

Step 3: Discount all of the cash flows back to time zero.

$$P_0 = \frac{D_1}{(1+k)} + \frac{D_2}{(1+k)^2} + \frac{P_2}{(1+k)^2} = \frac{1.20}{1.10} + \frac{1.44}{(1.10)^2} + \frac{41.40}{(1.10)^2} = \$36.50$$

(Study Session 14, LOS 50.e)

97. **C**   Semistrong-form market efficiency implies that fundamental analysis of publicly available information will not generate abnormal returns on average. Portfolio managers should help quantify a client's risk tolerances and return needs, offer portfolio policies and strategies to meet these needs, and construct a portfolio by allocating funds to appropriate asset classes. Portfolio managers can also create value by diversifying their clients' portfolios globally to reduce risk, monitoring and evaluating changing capital market conditions, monitoring their clients' needs and circumstances, and rebalancing their clients' portfolios when necessary. (Study Session 13, LOS 47.e)

98. **B**   Government bond trades typically settle in one day (T + 1) while corporate bond trades typically settle in three days (T + 3). Government and corporate bonds trade primarily in dealer markets. Bid-ask spreads depend on an issue's liquidity and may be wider for an illiquid government issue than for a liquid corporate issue. (Study Session 15, LOS 52.d)

99. **B**   Based on the relationship between Macaulay and modified duration, the bond's yield to maturity at the time of purchase is (15.0 / 14.5) − 1 = 3.45%. If the rate of return on reinvested coupon income is greater than 3.45%, the yield to maturity increased after the investor bought the bond. Over an investment horizon shorter than the Macaulay duration, an increase in YTM decreases the bond's market price by more than it increases reinvestment income. Therefore, the investor's annualized holding period return is less than the yield to maturity at issuance. (Study Session 16, LOS 55.b, k)

100. **B** The bond is sold at a premium. As time passes, the bond's price will move toward par. Thus, the price will fall.

   N = 10; FV = 1,000; PMT = 100; I = 8; CPT → PV = $1,134

   N = 9; FV = 1,000; PMT = 100; I = 8; CPT → PV = $1,125

   (Study Session 15, LOS 53.b)

101. **B** The bond is an inverse floater because the coupon rate will move opposite to any move in the reference rate. (Study Session 15, LOS 51.e)

102. **B** The two investments combine to form a 10-year, $1,000 face value, 8.0% semiannual coupon bond that would sell at par because the YTM (expressed as a BEY) equals the coupon rate. Thus the combined value is $1,000. The zero-coupon bond is worth $\frac{1,000}{1.04^{20}} = \$456.39,$ and the annuity payments are worth $543.61 (N = 10 × 2 = 20, PMT = 40, I/Y = 8/2 = 4, FV = 0, PV = −543.61).

   (Study Session 2, LOS 5.e, and Study Session 15, LOS 53.a, f)

103. **C** The benchmark yield increased, which suggests macroeconomic factors were unfavorable for bond prices overall. The corporate bond's spread to its benchmark decreased from 250 basis points to 225 basis points, which suggests microeconomic factors were favorable for the bond's price. (Study Session 15, LOS 53.i)

104. **C** The key term here is *coupon bond*. While an investor in a fixed-coupon bond can usually eliminate interest rate risk by holding a bond until maturity, the same is not true for reinvestment risk. The receipt of periodic coupon payments exposes the investor to reinvestment risk. A noncallable bond reduces reinvestment risk by reducing the risk of repayment. Thus, an investor most concerned with reinvestment risk would prefer a noncallable bond to a callable bond. Since lower coupon bonds have lower reinvestment risk, this same investor would prefer a lower coupon bond to a higher coupon bond. (Study Session 15, LOS 51.f, and Study Session 16, LOS 55.a)

   ©2014 Kaplan, Inc.

105. **B** A special purpose vehicle is a legal entity to which the assets used as collateral in an ABS issue are sold. This transaction separates the assets backing the ABS from the other assets of the company that creates the SPV. (Study Session 15, LOS 51.d, 54.b)

106. **B** $_2f_1 = \left[\dfrac{(1+z_3)^{1+2}}{(1+z_1)^1} \right]^{1/2} - 1 = \left[\dfrac{(1.12)^3}{(1.10)} \right]^{1/2} - 1 = 13.01\%$

   Note: $\dfrac{(3 \times 12) - (1 \times 10)}{2} = 13$ (Study Session 15, LOS 53.h)

107. **A** Portfolio duration as a weighted average of the individual bonds' durations is calculated assuming parallel shifts in the yield curve. Cash flow yield is used to calculate duration based on the weighted average time until a bond portfolio's cash flows are scheduled to be received. (Study Session 16, LOS 55.f)

108. **B** Secured creditors have priority of claims over unsecured creditors in a bankruptcy, rather than ranking pari passu with unsecured creditors. However, the priority of claims might not always be followed, either because the creditors have negotiated a different outcome or because a bankruptcy court has ordered one. (Study Session 16, LOS 56.b)

109. **C** A repurchase agreement is a form of short-term collateralized borrowing in which a bondholder sells a security and agrees to buy it back at a higher price. (Study Session 15, LOS 52.h)

110. **C** Carrying costs of holding the underlying asset increase the value of call options and decrease the value of put options. (Study Session 17, LOS 58.k)

111. **A** Open interest is the total number of contracts (long/short position pairs) outstanding. The number of contracts that change hands in a given period is volume, not open interest. (Study Session 17, LOS 57.c)

112. **B** The payoff diagram from owning stock and a long put on the stock is similar to that of a long call. (Study Session 17, LOS 59.a, b)

113. **B** At expiration, a forward contract has positive value to the short party (and an equal negative value to the long party) if the spot price of the underlying asset is less than the price specified in the forward contract. (Study Session 17, LOS 58.c)

114. **C** The time value of an option is zero at expiration. For an out-of-the-money option, the exercise value is zero at expiration. (Study Session 17, LOS 58.j)

115. **A** Writer of put's maximum loss = $50 – $4 = $46 (Study Session 17, LOS 59.a)

116. **B** Adding alternative investments to a traditional portfolio may increase expected returns because (1) some alternative investments are less efficiently priced than traditional assets, providing opportunities for skilled managers; (2) alternative investments may offer a premium for being illiquid; and (3) alternative investments often employ leverage. (Study Session 18, LOS 60.c)

117. **B** Collateral yield depends on the yield on T-bills posted as collateral (margin). Roll yield, or the gains and losses that result from entering into a new, longer-dated futures contract as previous contracts expire or are closed out, depends on whether the contract is in contango (futures price greater than spot price) or backwardation (futures price less than spot price). Futures markets for commodities with high convenience yield tend to be in backwardation, while futures markets for commodities with little to no convenience yield tend to be in contango. (Study Session 18, LOS 60.e)

118. **A** Mezzanine-stage venture capital financing provides capital during the period prior to an initial public offering. (Study Session 18, LOS 60.d)

119. **A** Historical mean and standard deviation of returns for hedge fund indexes are likely to overestimate expected return and underestimate risk due to survivorship and backfill biases. As a result, determining a portfolio asset allocation to hedge funds based on these measures is likely to overestimate the diversification benefits. (Study Session 18, LOS 60.c, g)

120. **C** Recapitalization is when the company issues debt to fund a dividend distribution to equity holders (the fund). It is not an exit, in that the fund still controls the company, but often is a intermediate step toward an exit. (Study Session 18, LOS 60.d)

 ©2014 Kaplan, Inc.

Exam 3
Afternoon Session Answer Key

To get valuable feedback on how your score compares to those of other Level I candidates, use your Username and Password to gain online access at Schweser.com and select "Performance Tracker" from your dashboard.

1. B	31. A	61. B	91. B
2. A	32. C	62. B	92. C
3. A	33. C	63. B	93. C
4. B	34. B	64. B	94. A
5. B	35. C	65. A	95. C
6. A	36. B	66. B	96. B
7. C	37. B	67. A	97. C
8. A	38. A	68. A	98. C
9. A	39. B	69. B	99. A
10. A	40. B	70. A	100. C
11. A	41. C	71. C	101. A
12. A	42. B	72. B	102. A
13. A	43. B	73. A	103. B
14. C	44. A	74. B	104. B
15. A	45. B	75. B	105. A
16. A	46. C	76. C	106. A
17. A	47. C	77. B	107. A
18. B	48. A	78. C	108. C
19. B	49. B	79. B	109. B
20. B	50. B	80. C	110. B
21. B	51. A	81. C	111. A
22. A	52. C	82. A	112. A
23. C	53. A	83. B	113. C
24. B	54. C	84. B	114. C
25. B	55. A	85. B	115. A
26. A	56. C	86. C	116. C
27. A	57. A	87. C	117. B
28. C	58. C	88. C	118. C
29. A	59. A	89. C	119. C
30. B	60. B	90. A	120. B

Exam 3
Afternoon Session Answers

Answers referencing the Standards of Practice address Study Session 1, LOS 1.b, c and LOS 2.a, b, c, except where noted.

1. **B** Standard I(A) Knowledge of the Law requires candidates and members comply with all applicable rules and regulations, including the CFA Institute Standards of Practice. Further, Standard I(A) requires that members and candidates must not knowingly participate in violations of applicable laws and Standards. Even though local law permits purchasing shares for personal accounts before purchasing IPO shares for client accounts, Standard VI(B) Priority of Transactions does not. The analyst knowingly violated the Code and Standards and, thus, violated Standard I(A). Since the analyst was unaware of the deceit in the valuation of the IPO stock [a violation of Standard I(D) Misconduct], his participation in publishing the IPO valuation did not constitute a violation.

2. **A** The chief financial officer and the portfolio manager are in violation of Standard VII(B) Reference to CFA Institute, the CFA Designation, and the CFA Program because they have improperly referenced the CFA designation or exaggerated its meaning (e.g., "group of the most qualified"). The marketing brochure is only stating factual information regarding the portfolio managers' success at passing the CFA exams on their first attempts.

3. **A** Standard V(B) Communication with Clients and Prospective Clients requires prompt disclosure of any change that might significantly affect the manager's investment processes. The disclosure need not be in writing.

4. **B** If an unsolicited trade is inconsistent with a client's IPS, a member or candidate should not execute the trade before discussing it with the client. According to Standard III(C) Suitability, if the trade will have only a minimal impact on the client's portfolio, the member or candidate should attempt to educate the client with regard to how it deviates from the IPS and then may follow her firm's policies for obtaining client approval for the trade. If the trade will have a material impact on the risk and return characteristics of the client's portfolio, the discussion should focus on changing the IPS.

5. **B** According to Standard II(A) Material Nonpublic Information, how specific the information is, how different it is from public information, and its nature are key factors in determining whether a particular piece of information fits the definition of material. An additional factor is reliability, which is often a function of the source of the information. While the liquidity of a security may be a factor in determining the materiality of advance knowledge of a large buy or sell order, in most cases, it would not be a factor in determining materiality.

6. **A** There is no requirement that a firm publicly release ratings changes by its analysts. Individuals outside the firm acting on this information after it is released to clients are not in violation of the Standard concerning nonpublic information. Purchases in a member's personal account are not subject to the requirements of the Standard concerning diligence and reasonable basis, so there is no violation indicated here.

©2014 Kaplan, Inc.

7. **C** Standard I(B) Independence and Objectivity allows investor-paid research but requires that members and candidates limit the type of compensation they accept for writing a research report so that it is not dependent on the conclusions of the research report. Best practice is for analysts to only accept a flat fee for such company-paid research reports. Such research should also include complete disclosure of the nature of the compensation received for writing such a report so that investors will not be misled as to the relationship between the analyst and the company. Paying for one's own transportation and lodging when the analyst is not employed by the subject firm is a recommended procedure for complying with Standard I(B), but it is not a requirement.

8. **A** In the absence of regulatory requirements, Standard V(C) Record Retention recommends maintaining records supporting investment recommendations and actions and records of investment-related communications with clients for at least seven years. Here, there is regulatory guidance, and seven years is a recommendation, not a requirement, in any case. Records can be maintained in electronic or hard copy format.

9. **A** Total firm assets must include all accounts whether discretionary or not and whether fee-paying or not. (Study Session 1, LOS 4.a)

10. **A** Under Standard III(B) Fair Dealing, clients placing orders contrary to the firm's changed recommendation should be advised of the change in recommendation before the firm accepts the orders.

11. **A** James is not in violation of the Standards. To comply with Standard VI(B) Priority of Transactions, members and candidates must give transactions for clients and employers priority over their personal transactions. In this instance, James did not adversely affect the client's interest because the client's trades were executed before James copied them. He has not acted fraudulently or deceitfully and, thus, has not violated Standard I(D) Misconduct.

12. **A** The circumstances of Hart's bankruptcy do not compromise his professional reputation. The bankruptcy did not involve fraudulent or deceitful business conduct; therefore, there is no violation of Standard I(D) Misconduct. The Standards do not require disclosing the bankruptcy to clients because it does not create any conflict of interest and is not relevant to Hart's professional activity.

13. **A** Marshall has an obligation to disclose that she receives special compensation based on the amount of client trading volume. Standard VI(A) Disclosure of Conflicts requires members to disclose to clients and prospects all matters that could potentially impair the member's ability to make investment decisions that are (and to give investment advice that is) objective and unbiased. The Standard on communications with clients addresses issues that involve clearly communicating investment recommendations and analysis. The Standard on additional compensation arrangements is concerned with accepting benefits that may create a conflict between a member's interests and her employer's interests.

14. **C** Lunar may claim compliance as long as it has met the reporting requirements necessary and is held out to clients (advertised) as a distinct business entity. Claiming partial compliance is not allowed. (Study Session 1, LOS 4.b)

15. **A** Of the choices given, seeking the advice of outside counsel about what actions Reilly may be required to take is the most appropriate. Under Standard III(E) Preservation of Confidentiality, members and candidates should maintain the confidentiality of information received in the course of their professional service relating to both current and former clients. In the case of illegal activity, however, Reilly may have a legal obligation to report the activity or, on the other hand, may have a legal obligation to maintain the client's confidentiality even if he suspects illegal activity.

16. **A** Standard II(A) Material Nonpublic Information requires that members and candidates who possess material nonpublic information not act or cause others to act on the information. Putting the stock on a restricted list or refusing the trade would violate this Standard because they involve acting or causing others to act on the nonpublic information he possesses. Dean should seek to have East Street make the information public. If East Street does not do so, Dean must act as he would have acted if he did not possess the information. Refusing to make the trade he was instructed to make would be "acting" on the information in this case. The obligation here is to the integrity of financial markets.

17. **A** Members and candidates should consider the knowledge and sophistication of those receiving the performance information. If only a brief presentation is given, members and candidates must make detailed information supporting the presentation available upon request. Individual account performance is permitted and no minimum number of years is recommended (these refer to GIPS, with which the Code and Standards do not require compliance). The primary requirement of Standard III(D) Performance Presentation is to not present false or misleading information.

18. **B** GIPS require that, to claim compliance, firms must present GIPS-compliant performance information for a minimum of five years or since inception if in existence less than five years. Firms may not link noncompliant performance information for any periods after January 1, 2000. (Study Session 1, LOS 3.a)

19. **B** This problem involves determining the present value of an annuity followed by finding the present value of a lump sum. Enter PMT = 10,000, N = 10, and I = 14. Compute PV = 52,161.16. That is the present value of the 10-year annuity, four years from today. Next, we need to discount that back to present for four years to find the amount of the investment today. Enter FV = –52,161.16, N = 4, I = 14, PMT = 0. Compute PV = 30,883.59. (Study Session 2, LOS 5.e)

20. **B** The cumulative absolute frequency of the fourth interval is 80, which is the sum of the absolute frequencies from the first to the fourth intervals. (Study Session 2, LOS 7.b)

21. **B** High levels of the VIX indicate that the outlook of investors is bearish. A contrarian interprets this as a bullish sign. Low mutual fund cash balances indicate that mutual fund managers are bullish, and, as a result, contrarians are bearish. A low put-call ratio indicates bullish investor sentiment, which a contrarian interprets as a bearish sign. (Study Session 3, LOS 12.e)

22. **A** The average annual compound growth rate is calculated as:

$$[(1 + 0.25)(1 - 0.25)(1 + 0.30)(1 - 0.30)]^{0.25} - 1 = 0.9611 - 1 = -0.0389 \text{ or } -3.89\%$$

(Study Session 2, LOS 7.e)

23. **C**   Mean = 120 / 10 = 12, median = 10, and mode = 10. The distribution is skewed to the right, so the mean is greater than the median and mode. Generally, for positively skewed distributions, the mode is less than the median, which is less than the mean. In this case, the mode and median are equal because the number of observations is small. (Study Session 2, LOS 7.e, k)

24. **B**   The coefficient of variation, CV = standard deviation / arithmetic mean, is a common measure of relative dispersion (risk). $CV_X = 0.7 / 0.9 = 0.78$; $CV_Y = 4.7 / 1.2 = 3.92$; and $CV_Z = 5.2 / 1.5 = 3.47$. Because a higher CV means higher relative risk, Security Y has the highest relative risk. (Study Session 2, LOS 7.i)

25. **B**   The median is the midpoint of a distribution, such that 50% of the observations are greater than the median and 50% are less than the median. This is equivalent to the second quartile (4 groups) and the fifth decile (10 groups). If a distribution is divided into quintiles (5 groups), 60% of the observations are less than the third quintile. (Study Session 2, LOS 7.f)

26. **A**   *Subjective probability* is based on personal judgement. A *joint probability* is a probability that two or more events happen concurrently. An *a priori probability* is one based on logical analysis rather than on observation or personal judgment. An *empirical probability* is calculated using historical data. A *conditional probability* is the probability of one event happening on the condition that another event is certain to occur. (Study Session 2, LOS 8.a, b, d)

27. **A**   Technical analysis assumes that supply and demand are governed by many factors, both rational and irrational. (Study Session 3, LOS 12.a)

28. **C**

	Selected by the Previous Portfolio Manager	*Selected by the Current Portfolio Manager*	*Total*
Value stocks	28 (28%)	12 (12%)	40
Growth stocks	48 (48%)	12 (12%)	60
Total	76	24	100

This problem involves the addition rule for probabilities, P(A or B) = P(A) + P(B) − P(AB).

P(A) is the probability that a randomly selected stock is a value stock, which is given as 40%.

P(B) is the probability that a stock was picked by the previous manager. That probability is (0.7)(0.4) + (0.8)(1 − 0.4) = 0.76. The previous manager selected 76% of the stocks in the portfolio.

P(AB) is the probability that a randomly selected stock is a value stock picked by the previous manager. Since the previous manager picked 70% of the 40% of the stocks that are value stocks, the probability that a randomly selected stock is a value stock picked by the previous manager is 40% × 70% = 28%.

From this, we have P(A or B) = 40% + 76% − 28% = 88%. (Study Session 2, LOS 8.f)

29. **A**   The *standard* normal distribution has a mean of 0 and a standard deviation of 1. (Study Session 2, LOS 8.g and Study Session 3, LOS 9.j)

30. **B** The 95% confidence interval is 10% ± 1.96(4%) or from 2.16% to 17.84%. The 90% confidence interval is 10% ± 1.65(4%) or from 3.4% to 16.6%. The probability of a return ± 1 standard deviation from the mean, between 6% and 14%, is approximately 68%. (Study Session 3, LOS 9.l)

31. **A** Using the standard normal probability distribution,

$z = \dfrac{observation - mean}{standard\ deviation} = \dfrac{0-10}{5} = -2.0$, the chance of getting zero or less return

(losing money) is 1 – 0.9772 = 0.0228% or 2.28%. An alternative explanation: the expected return is 10%. To lose money means the return must fall below zero. Zero is about two standard deviations to the left of the mean. 50% of the time, a return will be below the mean, and 2.5% of the observations are below two standard deviations down. About 97.5% of the time, the return will be above zero. Thus, only about a 2.5% chance exists of having a value below zero. (Study Session 3, LOS 9.m)

32. **C** According to the central limit theorem, the sample mean for large sample sizes will be distributed normally regardless of the distribution of the underlying population. (Study Session 3, LOS 10.c, d, e)

33. **C** The crowding-out effect refers to a reduction in private borrowing and investment as a result of higher interest rates generated by budget deficits that are financed by borrowing in the private loanable funds market. (Study Session 5, LOS 19.q)

34. **B** Arbitrage-free forward = 2.875 WSC/BDR × [(1 + 0.015 / 2) / (1 + 0.03 / 2)] = 2.8538 WSC/BDR. (Study Session 6, LOS 21.h)

35. **C** At competitive equilibrium, the sum of consumer and producer surplus is at its maximum level. Neither consumer nor producer surplus is necessarily at a maximum at the equilibrium output and price. Which surplus is larger or smaller depends on the elasticities of supply and demand. (Study Session 4, LOS 13.j)

36. **B** Open market operations are the U.S. Federal Reserve's most often used tool for changing the money supply. (Study Session 5, LOS 19.h)

37. **B** If quantity supplied does not respond to a change in price, supply is perfectly inelastic. For perfectly inelastic supply, elasticity equals zero. (Study Session 4, LOS 13.m)

38. **A** In the short run, an increase in the money supply will increase aggregate demand. The new short-run equilibrium will be at a higher price level and a greater level of real output (GDP). (Study Session 5, LOS 17.i)

39. **B** The law of diminishing returns states that at some point, as more of a resource is used in a production process, holding other inputs constant, output increases at a decreasing rate. This accounts for the upward slope of the SRMC curve beyond that point. Returns to scale determine the shape of the long-run cost curves. (Study Session 4, LOS 15.d)

40. **B** Under perfect competition, each firm faces a flat demand curve. This means the price is constant and the marginal revenue line is flat. A company will continue to produce as long as MR > MC, so the competitive company will produce as long as P > MC. It will stop when MC = MR = P. (Study Session 4, LOS 15.f, 16.d)

41. **C** Customs unions adopt uniform trade restrictions with non-members. Customs union members do not adopt a single currency. Both free trade areas and customs unions remove trade barriers among their members. (Study Session 6, LOS 20.f)

©2014 Kaplan, Inc.

42. **B**   Based on utility analysis, the optimum bundle of goods lies on the consumer's highest attainable indifference curve, at the point where this indifference curve is tangent to the consumer's budget line. The point of tangency is the only point at which this indifference curve intersects the consumer's opportunity set of attainable bundles. The consumer would prefer bundles that lie on higher indifference curves, but those bundles are unaffordable given the consumer's budget constraint. (Study Session 4, LOS 14.b, d)

43. **B**   Unemployment insurance is an example of an automatic stabilizer that is not subject to the action lag of discretionary fiscal policy tools. One reason why the unemployment rate is a lagging indicator is the fact that employers are slow to lay off employees early in recessions and slow to add employees early in expansions, because frequent hiring and firing has high costs. Another reason is that early in expansions, more discouraged workers (who are not counted as unemployed because they are out of the labor force) may begin seeking work (thereby re-entering the labor force) than the number of new jobs that are available, which increases the unemployment rate. (Study Session 5, LOS 18.b, d, i, 19.p)

44. **A**   A natural monopoly may exist when economies of scale are great. The large economies of scale mean that a single producer results in the lowest production costs. (Study Session 4, LOS 16.a, b)

45. **B**   Extraordinary items are unusual and infrequent items that are reported separately, net of tax, after net income from continuing operations. (Study Session 8, LOS 25.e)

46. **C**

original shares of common stock	= 1,000,000(12)	= 12,000,000
stock dividend	= 100,000(12)	= 1,200,000
new shares of common stock	= 400,000(3)	= 1,200,000
total shares of common stock	$= \dfrac{14,400,000}{12}$	= 1,200,000

Stock dividends are assumed to have been outstanding since the beginning of the year. (Study Session 8, LOS 25.g)

47. **C**   Under FIFO, Snow Blower will report lower cost of goods sold because the first items bought are assumed to be the units sold, and these have the lowest cost in a rising price environment. Net income is higher under FIFO in an increasing price environment because lower cost of goods sold results in higher income. Ending inventory is higher under FIFO in an increasing price environment. (Study Session 9, LOS 29.e and Study Session 10, LOS 33.h)

48. **A**   The debt ratio is total debt to total assets. Because common-size balance sheet data are stated as percentages of total assets, the debt ratio can be determined from the data given.

20X3: 10% + 24% = 34%
20X4: 11% + 21% = 32%
20X5: 12% + 18% = 30%

The debt ratio is decreasing over the period shown. Neither the inventory/sales ratio nor the quick ratio can be determined from the data given because the data do not include sales or current liabilities. (Study Session 8, LOS 26.g, h)

49. **B**   When using the direct method of calculating operating cash flows, depreciation and amortization are not "added back" (to net income) because we don't begin with net income under the direct method. Depreciation and amortization are noncash changes and are not used under the direct method. The other statements are true. Interest payments on debt affect cash flow from operations. When using the indirect method, an analyst should add any losses on sales of fixed assets to net income since they are not operating cash flows. (Study Session 8, LOS 27.c, f)

50. **B**   Under U.S. GAAP, a change to LIFO from another inventory cost method is an exception to the requirement of retrospective application of changes in an accounting principle. Instead of restating prior years' data, the firm uses the carrying value of inventory at the time of the change as the first LIFO layer. U.S. GAAP requires a company that is changing its inventory cost assumption to explain, in its financial statement disclosures, why the new method is preferable to the old method. (Study Session 9, LOS 29.g)

51. **A**   ROE 20X6 = (0.7)(0.85)(0.15)(1.5)(1.5) = 0.2008

ROE 20X7 = (0.7)(0.85)(0.10)(1.8)(1.6) = 0.1714

Profit margin fell, and the increase in the total asset turnover ratio and the leverage multiplier were not enough to offset the decline, so ROE decreased. (Study Session 8, LOS 28.d)

52. **C**   Options are derivatives, which are reported at fair value on the balance sheet with unrealized gains and losses recognized on the income statement. Available-for-sale securities are marked to market on the balance sheet, but unrealized gains and losses are reported in owners' equity as other comprehensive income. Bonds purchased in a private placement cannot be resold to the public and therefore are likely to be classified as held-to-maturity, in which case the firm does not recognize unrealized gains or losses. (Study Session 8, LOS 26.e; Study Session 13, LOS 45.i; Study Session 17, LOS 57.a)

53. **A**   If equity equals 45% of assets and current liabilities equal 20%, long-term debt must be 35%.

$$\text{long-term debt-to-equity ratio} = \frac{\text{long-term debt}}{\text{total equity}} = \frac{0.35}{0.45} = 0.778 = 77.8\%$$

CA = 0.1 + 0.15 + 0.20 = 0.45

$$\text{current ratio} = \frac{\text{CA}}{\text{CL}} = \frac{45}{20} = 2.25 \text{x}$$

(Study Session 8, LOS 28.b)

54. **C**   Interest expense is shown as a non-operating component of net income for a manufacturing company but would typically be classified as an operating expense for a financial services company. (Study Session 8, LOS 25.f)

55. **A**   In the IFRS framework, the two assumptions that underlie the preparation of financial statements are the accrual basis and the going concern assumption. (Study Session 7, LOS 24.d)

   ©2014 Kaplan, Inc.

56. **C** With an operating lease, the entire lease payment (rent expense) is subtracted from operating income. With a capital lease, only depreciation is subtracted from operating income, so operating income is higher with a capital lease. Net income in the first year is lower with a capital lease because the sum of depreciation (operating expense) and interest (non-operating expense) is greater than the lease payment. (Study Session 9, LOS 32.g)

57. **A** The warrants are dilutive because their exercise price is less than the average market price.

    shares issued to warrant holders = 100

    warrants generate cash of 100(50) = $5,000

    $$\text{repurchased shares} = \frac{5,000}{60} = 83$$

    net new shares created = 100 − 83 = 17

    Alternatively, $\dfrac{60-50}{60} \times 100 \approx 17$

    $$\text{diluted EPS} = \frac{\text{NI} - \text{preferred dividends}}{\text{weighted average \# shares} + \text{warrant adjust}}$$

    $$\text{diluted EPS} = \frac{5,000 - 500}{1,017} = \$4.42$$

    (Study Session 8, LOS 25.g, h)

58. **C** Corporate press releases are written by management and are often viewed as public relations or sales materials because of the great possibility of inherent management bias in such documents. Often, little or none of the material is independently reviewed by outside auditors. Such documents are not mandated by the securities regulators. Form 10-Q (quarterly financial statements) and proxy statements are mandatory SEC filings in the United States, which inherently increases their reliability given the penalties that can be imposed by the SEC if any serious irregularities are subsequently found. (Study Session 7, LOS 22.e)

59. **A** The impairment writedown in 20X3 will reduce depreciation expense in 20X4, which will increase 20X4 EBIT and net income. Operating cash flow and taxes payable are not affected because an impairment cannot be deducted from income for tax reporting purposes until the asset is sold or otherwise disposed of. (Study Session 9, LOS 30.h)

60. **B** There is a 20% reduction in the tax rate [(40% − 50%) / 50% = −0.2]. Hence, the deferred tax asset will be $800 = $1,000(1 − 0.2), the deferred tax liability will be $4,000 = $5,000(1 − 0.2), and the income tax expense will fall by the net amount of the decline in the asset and liability balances ($1,000 − $200 = $800). (Study Session 9, LOS 31.d)

61. **B** The improved benefit for existing employees will be shown as past service costs. Because past service costs are included in their full amount as pension expense under IFRS, net income will be lower under IFRS. Under U.S. GAAP, past service costs are included in other comprehensive income and amortized to pension expense over time so the first year impact on net income is less than under IFRS. (Study Session 9, LOS 32.j)

62. **B**   Capitalizing costs tends to smooth earnings and reduces investment cash flows. It will also increase cash flows from operations and increase profitability in the early years. (Study Session 9, LOS 30.a)

63. **B**   When cash is paid before the expense is recognized in the income statement, a prepaid asset for this expense is increased and cash is decreased by the amount paid. A prepaid liability account would not be set up unless the expense is recorded before the cash payment is made. (Study Session 7, LOS 23.d)

64. **B**   Based on the data given, use the basic DuPont equation and solve for expected net income.

ROE = (net income / revenues) × (revenues / total assets) × (total assets / total equity)

0.15 = (net income / $3 billion) × ($3 billion / $5 billion) × 2.5

net income / $3 billion = 0.1

net income = $300 million

Alternatively, A/E = 2.5 and assets = $5 billion, so equity = $2 billion.

net income / equity = 15%, so net income = 0.15($2 Billion) = $300 million
(Study Session 10, LOS 34.b)

65. **A**   PMT = 800,000; FV = 10,000,000; N = 5; I/Y = 8.25; CPT → PV = $9,900,837

interest expense = 9,900,836.51 × 0.0825 = $816,819.01

year-end adjustment = 816,819.01 − 800,000 = $16,819.01

year-end debt = $9,900,836.51 + $16,819.01 = $9,917,655.52

Note: Since this is a discount bond, we know the initial liability will be less than the face value, so we really didn't have to do any calculations to answer this question.
(Study Session 9, LOS 32.a, b)

66. **B**   Unrealized gains and losses from trading securities are reflected in the income statement and affect owners' equity. However, unrealized gains and losses from available-for-sale securities are included in other comprehensive income. Transactions included in other comprehensive income affect equity but not net income. Dividends paid to shareholders reduce owners' equity but not net income. (Study Session 8, LOS 25.l)

67. **A**   Conversion of bonds into common stock is a non-cash transaction, but the conversion should be disclosed in a footnote to the statement of cash flows.
(Study Session 8, LOS 27.f)

68. **A**   With LIFO, more recent, lower costs would be used for COGS. A reduction in COGS will increase gross profits and net income, other things equal. (Study Session 9, LOS 29.b)

©2014 Kaplan, Inc.

69. **B**

Year	0	1	2	3	4
Net cash flow	−$5,000.00	$1,900.00	$1,900.00	$2,500.00	$2,000.00
Net cash flow discounted at 12%	−$5,000.00	$1,696.43	$1,514.67	$1,779.45	$1,271.04
Cumulative discounted net cash flows	−$5,000.00	−$3,303.57	−$1,788.90	−$9.45	$1,261.59

$$\text{discounted payback period} = 3 + \frac{9.45}{1,271.04} = 3.01 \text{ years.}$$

(Study Session 11, LOS 35.d)

70. **A** To compare these short-term securities, state the return on each as a bond-equivalent yield. For the commercial paper, the BEY is given as 5.10%. The BEY for the certificate of deposit is 2.5% × 365 / 180 = 5.07%. For the Treasury bill, the BEY is [(100 − 97.5) / 97.5] × 365 / 180 = 5.20%. Miller should purchase the Treasury bill. (Study Session 11, LOS 39.e)

71. **C** Current market yields, not the coupon rate, should be used to estimate the cost of debt capital. (Study Session 11, LOS 36.f)

72. **B** To calculate the asset beta, the analyst will need to estimate the firm's beta, its debt-to-equity ratio, and its tax rate. (Study Session 11, LOS 36.i)

73. **A** Investors should take steps to discourage the use of the corporate funds to pay "greenmail." (Study Session 11, LOS 40.g)

74. **B** Good corporate governance practices will discourage or prohibit both the payment of finder's fees to board members for identifying attractive merger or acquisition targets and the use of corporate assets by board members or their families. (Study Session 11, LOS 40.f)

75. **B** IRR and NPV lead to the same decision when choosing independent projects but may lead to different decisions when choosing between projects. (Study Session 11, LOS 35.e)

76. **C** Break points in the marginal cost of capital structure occur at the levels where the cost of one of the components of the company's capital structure increases, increasing its weighted average cost of capital. (Study Session 11, LOS 36.k)

77. **B** Neither statement is accurate. The stock should decline in value by the amount of the dividend on the ex-dividend date, not the payment date. The holder-of-record date occurs two business days *after* the ex-dividend date. (Study Session 11, LOS 38.b)

78. **C** The diversification ratio of a portfolio equals its standard deviation of returns divided by the average standard deviation of the individual securities in the portfolio. Therefore, a more diversified portfolio will have a lower diversification ratio than a less diversified portfolio. A portfolio containing the highest number of securities from different industries will be the most diversified and will have the lowest diversification ratio. A portfolio of stocks from the same industry is likely to have a higher diversification ratio (reflecting less diversification) than a portfolio of stocks from different industries. (Study Session 12, LOS 41.a)

79. **B** In a situation where the client's expressed willingness to bear investment risk is significantly greater than the client's ability to bear investment risk, the advisor's assessment of the client's risk tolerance in the IPS should reflect the client's ability to bear investment risk. (Study Session 12, LOS 44.d)

80. **C** The capital market line plots expected return against standard deviation of returns for efficient portfolios. The efficient frontier plots expected return against the standard deviation of return, a measure of total risk. (Study Session 12, LOS 42.g, 43.b, f)

81. **C** As randomly selected securities are added to a portfolio, the diversifiable (unsystematic) risk decreases, and the expected level of nondiversifiable (systematic) risk remains the same. (Study Session 12, LOS 43.c)

82. **A** Based on the CAPM, the portfolio should earn: E(R) = 0.05 + 1.5(0.15 − 0.05) = 0.20 or 20%. On a risk-adjusted basis, this portfolio lies on the SML and is, thus, properly valued. (Study Session 12, LOS 43.h)

83. **B** These ethical issues fall under the heading of unique needs and preferences. Some investors would exclude these types of investments due to their own personal preferences. Legal restrictions and regulatory factors have to do with the type of account and its supporting legal documents. (Study Session 12, LOS 44.e)

84. **B** Since the portfolio manager is not directing the flow of cash into and out of the account, the time-weighted annual rate of return is the appropriate performance measure. Calculate the 2-year holding period return +1, then take the square root and subtract 1 to get the annual time-weighted rate of return:
$[(11.2 / 10)(12.5 / 12.4)(15 / 11.9)]^{1/2} − 1 = 19.29\%$. (Study Session 12, LOS 42.a)

85. **B** Shares of open-end mutual funds trade at NAV. The others may deviate from NAV. (Study Session 12, LOS 41.e)

86. **C** A *stop buy order* is a conditional market order by which an investor directs the purchase of a stock if it rises to a certain price. Stop buys are placed above the current market price. Limit orders can have market price as the limit, used when lack of liquidity is a concern. (Study Session 13, LOS 45.g, h)

87. **C** $P/E = \dfrac{\text{dividend payout ratio}}{k - g}$

dividend payout ratio = 1 − retention ratio = 1 − 0.4 = 0.6

growth rate (g) = retention rate × ROE = 0.4 × 15% = 6%

$P/E = \dfrac{0.6}{0.14 - 0.06} = 7.5$

(Study Session 14, LOS 50.h)

88. **C** The expected growth rate in dividends is an input into the dividend discount model, but the real risk-free rate, the expected inflation rate, and the risk premium are the components of the required rate of return. (Study Session 14, LOS 50.c)

89. **C** High return on invested capital and high pricing power are associated with high industry concentration (i.e., small number of firms), high barriers to entry, and low industry capacity. (Study Session 14, LOS 49.g)

  ©2014 Kaplan, Inc.

90. **A**   If capital markets are weak-form efficient and semistrong-form efficient, no publicly available information can be used to earn abnormal (risk-adjusted) returns. (Study Session 13, LOS 47.e)

91. **B**   Time line = $0 now; $0 in year 1; $0 in year 2; $1 in year 3.

$$P_2 = \frac{D_3}{(k-g)} = \frac{1}{(0.17-0.07)} = \$10$$

Note that the price is always one year before the dividend date. Solve for the PV of $10 to be received in two years.

FV = 10; N = 2; I = 17; CPT → PV = $7.31. (Study Session 14, LOS 50.e)

92. **C**   The forecast year-end price, *P*, is:

$$P = EPS \times \left(\frac{P}{E}\right) = 10(12) = 120$$

$$\text{expected return} = \frac{\text{dividend} + (\text{ending price} - \text{beginning price})}{\text{beginning price}} = \frac{\$5 + \$120 - \$100}{\$100} = 0.25 \text{ or } 25\%$$

(Study Session 14, LOS 50.e, h)

93. **C**   There is no maximum time for which a security can be borrowed. It must be returned whenever the lender requires it to be. (Study Session 13, LOS 45.e)

94. **A**   Consumers buy fewer durable goods, such as furniture, during recessions and buy more during expansions. As a result, producers of these goods tend to have cyclical demand, revenues, and earnings. Operating leverage (high fixed costs as a proportion of total costs) also contributes to cyclicality of earnings. (Study Session 14, LOS 49.c)

95. **C**   Under cumulative voting, shareholders receive one vote per share for each board position election but can vote them for any board candidate or spread them over multiple candidates. This allows, for example, a holder of 20% of the shares to elect one of five board members. Under statutory voting, a minority shareholder could not elect any board members based only on their share voting rights. (Study Session 14, LOS 48.b)

96. **B**   Equal-weighted indexes require regular and frequent rebalancing, because price changes of their component securities will cause component weights to drift away from their target weights. Price-weighted indexes and market-capitalization weighted indexes generally do not require regular rebalancing, because both the target weight and actual weight of each security varies with the price of that security. (Study Session 13, LOS 46.f)

97. **C**   The shakeout phase of the industry life cycle is characterized by slowing growth, intense competition, and declining profitability. The mature phase is characterized by industry consolidation and little or no growth. In the decline phase of the industry lifecycle, growth is negative and excess capacity results. (Study Session 14, LOS 49.h)

98. **C**   Resetting interest rates makes the bond less, not more, susceptible to interest rate changes. (Study Session 15, LOS 51.e, 53.f)

99. **A**   Modified duration = Macaulay duration / (1 + YTM). Modified duration is lower than Macaulay duration unless YTM equals zero. (Study Session 16, LOS 55.b)

100. **C** Given the two-year forward rate two years from now, the next point on an annual forward rate curve is the two-year forward rate three years from now, 3y2y. This rate can be derived from the three-year and five-year spot rates as follows: $(1 + S_5)^5 = (1 + S_3)^3(1 + 3y2y)^2$. (Study Session 15, LOS 53.g, h)

101. **A** "Notching" refers to the credit rating agency practice of assigning ratings to debt issues that differ from the issuer's credit rating. An issuer credit rating applies to a firm's senior unsecured debt. Debt issues with different seniority or covenants may be notched to a higher or lower issue credit rating. (Study Session 16, LOS 56.c)

102. **A** $$\frac{\Delta P}{P} = -\text{Duration}\,\Delta YTM + \frac{1}{2}\text{Convexity}\,(\Delta YTM)^2$$

$$\frac{\Delta P}{P} = (-)(8)(-0.005) + \frac{1}{2}(100)(-0.005)^2 = +0.0400 + 0.00125 = +0.04125, \text{ or up } 4.125\%$$

The price would thus be $\$1,000 \times 1.04125 = \$1,041.25$. (Study Session 16, LOS 55.i)

103. **B** Matrix pricing for untraded or infrequently traded bonds should be based on yields of more frequently traded bonds with similar credit ratings. (Study Session 15, LOS 53.e)

104. **B** Acme's financial ratios suggest its credit rating should be between BB and B, which is below investment grade. (Study Session 16, LOS 56.g)

105. **A** Any type of call protection structured into the loan itself (in this case, yield maintenance charges) increases the overall call protection of the CMBS. Agency MBS do not provide call protection at the individual loan level. (Study Session 15, LOS 54.f)

106. **A** Bonds with a bullet structure are non-amortizing and return their entire principal to the bondholder at the maturity date. A non-amortizing bond makes a bullet *payment* at maturity. (Study Session 15, LOS 51.e)

107. **A** When the foreign currency appreciates, each foreign currency-denominated cash flow buys more domestic currency units—increasing the domestic currency return from the investment. The appreciation of the foreign asset benefits the investor as well. (Study Session 6, LOS 21.c, and Study Session 15, LOS 51.a, d)

108. **C** Reinvestment risk becomes more problematic when the current coupons being reinvested are relatively large. (Study Session 16, LOS 55.a)

109. **B** "Duration gap" refers to a difference between a bond's Macaulay duration and the bondholder's investment horizon. (Study Session 16, LOS 55.k)

110. **B** The intrinsic value of a put is the difference between strike price and stock price if stock price is less than strike price ($80 - 78 = 2$). The loss is equal to the intrinsic value minus the premium paid ($2 - 5 = -3$). (Study Session 17, LOS 59.a)

111. **A** Call options represent an obligation to perform in the case of the seller. The owner of the option (buy) has the right, but not an obligation, to purchase an underlying good at a specified price for a specified time from the seller. (Study Session 17, LOS 57.c, 58.j, k)

112. **A** If a bank borrows for 360 days and simultaneously lends the proceeds for 90 days, it creates a synthetic long (borrower) position in a 90-day FRA on 270-day LIBOR. The bank has no net position for the first 90 days and a borrowing position at a fixed rate of interest for the subsequent 270 days. (Study Session 17, LOS 58.e)

©2014 Kaplan, Inc.

113. **C** This is an out-of-the-money covered call. The net cost is $37 (40 − 3) and the maximum payoff on the position is the exercise price, $42. Thus, the maximum profit is $5. (Study Session 17, LOS 59.b)

114. **C** *Forwards* are subject to default risk, but *futures* are not. *Forwards* are individualized contracts, but *futures* are standardized. (Study Session 17, LOS 57.b)

115. **A** The key advantages of derivatives markets are providing price information, reducing transactions costs, and shifting risks among market participants. Derivatives markets are highly efficient and arbitrage opportunities rarely exist or are quickly eliminated. (Study Session 17, LOS 57.d)

116. **C** A trade sale involves selling a portfolio company to a competitor or another strategic buyer. An IPO involves selling all or some shares of a portfolio company to the public. A secondary sale involves selling a portfolio company to another private equity firm or a group of investors. (Study Session 18, LOS 60.d)

117. **B** By investing in a mortgage-backed security, an investor gains exposure to real estate, a category of alternative investments. Emerging markets are not classified as alternative investments. Neither convertible bonds nor high-yield bonds in general are classified as alternative investments, although some hedge funds (a class of alternative investments) invest in these assets. (Study Session 18, LOS 60.a, b)

118. **C** The fee may actually be substantial since, in addition to paying the manager of the FOF, a fee must be paid to each hedge fund within the FOF. (Study Session 18, LOS 60.d)

119. **C** Private investment in public equities refers to a private equity firm providing equity financing to publicly traded companies. Angel investing refers to financing the formation of a business. Mezzanine financing refers to subordinated equity-linked debt or preferred shares issued to finance a leveraged buyout. (Study Session 18, LOS 60.d)

120. **B** If a hedge fund has a high water mark, incentive fees are based on increases in investors' accounts above their highest previous values. As a result, fund managers do not receive incentive fees on returns that reverse previous losses. A hurdle rate is a minimum return a fund must achieve in a given period before fund managers receive incentive fees. A 2-and-20 structure means fund managers receive a 2% management fee and a 20% incentive fee; other provisions determine the base amounts on which these fees are calculated. (Study Session 18, LOS 60.f)

Notes

Notes

Notes

Notes

Notes

Notes

Notes